1 WAY 2 C THE WORLD:
WRITINGS 1984–2006

Internationally acclaimed author Marilyn Waring is highly regarded as a public intellectual, feminist leader, environmentalist, and social justice activist. Elected to New Zealand's Parliament at age twenty-three, she quickly rose to prominence on the political world stage. Since leaving Parliament in 1984, she has published numerous books and articles. This collection of essays, a selection of her popular journalism as well as new material, reflects on many important issues of our time. Here Waring provides incisive and illuminating commentary on a wide range of topics such as human rights, gay marriage, globalization, the environment, and international relations and development.

At home and abroad, Waring is a lively travel guide and astute observer, whether she is discussing global warming, women's rights, or life on a farm in New Zealand. Her work has stood the test of time: her accounts of being in India when Indira Gandhi was assassinated and in Ethiopia during the 1984 famine remain as vivid and relevant as her more recent writings on the post-9/11 world. Brimming with Waring's characteristic wit, compassion, and insight, *1 Way 2 C the World* is bound to fascinate and inspire.

MARILYN WARING is a professor in the Institute of Public Policy at the Auckland University of Technology.

1 Way 2 C the World

Writings 1984–2006

Marilyn Waring

To Susan,

With best wishes,

Marilyn J Waring.

UNIVERSITY OF TORONTO PRESS
Toronto Buffalo London

www.utppublishing.com
Printed in Canada

ISBN 978-0-8020-9034-8 (cloth)
ISBN 978-0-8020-9375-2 (paper)

Printed on acid-free paper

Library and Archives Canada Cataloguing in Publication

Waring, Marilyn, 1952–
1 way to C the world: writings 1984–2006/Marilyn J. Waring.

Updated, revised North American ed. of: In the lifetime of a goat.
ISBN 978-0-8020-9034-8 (bound). – ISBN 978-0-8020-9375-2 (pbk.)

1. Waring, Marilyn, 1952–. 2. Women in politics. 3. World politics.
4. New Zealand – Politics and government – 1972–. I. Title.

AC8.W37 2009   081   C2008-906921-8

University of Toronto Press acknowledges the financial assistance to its publishing
program of the Canada Council for the Arts and the Ontario Arts Council.

University of Toronto Press acknowledges the financial support for its publishing activities of the Government of Canada through the Book Publishing
Industry Development Program (BPIDP).

For my dear Canadian friends
Terre and Gerry and Peggy
and
Joanna and Brettel and Ange

Contents

Acknowledgments

Canada has been a very special country for me. It embraced my early work *Counting for Nothing/If Women Counted* in school and university curricula, and in the National Film Board of Canada documentary *Who's Counting? Marilyn Waring on Sex, Lies, and Global Economics.* I have been invited to and spoken in a good deal more of this beautiful country than most of its citizens get to in their lifetime. I have developed deep lifelong friendships there, and I have been given the opportunity to think and work with many people in Canada. Significant new work collected in this book had its birth in Canada, and the book's dedication is to a group of very special Canadians.

I began writing in 1984 when David Beatson, then editor of the New Zealand *Listener,* asked if I would like to write a fortnightly column for the magazine after my retirement from the New Zealand Parliament. I didn't want to commit myself to anything at all. 'But,' he reasoned with me, 'you may find you need the place for political catharsis, and you could probably do with the money, small as it is.'

He was right on both counts. I never knew how many short essays would appear over the next five years. Much to the chagrin of the subeditors (who complained with increasing intensity over time), many of them were hand written and faxed from far-flung places on the planet, arriving marginally before deadline, still needing to be typed and set. I never kept copies of what finally numbered more than 100 pieces.

I had also written columns for a brief time for the editor of the Wellington daily newspaper, the *Evening Post.* Computer literate by that time, I had retained these scripts.

x Acknowledgments

Neither the *Listener* nor the *Evening Post* ran footnotes or citations. I have done my best to recover or find many of these, but some have completely evaded my memory or more recent search engines.

The University of Toronto Press sent the text of this work to North American readers whose feedback on what they enjoyed influenced the major cull: what was in or out, and in what order.

Many other people have provided different sorts of material for my comments over the years. Some of them have been happy when they have recognized themselves, others have been offended. Most were just fellow citizens of the planet with whom I shared a moment and a place in time.

Portions of this book first appeared in the *New Zealand Listener* as part of the series of columns 'Letters to My Sisters.' Several pieces were published in the *Evening Post,* and one in the *Waikato Times.* The essay 'Civil Society: Community Participation and Empowerment in the Era of Globalisation' was published as an Occasional Paper for the Association of Women's Rights in Development (AWID) when I was a visiting scholar in their Toronto office in 2004. The essay on 'The Pacific Region' was first published in the book *Voix Rebelles du Monde* by French NGO ATTAC in 2007. Most of the essay 'Do Unpaid Workers Have Rights?' was also published in *Managing Mayhem: Work-Life Balance in New Zealand,* edited by Marilyn Waring and Christa Fouché (Wellington, NZ: Dunmore Publishing, 2007).

Marilyn J. Waring
Aotearoa/New Zealand
February 2008

Acronyms

ADB	Asian Development Bank
ALRANZ	Abortion Law Reform Association
ATTAC	Association for the Taxation of Financial Transactions for the Aid of Citizens
BPW	Business and Professional Women
CEDAW	Convention on the Elimination of All Forms of Discrimination Against Women
CHOGM	Commonwealth Heads of Government Meeting
CUB	Civil Union Bill
EEC	European Economic Union
EEZ	Economic Exclusion Zone
EU	European Union
FAO	Food and Agricultural Organization
FPP	First past the post
GATS	General Agreement on Trade in Services
GDP	Gross domestic product
G7	Group of Seven (Canada, France, Germany, Italy, Japan, UK, U.S.)
ICCPR	International Covenant on Civil and Political Rights
IHC	Intellectually handicapped Children
ILO	International Labour Organization
JICA	Japanese International Cooperation Agency

MDG   Millennium Development Goals
MP   Member of Parliament
NCW   National Council of Women
NDP   New Democratic Party
NGO   Non-government organization
NOW   National Organization of Women
NZFU   New Zealand Federation of University Women
NZRFU   New Zealand Rugby Football Union
OECD   Organization for Economic Cooperation and Development
RAMSI   Regional Assistance Mission to the Solomon Islands
SIS   Security Intelligence Service
SLORC   State Law and Order Restoration Council
SNA   System of National Accounts
SNI   System of National Income Accounts
SOS   Sisters Overseas Service
SPUC   Society for the Protection of the Unborn Child
SROW   Society for Research on Women
STV   Single transferable vote
UNDP   United Nations Development Programme
UNESCO   United Nations Educational Scientific and Cultural
           Organization
UNICEF   United Nations Children's Fund
UNITAR   United Nations Institute for Training and Research
UNSNA   United Nations System of National Accounts
USAID   United States Agency for International Development
USIS   Unites States Information Service
WEDO   Women's Environment and Development Organization
WEL   Women's Electoral Lobby
WHO   World Health Organization
WONAAC   Women's National Abortion Action Campaign

1 Way 2 C the World

Introduction

The previously published writing in this collection appeared in the New Zealand *Listener* as 'Letters To My Sisters' between mid-1984 and early 1989. Sometimes there were stories behind my story, but ones I dared not tell at the time because of my circumstances. I could never be sure about the security of the public fax that relayed the fortnightly writing to Wellington, whether in India when Ghandi was assassinated, or in Ethiopia at the height of the 1984 famine. I have taken the liberty of adding some of this previously unpublished material.

Series One collects five essays from very different contexts providing some guidance for the way I see the world, and perhaps some of the reasons why my lens is focused, as it is, on New Zealand and the South Pacific region. The pieces include elements of my childhood in the 1950s and observations of another childhood some forty years later. I explore my feeling of belonging to Aotearoa/New Zealand as a fourth generation Pakeha. I remember the feminist politics of the seventies and the outrageous discrimination in women's lives. The series also includes the letter that began the *Listener* columns, written in 1984 while I was still a Member of Parliament, and from a place and experience that would forever shift my perceptions of power, politics, abuse – and feminism. Indeed the adaptation of the letter form was a deliberate response to all that. I was prepared to write of how it had been for me there, but I made no apology for addressing a selected audience as 'My Dear Sisters.' I did not care to bother to explain myself to men anymore. The last essay in this series is on the Pacific – a region of patriarchal violence and endemic corruption – a region where few outside of it can name the countries of which I write.

Series Two contains three small vignettes on women of influence, moments captured in the time of the essays. Bella Abzug, Maria de

Lourdes Pintasilgo, and Gertrude Mongella are honoured here, but none of these essays speaks to the broad strokes of influence these women have had in their communities, in the political life of their countries, and on the world stage.

Being invited to conferences, or on fact-finding or advocacy missions is '1 Way 2 C the World,' which is the subject of Series Three. In 1984 I was invited to a 'Roundtable' in New York, sponsored by the Sisterhood Is Global Institute. I thought it might be a good idea to travel via Thailand, Burma, India, and Ethiopia to be better briefed for the meeting. I thought it might 'do me good' to investigate some of the more harrowing circumstances in which my sisters lived. So this was not a tourist jaunt, and I did not set out to have a good time.

The trip to China in 1985 was as one of a six-person team travelling under the auspices of the New Zealand China Friendship Association. In retrospect we were scenting and sensing some of the undercurrents that led to the democracy movement and its end in Tiananmen Square some three years later. My trip to Brazil was as one of a team invited by Ruth Escobar, Brazil's representative on CEDAW. Brazil was holding hearings on its new constitution, and we lobbied, spoke, advocated according to the wishes of our hosts. It wasn't all work: one weekend I did manage my only stay in a beach home designed by Frank Lloyd Wright. In the Philippines, I was one of a team asked to write a report on human rights. We were guests of Gabriela, the superb Filipina women's organization.

Series Four has its focus on two issues: relationships between New Zealand and the U.S. when New Zealand committed to its nuclear free policy, and the changes in the form of the parliamentary electoral systems in New Zealand, from first past the post (FPP) to the mixed member proportional (MMP) system. The last in the series, a letter to then prime minister Bolger, concerns relationships with Indonesia at the end of the Suharto regime, but the matters raised are constant for all trade, diplomatic, and development relationships.

For fifteen years I spoke about being at home on the farm as 'my real life,' so this is Series Five. Life wasn't, and isn't, all just earnest serious politics for me. I love good books, great music, and life outside office or hotel walls. I love to ski, play golf, bodysurf, and walk carefree on long beaches. From 1986 onward, when I bought the first farm and the goats came 'home,' I would have preferred to have written about daily activities there and the fun things in life. But unless one is Vita Sackville West or May Sarton, this is not a commercial prospect. These are just a taste of such times, and I hope that the joy that they brought me can be shared by the reader. The vigilance required to sustain the environment of our precious planet is the last of the subjects in this series.

Sometimes this happens: feminist Michelle Landsberg reviewed *Counting for Nothing/If Women Counted* for the *Globe and Mail*, and this drew it to the attention of Pamela Adamson who saw the possibilities of a film documentary. Terre Nash came on board as director, and the result, *Who's Counting? Marilyn Waring on Sex, Lies, and Global Economics*, became one of the best selling NFB documentaries, and young Canadians have had to watch it in many academic courses since.

Hans Messenger was working at Statistics Canada and saw my work as a challenge not a criticism, and he did much to enhance the visibility of unpaid work and the environment in the work of Statistics Canada. Women activists and academics sought to use the arguments and analyses and construct their own research. Innovators such a Mark Anielski in Alberta and Ron Colman in Nova Scotia were working on alternative indicators.

For many years I have been stimulated by the response of Canadians to my work and the opportunities to write and lecture during my visits to Canada. I have spent some of the best times of my life in Canada and with Canadians, and all of the essays in Series Six owe their genesis to Canadian people and events.

The Grounds for the Lens

In 1999, the Waikato Times *newspaper wished to begin a series of articles from 'old' local identities with the theme of nostalgia. I was asked to write the first of these, and I chose to write about the small village of Taupiri, where I lived the first fourteen years of my life.*

1 Under the Mountain

Nostalgia is associated with homesickness and a yearning for the past. Whenever I leave New Zealand I am homesick, not for anywhere in particular but for a light and colours and topography and air, for what my senses expect of Aotearoa.[1] Any yearning I have for the past is associated with those senses fully expressed as a child, and thus associated with Taupiri.

Some of the stories I most remember are those told by my maternal grandmother remembering her childhood there. About the morning when there was snow on the Hakarimata ranges. About being dressed in her finest clothes by her mother and put in the gig for the two of them to drive to Taupiri where my great-grandmother cast her first vote in the election following the 1893 suffrage victory. About the heavily tattooed Maori bearers who would emerge from the paths through the tea-tree-laden swampland carrying the dead to the burial grounds on the hill beside the Waikato River.

Taupiri is a sacred place, and Tainui[2] people are brought home to be buried there. For many years I was surrounded by the calling and prayers and protocol that surrounded the tangi, or funeral processions, close to my home, in the shadow of the mountain. Taupiri has a special place in the kingitanga movement, which emerged in the 1850s as Maori came under increasing pressure to sell land. They determined on unity under a king to assist resistance to confiscation, land wars, and sale. So we kids knew about Te Putu and Tawhia ki te rangi and Potatau Te Wherowhero, the first Maori king. We knew that the first school had

---

1 Aotearoa is the original Maori name for New Zealand. Maori is an official language of New Zealand. Many New Zealanders use 'Aotearoa' instead of, or along with, 'New Zealand' to describe where we are from.
2 Tainui are a major indigenous Maori iwi or tribe.

been the mission station school across the river at Kaitotehe, and that William Colenso's[3] deserted wife and children had lived there.

On my paternal side, Harry Waring had opened his first butchering business in Taupiri in the 1880s and his grandson, my dad, was working there when I was born. It was still a small village, and the population has always numbered in the hundreds. So everyone knew everyone else.

For most travellers, Taupiri is a blur on the map, with nothing to distinguish it from a myriad of similar towns around the country. But for me as a child, the whole place was a playground. We could rove and roam pathways, riverbanks, school fields, sports grounds, backyards, and paddocks freely, as if they were our own. I remember the shock of the UK immigrant newcomers, who were building their house, telling us we were trespassing and couldn't take the shortcut through their property from the dairy factory on our way home from school. Trespass wasn't the sort of word you used in Taupiri.

We climbed what we called the 'mountain' regularly in my childhood, avoiding the sacred burial ground on the western side. In the 1840s it was described as a 'beautiful hill, one mass of living verdure, towering upwards, a perfect cone,' and, in the 1950s, it was still worthy of that description. After pushing through the bracken and gorse of the bottom slopes, the path carved through beautiful bush. Occasionally, there were fires that would raze the southern side after some stoker on a steam train had hurled his coals from the train to the tracks on the mountain's edge. Over the years, these outbreaks took their toll and, even before the pines took over, the forest remnants were all but lost.

I lived right under the mountain, but there were days in the winter I couldn't see it at all. Between the Waikato and Mangawara Rivers a thick fog would descend and often not lift at all. Some of the locals associated this with the spirits of the buried Tainui people, but for me it was just damp. You could leave Taupiri and be in sunlight five minutes either side of the village, but be fogged in all day at home. I hated this, and the memories of fog and its continued presence in later years finally drove me from the Waikato. At other times of the year the river was the centre of attention. We waterskied there, went eeling, played in leaking canoes fashioned out of corrugated iron.

---

3 Colenso was a missionary, botanist, and historian who was responsible for the first printing press and first printing in New Zealand.

The other centre of town was the Taupiri Domain. The highway runs right through that space now, but it was my field of dreams. We lived directly opposite the Domain, beside the bowling and croquet clubs. The tennis, netball, rugby, cricket, and athletics clubs met weekly at the Domain, dependent on the season. My brother and I played everything, not just because we wanted to but because if any team was ever short they came over to 'see if one of the Warings could play.' As well, we kids played softball and soccer and built rope swings on the old oak trees in preference to the regular playground constructions there.

Everyone knew everyone. Several times a year I knocked on every door in town, selling Girl Guide biscuits or the gestetnered school magazine or tennis club raffle tickets. And every year the local Seventh Day Adventists, the local IHC (Intellectually Handicapped Children)[4] collectors, and the local (Beijing-aligned) member of the Communist Party of New Zealand would knock on our door. My father bought me Bertrand Russell's *Common Sense and Nuclear Warfare*[5] from one of these visitors when I was a teenager. None of us could have envisaged the role that small book would play in New Zealand politics in 1984.

We had native trees planted around the perimeter of the school grounds and we all knew their names. Anyone who could sing was in the school choir and in the Maori concert group coached by one of the local kuia, an older Maori woman steeped in cultural knowledge. We took these things for granted.

The pub closed at 6 p.m., so everyone knew who was there every night and wobbled home. We knew who got pregnant and who the dad was. We knew solo mothers and transvestites and boys who would be in trouble with the coppers. We knew who got slapped around at home, and who had no school lunch. If the local factory or the abattoir works didn't have a job for your boy, someone around the town managed something. We watched out for each other.

We went blackberrying and mushrooming in teams, and the whole town seemed to go to one of my relative's farms every Guy Fawkes Night for a huge bonfire and barbecue. If you held anything in the big hall, say a school concert, the whole town came, even people with no children at school.

---

4 IHC is New Zealand's largest provider of services to people with intellectual disabilities and their families.
5 Brooklyn, NY: AMS Press (1968).

I don't have any trouble being nostalgic for all that sort of life. It seems long gone. I know in later years I chose to live rurally because there was still the possibility of capturing some of that sense of community.

I don't know if any of that is still possible in Taupiri. I walked the streets there in 1999 with my brother when the Waring family held their reunion. We talked to some of the locals we had known as kids. They hadn't changed, but they said the town had.

So has the country. I write this in a school vacation where the media urges children to have their senses assaulted with electronic lights and noise and at great expense.

How rich and safe my childhood freedoms in Taupiri appear by comparison.

2 The Seventies: A Feminist Perspective

In 2004, Te Papa, New Zealand's National Museum and Gallery, held an exhibition called 'Out on the Street: New Zealand in the 1970s.' A conference on 'The Seventies in New Zealand: A Decade of Change' was organized to coincide with its opening, and I was asked to give one of the plenary opening addresses. I wrote this as memoir.

I 'appeared' twice in the exhibition: the first was as the subject of the head-line front cover of the 'expose' story in the Truth *newspaper in 1975, 'MP's Strange Love Life,' which was part of the exhibition's coverage of gay and lesbian issues in the seventies. The second was a photograph of my parliamen-tary colleague Ann Hercus and me, leaping in a staged moment, before taking our places in the parliamentary cricket team for the annual game against the Press Gallery. There were four women MPs in the House at the time. As part of my 'uniform' I was wearing a white T-shirt emblazoned with the large message 'Abortion – A Woman's Right to Choose.'*

Eva Rickard, Tainui Maori land activist for the Raglan Golf Course; Mira Szaszy, first Maori woman graduate, feminist fighter, and social worker; Whina Cooper, founding president of Te Rarawa, Maori Women's Welfare League, and Maori land activist; Elsie Locke, writer, historian, campaigner for peace and nuclear disarmament, and a life-long women's activist; Louisa Crawley, founding member and presi-dent of Pacifica, the nationwide Pacific Islands' women's organization;

and Sharon Alston, lesbian feminist activist and artist – I could fill
these pages with a recitation of the names of New Zealand women
who lived political lives of influence, and who can be particularly associated with the politics of the seventies.

In 1970 I was seventeen years old and beginning my first year of
study at Victoria University in Wellington. I have spent some time
remembering what influences I took with me to university: the protests
against the Vietnam War, the lyrics of Cohen and Baez and Donovan's
Universal Soldier, Peter Watkins's *The War Game*,[6] Bertrand Russell's
Common Sense and Nuclear Warfare.

For me the politics were everywhere and the adrenalin was racing for
a girl from Taupiri. There was the great night of noise and protest on
Willis Street outside the Grand Hotel beating the drum to 'No Maoris No
Tour' in 1970. The New Zealand rugby team, the All Blacks, were in the
hotel, and due to leave for a tour of South Africa, in which the Maori
members of the team would be treated as 'honorary whites' for the duration of their time in South Africa. On 21 March each year I would walk
through Lambton Quay and Willis Street in a line of twelve or so, carrying small white crosses to remember the Sharpsville Day massacre of
1960. Later, the 1973 South African rugby tour to New Zealand was as
called off by Prime Minister Norman Kirk, on the basis that it would
result in riots and violence unprecedented in New Zealand. He was
right; this was the result when a tour went ahead in 1981.

Now you might be thinking that these were not issues for Women's
Liberation. But they meant we went searching in the silences. We
found black South African anti-apartheid activist Miriam Makeba, and
her music, exiled in London. Instead of Joe Slovo,[7] we learned about
Ruth First – the investigative South African journalist held in solitary
confinement and finally murdered by a letter bomb in 1982 – because
we went looking. We would make sure that women weren't hidden
from history anymore.

 We marched against French nuclear testing in the South Pacific. From
1966 to 1990, 167 nuclear test explosions were performed on Moruroa
and Fangataufa atolls, tests used for the development of at least eight

---

6 A BBC TV movie made in 1965, *The War Game* was a fictional, worst-case-scenario
   docu-drama about nuclear war and its aftermath in and around a typical English city.
7 Slovo was long time leader of the Communist Party of South Africa and a leading
   member of the African National Congress. He and First were married in 1949.

types of nuclear warheads. The first atmospheric test was performed on Mururoa on 2 July 1966, the last on 15 September 1974. In 1974 New Zealand sent a naval frigate to the test site. Much was made of the fact that there was a New Zealand cabinet minister on board. However, after June 1975, all tests went underground. We established links with the women of New Caledonia and Micronesia to hear their stories of the health and other effects of American and French testing.

We knew about the quite literal 'rape' of Bangladesh. In 1971, the mass killings of more than one million people by the Western Pakistan military was accompanied by the systematic multiple rape of more than 200,000 Bangladeshi women. At the same time, Australian women were prevented from laying wreaths at the cenotaph in Canberra on Anzac Day when they wanted to remember the civilian women and children raped, killed, or brutalized by war. In the U.S., the Watergate affair – the burglaries of the Democratic Party's National Committee rooms, which led to the resignation of President Nixon – exploded in 1972 and, for a political science student, it was magnificent. In 1971, *The Pentagon Papers* began to be published by the *New York Times*, and Daniel Ellsberg, who leaked them from the State Department, was the next hero. The *Papers* showed that the U.S. government had deliberately expanded the Vietnam War by conducting air strikes over Laos, raids along the coast of North Vietnam, and offensive actions taken by U.S. Marines, and that the U.S. public had been misled by the Administration in respect of the war. In an honours year in political science I read these along with Charlotte Perkins Gilman's *The Yellow Wallpaper*, Kate Millett's *Sexual Politics*, and Mary Daly's *Beyond God the Father*[8] in a class on political sociology.

On my way to and from the university each day I passed the Hill Street University Bookshop. Here I first saw Robin Morgan's anthology *Sisterhood Is Powerful*, Shulamith Firestone's *The Dialectic of Sex*, Andrea Dworkin's *Women Hating*,[9] and the copies of the UK magazine *Spare Rib*. I used to go to that table and look in awe at these books and journals: that women had the courage to write them and to say all this 'out loud'; that anyone published them; that it was possible for some of

---

8 (London: Virago, 1973); (London: Vigaro, 1977); and (Boston: Beacon Press, 1973), respectively.
9 (New York: Vintage Books, 1970); (New York: William Morris, 1970); and (New York: E.P. Dutton, 1974), respectively.

the women I knew to have enough money to purchase each of them as they arrived, one every month or so.

The latest wave of the international women's movement was U.S. dominated, but the content had international resonance. There were political women in the news. They weren't all politically pretty, but they were there. There was Bella Abzug, who represented Manhattan in the U.S. House of Representatives from 1971 to 1977; and Margaret Thatcher, UK Secretary of State for Education and Science in the Heath government of 1970, leader of the opposition in 1975, and becoming UK's prime minister in 1979. Bernadette Devlin became the youngest women elected to the UK House of Commons at the age of twenty-one in 1969, representing the mid-Ulster constituency as a political activist from the Northern Ireland Republic. In France, there was Simone Veil, minister of health from 1976 to 1979 during which time she promoted access to abortion; and Francoise Giroud, who was first French Secretary of State for Women from 1974 to 1976, serving as minister of culture in the cabinet from 1976 to 1977. In Canada, Flora MacDonald was elected to the House of Commons as a 'Red Tory' in 1972, and in 1979 was appointed Secretary of State for External Affairs under the Clark government, making her one of the first female foreign ministers anywhere in the world. In the U.S., Elaine Noble became the first out lesbian elected to the Massachusetts House of Representatives in 1974, serving until 1976.

In terms of sexuality, I was pretty closeted. Venn Young had introduced a private member's bill for homosexual law reform into the New Zealand Parliament in 1974, to decriminalize sexual activities between consenting male adults in private. The bill lost, but it also meant an outbreak of homophobia. While the university environment was relatively safe for me, the larger social environment certainly wasn't.

Publicly, Billie Jean King was in denial. This world leading tennis figure did not publicly acknowledge her sexuality until 1981. The media images of the late 1960s and early 1970s wave of the lesbian feminist movement were not promising – boots, boiler suits, bikes, and anger were not particularly enticing. To see several dozen women who were neither suicidal nor leather kitted dykes on bikes, under a Lesbian Nation banner at the 1975 United Women's Convention, was the first public and celebratory exposure I had to alternatives.

I didn't ever join one of the formal women's liberation groups. For some years there seemed to be an esoteric argument, which I am afraid was completely lost on me, about the virtues or differences between feminists and members of the women's liberation movement. But I had no problems with the issues at the first national Women's Liberation Conference held in 1972 in Wellington. Claudia Mason led the workshop on abortion, Ann Ruth that on equal pay. Sonya Davies gave the report from the childcare workshop, Joan Rotherham that on legal rights, and Ngahuia te Awekotuku that on gay liberation. There were workshops for student women, high school women, working women, housewives, and issues around women in the union movement, school curricula, and leave to care for sick family members. Women's liberation groups formed in Auckland and Wellington, and in Dunedin the amazing Collective for Women began. I remember the Wellington group used to meet regularly in the student union building. I know I wanted to go many times, but these gals were scary. I remember Teresa O'Connell, Deborah Jones, Linda Evans, and others as a moving throng of togetherness clad in black and not really inviting. They didn't look as though they ever had fun.

Broadsheet started publication in Auckland in 1972; Wellington circulated a publication called *Up From Under*. In March 1972 Germaine Greer, Australian feminist and author of *The Female Eunuch*,[10] filled the Student Union to overflowing and was terrific entertainment. New Zealand–born Juliet Mitchell returned to Wellington to give the chancellor's series lectures at Victoria University and was earnest on *Psychoanalysis and Feminism*.[11]

What were we up against? John Bowlby's writing on fathers and maternal deprivation theory was first published in the 1950s, but the media and women's magazines in particular pushed the game and cited far-reaching effects on the whole future of the young child who experienced 'prolonged deprivation' of maternal care. Bowlby's attachment theories were used well out of context to pressure women to stay at home and fulfil the wifely stereotype.

Here's another taste from the Wellington *Evening Post* of 12 October 1972. It's an interview with Julie Cameron, who was setting up the Homemaker's Union:

> Obviously if such a union was going to start it had to be begun by someone intelligent, but somehow Julie Cameron is the antithesis of the ideal

---

10 (London: Mac Gibbon and Key, 1970).
11 (London: Allen Lane, 1974).

member one might imagine. She's attractive and bright, in that flinty way that some women are; she has an MA in English and is studying so that she can set up a farm accounting business. She's on the Wairarapa Hospital Board, and for a farmer's wife she has to be considered radical.

And that's another thing. Julie is not a typical farming wife. While she helps her husband on his 2000-acre farm, while she farmhouse bakes and freezes, looks after her pre school son John, in a curious way she looks as if she doesn't really belong on a farm. She hasn't settled down to a rural existence. And certainly she hasn't stopped thinking. Perhaps it is the area in which she lives – 23 miles from Featherstone above Lake Onoke, a windswept region in which many women would feel stranded and abandoned – that has made her aware enough of other people's needs to start the Homemaker's Union.

While the feminist movement was everywhere, there were some self-appointed central-committee folks about making life difficult, in addition to the usual paternal tokenistic treatment. An early example was when Dorothy Jelicich, newly elected as Labour MP for Hamilton West, was asked to lead the New Zealand Parliament's Address in Reply Debate on 20 January 1973, the first time a woman had had this opportunity. (That wasn't hard – there had only been a dozen women Members of Parliament at that stage.) The *Otago Daily Times* reported that:

> wearing an autumn toned dinner dress, she ranged over a number of subjects, both local issues and social welfare questions, but placed most emphasis in her address to equality for women and measures to ensure them equality both at home and in employment.

In her address Jelicich, who had a union background, had said: 'equal opportunity for women is as important as equal pay or remuneration.' In context that was a breakthrough phrase. There were only four women members of the House and this was 1972. But Dorothy had gone on to say: 'Just as women demand recognition for equal rights, so they too must be prepared to shoulder responsibilities of government and become the companion of man.' That was too much to ask. Writing in *Broadsheet*, Fern Mercier wanted to know:

> Why do we have to be the companions of man? ... What (the men) do like, is [sic] the reformists whom they choose to call Women's Liberationists ... Why, Mrs Jelicich even made front page news, a sure sign of establishment

approval, when you get into the media. Men approve of the reformist
women, the companions – because they will help them bolster their selves
still, help them continue their games of self-deception and delusions of
grandeur and all their jolly, boyish games that are destroying humankind
and our Earth too … and so on and on it goes.[12]

Men loved it – the squabbling women. And if they could find one to
set up against another, they had a victory: the Abortion Law Reform
Association (ALRANZ) versus the Society for the Protection of the
Unborn Child (SPUC); United Women's Conventions versus Save Our
Homes. At the first United Women's Convention in Auckland in 1973,
union organizer Connie Purdue led a walkout when women's reproductive freedom and the right to abortion was the majority opinion of
the women at the gathering. In 1974, MP Gerry Wall introduced a private member's bill in the New Zealand Parliament to outlaw abortion,
and in 1976 a Royal Commission on Contraception, Sterilization, and
Abortion was set up. In the subsequent legislation before Parliament,
even rape was removed as grounds for the termination of pregnancy.
The Sisters Overseas Service (SOS) was established to fly women who
needed terminations to clinics in Australia.

If there were small gains, there had to be silence. When the women
clerical workers at Associated Motor Industries Panmure won a victory
for equal pay (the whole factory had gone on strike in support of their
demands), the Clerical Workers Union had negotiated for them. They
finally accepted a promise of equal pay in twelve months, and 60 per
cent of the existing difference immediately. The spokesman for the clerical workers union said that they had agreed not to publicize the settle-
ment, because the Labour government was afraid it would lead to more
strikes and more wage increases. There was a wage freeze on at the time,
which didn't apply to equal pay cases. Under the Equal Pay Act 1972,
women had to wait four years before they would be granted equal pay,
but there was nothing to stop them getting it earlier.[13]

'All issues are women's issues' was the reply Her Royal Highness
The Princess Anne gave Prime Minister Robert Muldoon when he
introduced me to her as being interested in 'women's issues.' Indeed,
we began to be everywhere, bringing our analyses to any debates or

---

12 Fern Mercier, 'Dear Mrs Jelicich,' *Broadsheet*, no. 7 (March 1973), 6–7.
13 'Hush Up on Equal Pay Victory,' *Broadsheet*, no. 13 (September 1973), 16.

stages we could occupy. Radio and television journalist Cherry Raymond addressed the Commonwealth South Pacific Regional Conference on Human Settlements in Auckland in February 1976:

> Auckland women are under house arrest in badly planned suburbs. Many women in the suburbs and in new housing areas had a feeling of isolation; there were few community centres, almost no day care centres, few parks, few day time cultural activities and little opportunity for casual social contact. Planners needed to consider women as 'individuals' rather than as instruments of social and economic policy.

In 1974 a course in women's studies was established at the University of Waikato, with Jane Ritchie and Rosemary Seymour working hard for that. Victoria University in Wellington followed a year later. Women held Take Back the Night marches. We protested at beauty contests, and in one incident mice were released on to the stage during the parade of objectification. Other sexual stereotyping was targeted, including that in advertisements and textbooks. We argued about the honorific Mrs and introduced Ms. Where this wasn't acceptable – and in the press and in Parliament in 1975 this was certainly not acceptable – I gave instructions that I was to be called Marilyn Waring without any title. We struggled with the forms that designated women the vicarious liabilities of their husbands: forms for mortgage lending, credit in business, the language of the Census asking for the 'head of the household' to fill it in. We struggled with language that abused and language that made us invisible and language that assumed we were like men.

Mary Batchelor introduced a private member's bill on domestic violence into the New Zealand Parliament. In fact I think Mary introduced this bill three times before it was ever adopted by any government, but in the early seventies it was one of the triggers that led to the establishment of the parliamentary Select Committee on the Role of Women in New Zealand Society. The 1970 Royal Commission on the Status of Women in Canada was a precedent for such an inquiry, which was helpful. The submissions to this committee were extensive and covered a vast scope of issues, though to participate in the hearings in any way was seen as institutionalized co-option by some elements of the women's movement.

In 1973 the Domestic Purposes Benefit (DPB) had been introduced, but there is no doubt that the select committee provided the impetus for further legislative changes. The first was the Matrimonial Property Act of 1976. Legislation was introduced by the Labour government in 1975 but held over through the election that year. The need for change was heavily influenced by the *Haldane* case,[14] which went to the Privy Council. The decision was forced on the courts because the state of the law was most iniquitous, and the judgment said as much. The result was a leading piece of legislation in the world, a fifty-fifty split of property, including separate property, unless such a division would be 'repugnant to justice.'

In the mainstream, battles were being fought over whether the middle of the road National Council of Women (NCW) could be co-opted against these dreadful radical feminists. I think back to the skilful political manoeuvring of those women a generation older than I. Mavis Tiller, Joyce Herd, Dorothy Winstone, Laurie Salas, Miriam Dell, Vivien Boyd: these were the core of the 'safe' women so the politicians thought, and these were the 'only woman' so often. But they influenced a great deal. They provided membership for the Commission on Social Security, the National Development Council, the Equal Pay Commission, the Consumer Council, the National Consultative Committee on Disarmament, and the Royal Commission on Nuclear Power Generation. Mavis Tiller was a president of NCW and between 1973 and 1982 was vice-convenor, then convenor, of the International Council of Women Standing Committee on International Relations and Peace. She was a Commissioner on the Royal Commission on Social Security in New Zealand, which reported in 1972.

While a member of NCW, Joyce Herd wrote the parliamentary submissions jury service, childcare, equal pay, maternity services, contraception, sterilization, abortion, and homosexual law reform. She was also an active member of the Federation of Graduate Women, Ecology Action and the Historic Places Trust.

Dame Dorothy Winstone was a leader in the Federation of Graduate Women and an activist and philanthropist for many women and women's groups.

Laurie Salas was a peace activist, a member of the National Consultative Committee on Disarmament (NCCD), the Women's International League for Peace and Freedom, and the New Zealand Associations for the United Nations and UNESCO.

---

14 *Haldane v. Haldane* [1976] 2NZLR 715. This matrimonial property case had such an appalling and unjust outcome for the wife, who had done all the housework and child-rearing duties, and the greatest part of farm work and maintenance. It caused a major change in the law that led to the fifty-fifty split of matrimonial property.

Miriam Dell was national president of NCW in 1970. In 1974 she became chairperson of the New Zealand's Committee on Women and was coordinator for International Women's Year, and a member of the New Zealand Government delegation at all three of the United Nations Conferences for the Decade of Women. She was elected to the Board of Officers of the International Council of Women (ICW) in 1976 and was international president 1979–86.

Vivien Boyd chaired the Consumer Council for six years and was the only woman on the Royal Commission on Nuclear Power Generation.

They had an outward pretence of conservatism, and they played a game of never divulging a party preference for Labour or National, and taking pride in this. But they were also drivers of church organizations and environmental movements – and they were pushed along by their constituencies, those groups under the umbrella of the NCW such as Business and Professional Women (BPW), the Federation of University Women (NZFU), the Society for Research on Women, (SROW), the Women's Electoral Lobby (WEL), the National Organization of Women (NOW) – at one stage in the seventies there were more than 100 affiliated groups – who had leaders emerge who were very happy to be known as feminists. Paddy Walker in Auckland and Fanaura Kingstone in Tokoroa were building the women's organization Pacifica, and Edie Tawhiwhirangi was piloting the first Te Kohanga Reo, a full-immersion Maori language pre-school centre.

But there was plenty to deal with. Women could not be firefighters, jockeys, air force pilots, knife hands. At the beginning of the seventies we couldn't drive taxis. Under the Factories Act, we could not be employed after 11:00 p.m. and before 7:00 a.m. Of course we could be nurses at those times, because hospitals were not covered by the Factories Act, and as Professor Margaret Wilson pointed out in 1973, seventeen-year-old strippers could perform until the early hours without a threat of prosecution for their employer. Even where women seemed to make ground, they were stopped in their tracks by male unions. The male-dominated Cooks and Stewards Union ensured for many years that Air New Zealand staff hired as hostesses could not become 'pursers,' and this stand-off, in which Air New Zealand supported the union, was to become the first major test of the Human Rights Act passed in 1977 and the subject of Gaylene Preston's beautiful documentary, *Coffee Tea or Me*.

In 1976, Parliament decided to have a Select Committee on Violence as a way of looking at gang behaviour, but by now women were getting very smart and turned many of the hearings into a detailed

account of male violence against women. The Evidence Amendment
Act was passed in 1977. Rape victims could no longer be questioned in
court about their sexual history. I remember going to a day's workshop
at this time held in Auckland. It's strange to think of it now, but most
of the attendees – we were all invited – were men. They were the
police, the examining doctors, the prosecutors, the judges. There was a
small group of women there and we sort of found each other to sit
with. There were discussions on the virtues or otherwise of this
intended piece of legislation. I remember the 'Police Doctor' telling the
assembly that it was a silly piece of legislation, because when he conducted examinations of some women who claimed they had been
raped, their vaginal walls were so distended the speculum fell out. He
thought this proved they must have wanted it, and most of the audience laughed! It was not surprising. Rape numbers according to police
reports at the beginning of the seventies were as follows:

	Reported	Prosecuted	Groundless
1971	160	56	66
1972	210	68	100
1973	251	80	126

But 1973 also saw the establishment of the first rape crisis centre, and
four years later we had rape crisis telephone lines, the very first
women's refuges run for and by women, and Sue Lytollis started the
YWCA self-defence courses. The mainstream women's magazines
deserted Bowlby, and in 1977 the New Zealand *Women's Weekly* ran a
rape survey for NOW; in 1978 it ran a survey questionnaire on battered
wives for feminist researcher Miriam Saphira.
    In 1977 the first Human Rights Act was passed. It began with small
changes. It is hard to believe that hospital boards still had a 'husbands
only' visiting policy in the evenings in neo-natal units. The Human
Rights Commission boldly requested a change to 'one adult visitor
only.' The International Labour Organisation (ILO) provision on night
work was denounced and access to workforce positions for women
grew, assisted by the earnest work of Sonya Davies and other women
in the front line of the union movement.
    By the late seventies opponents of feminism took to arson tactics.
Fires were lit at the offices of Sisters Overseas Services in Auckland,
and the Auckland Medical Aid Centre, which performed terminations
of pregnancy, was also set on fire.

I was one of the coordinators of the 1979 United Women's Convention in Hamilton. The conventions were always challenging environments, and in Hamilton pressure came on the lesbian performers not to participate. This 1979 convention marked the first time entertainers were being paid to perform. Political stands were taken. Maggie Eyre recalled:

> We were being told by other lesbians that we couldn't perform for non-lesbian women. I was told not to dance for heterosexual women. That infuriated me, because all my work in workshops had shown me just how positive my position as a lesbian was when working with them. It just brought them to a feeling of self confidence that was invaluable.[15]

Lynda and Jools Topp, The Topp Twins, were attending a convention for the first time, and were given the same instructions. Jools got angry and Lynda reports her as saying: 'No one's going to tell me where to sing and who to sing to – so we went and sang. And the funny thing was, all the lesbians who'd been so heavy to us were there at the concert anyway – at the back, but there.'[16]

We screamed in the middle of the night with Dory Previn, knew what Lesley Gore meant when she sang 'You don't own me,' and owned LP records called *Lavender Jane Loves Women*. We read Erica Jong's *Fear of Flying*, Marilyn French's *The Women's Room*,[17] and articles such as 'The Myth of Vaginal Orgasm' and 'Combat in the Erogenous Zone.'[18]

Overnight we painted all the buses in Wellington for one International Women's Day and they had to drive around covered in feminist slogans because there was no time to clean them. In the abortion debates in 1977 a crowd of Women's National Abortion Action Campaign (WONAAC) activists arrived in Parliament all looking like pregnant women. They sat in the parliamentary gallery and at an appointed time let go of the helium balloons they had under their clothing. They were purple, and stamped with 'A women's right to choose,' and they floated in the debating chamber for over a week until they slowly descended as the helium escaped. When the U.S. Navy sent its frigates for R and R in

---

15 Maggie Eyre, personal communication with author, January 2008.
16 Ibid.
17 (New York: Signet, 1973); (New York: Summit, 1977).
18 See Anne Koedt, 'The Myth of the Vaginal Orgasm' (1970), available online at the CWLU Herstory Archive Website, www.uic.edu/orgs/cwluherstory/CWLUArchive/vaginalmyth.html; and Ingrid Bengis, 'Combat in the Erogenous Zone,' *in Combat in the Erogenous Zone: Writings on Love, Hate and Sex* (New York: Knopf, 1972).

Wellington, we dialled sailors and invited them to dinner at addresses that were miles from nowhere and where they would find no home. Well before the nuclear free New Zealand stand-off, the U.S. sailors preferred to take their R and R somewhere else.

Feminists established the *Double Standard* and the *Virgin Chronicle*, fictitious newspaper titles that would have banner headlines up all over Wellington each week. The prime minister used to be known as Piggy Muldoon. One banner read 'Rutting Pig Shot in Ngaio: PM Safe.'

Slowly, through the seventies, other voices entered our New Zealand world – novelist Ama Ata Aidoo from Ghana, theorist Christine Delphy from France, voices like Naila Khabeer from Bangladesh and Fatima Mernissi from Morocco. Margareta von Strade and Agnes Varda and Marlene Gorris made stunning political movies, and Judy Chicago's art installation *The Dinner Party* was a breathtaking, moving, and artistically unmatched acknowledgment of women's lives and artistic skill over the centuries.

We worked damned hard, and we had the political potluck dinner down to a fine art. It got easier as some women realized there wasn't a central committee or a little red book in this movement. Our fashion sense was appalling, but we made great politics. And we laughed a lot, and we were very funny. If I leave out the parliamentary part, these were many of the best days of my life!

3 On Leaving Parliament

In March 1984 I had announced that I would not be seeking re-election as a Member of Parliament in November. I was asked by the Listener *to write something for them about my experience. 'Letter to My Sisters' was written in early May, when the expectation was that there would be a general election in November, and I still had six months to run as a sitting parliamentarian.*

26 May 1984

My dear sisters,

Now that I am to leave Parliament, I suppose I should be flattered that so many want my opinion and ask that I write for them. Among those letters comes one from the *Listener* requesting 'a frank personal account of what it is really like to be an MP in the New Zealand Parliament, especially from the point of view of a young woman.' (It is difficult to see how it might be from any other point of view.) 'Perhaps the article could take the form of a kind of odyssey from 1975 ...'

So much that is past should be left that way. I address you to avoid playing games, to keep myself honest, remembering how easy it would be to package only the retail item. The editor of the *Waikato Times* told me on my first visit to him as a candidate in 1975: 'I am a salesman. I have a daily product. I am not here to educate, I am here to sell.' And I have never forgotten it.

I address you, too, remembering Adrienne Rich writing in *Women and Honour: Some Notes on Lying*:

> We assume that politicians are without honour. We read their statements trying to crack the code. The scandal of their politics is not that men in high places lie, only that they do so with such indifference, so endlessly, still expecting to be believed. We are accustomed to the contempt inherent in the political life.[19]

And if I must write, then I am comfortable and comforted in addressing you. It has been important to feel thus, reinforced by my predecessor, Sir Douglas Carter, saying to me: 'At the end of every day you are the person you have to live with' – advice for the mind and the spirit – as he marched me one hot December day in 1975 in and out of every government department in Hamilton, saying: 'This is where your work is, this is where you help your constituents; ministers and ministerials are last resorts' – advice for praxis.

Armed with little else but advice I went to serve Raglan, and you, though I knew so little of your lives and still saw our multiple oppressions in trivial ways, consumed with the myths of objectivity and measuring our invisibility by numbers.

In 1975 we were four of eighty-seven in Parliament, with a male cabinet of nineteen, and five male parliamentary undersecretaries. All heads of government departments were men, and while there were nine women private secretaries to ministers, all forty-three principal private secretaries were men. Thirty-one men and eight women members of the

---

19 Adrienne Rich, *Women and Honour: Some Notes on Lying* (London: Only women Press, 1979), n.p.

Parliamentary Press Gallery fed their views from central government to thirty-seven major metropolitan and provincial daily newspapers, all edited by men. The law courts were presided over by twenty-three male judges and only three of the twenty-six major city councils by women mayors.

(In 1984 [at the time of this letter], we have 8/92 in Parliament, 12/55 private secretaries to ministers, 7/26 members of the Press Gallery, 12/26 mayors of major cities, one head of a government department. There are still no women cabinet ministers, judges, or editors of metropolitan dailies.)

Such lists were (and still are) endless – but I see them as illustrative of only a fragment of our powerlessness. Our oppressions far exceed any succinct numberings of our absence; they run deeper than our ability to count, and too frequently beyond our ability to express them.

I write my first letter to the Clerk of the House requesting a crèche or childcare facility in the buildings – not just for staff and members but also for the parents who come to watch and hear Parliament, who must stand waiting in corridors with their younger children while the rest of the family go in to watch, because children under eight cannot be admitted to the House. It would not surprise you to see which parent that inevitably is.

I watch the games and lines of caucus for the first time not recognizing them; taken in, not realizing I would become used to these moves. The most testing agenda items left until 12:45 p.m., with a conclusion of 1:00 p.m.; issues like a national price for milk, or national two-channel coverage for television popping up and being a safe bet for an inconclusive and wasted hour when there was major electoral discontent that should have been aired.

The good old pre-budget kite-flyers, to make the backbenchers feel they've been consulted: prescription charges, indirect taxes ... When just enough new members enter every three years, and just enough older members think they might jeopardize promotion chances by getting involved, and just enough don't want to get involved, and just enough think it's a pointless waste of energy anyway, old dogs don't need new tricks.

I become involved in my first abortion debate and it highlights what I have slowly learned of the diversion of being beset by sisters ... and the abject humility of being understood.

There is the rewriting of the Security Intelligence Service legislation, and [fellow back bench MP] Michael Minogue wins a commitment to an Official Information Act. I take down every word of caucus for this year and keep it with a copy of the official caucus minutes – still the student, I think the comparison may be of interest some day.

There is too much to do, so much to learn, so much I don't see clearly, so much I don't say – but Huntly [my constituency] needs $1 million of energy resources levy, and a National Roads Board priority for a bypass, and a poll [about establishing] a Trust tavern [so that the profits from the sales go to the community and not the breweries], and I am meeting with Eva Rickard about the return of the Raglan golf course …

I do as much as I can … I arm myself with Katherine Mansfield for bold encouragement, and on my wall I write: 'Risk. Risk anything. Care no more for the opinions of others, for those voices. Do the thing hardest on earth for you to do. Act for yourself. Face the truth.'[20]

It joins T.S. Eliot's:

And right action is freedom
From past and future also,
For most of us, this is the aim
Never here to be realised;
Who are only undefeated
Because we have gone on trying …[21]

I go to Public Expenditure Committee meetings and ask about all the unutilized and underutilized departmental housing. It is considered unimportant. A subcommittee of one – me – is appointed to investigate while the full committee spends weeks on a complaint about a consumer report on Hobbs kettles. I find 200 houses all over the country that should, I argue, be handed to the Housing Corporation for tenancy. There is no interest and no support. Eight years later, in quite different socio-economic circumstances, and with no small amount of insensitivity, such a policy is adopted.

I ask why we don't have a management audit of the legislative department. This is tantamount to treason – I am transferred from the Public Expenditure Committee to the Statutes Revision Committee for hearings and deliberations on the matrimonial property legislation.

---

20 C.K. Stead, ed., *The Letters and Journals of Katherine Mansfield: A Selection* (Harmondsworth, UK: Penguin, 1977).
21 T.S. Eliot, *The Dry Salvages in Four Quartets* (New York: Harcourt Brace, 1943).

The management audit goes ahead seven years later, initiated elsewhere, and its conclusions bring considerable savings.

But on the Statutes Revision Committee I celebrate that the quality, argument, and persuasiveness of the submission by the Women's Electoral Lobby with advocate Ruth Richardson is heard by a willing committee. A major change in the division of property after a marriage is on the way. A fifty-fifty division, to be altered only if such a division is repugnant to justice, changes not just the lives and chances of many of you, but your status, and without a great battle.

Meanwhile, the Boundaries Commission abolishes my parliamentary seat of Raglan and sends it spinning in three different directions. The conservative women of Waipa mobilize, and I am selected as party candidate on the first ballot, and elected as MP for Waipa in November 1978.

In this second term I am the only woman in government. I feel the aloneness – and not just that form of aloneness. We return to the government caucus depleted in number, all humming the same tune. The prime minister made life easy in the 1975 campaign; in 1978, every candidate wore him as the albatross around their neck. They all say it – especially those who have been defeated, who return to this first caucus rehearsing how they might say so when asked for their last few words. But they are dazzled by the presentations of silver trays, and their tongues are still on the subject. 'Lying is done with words, and also with silence,' says Adrienne Rich.

I'm not a martyr, and I don't find it easy to take personal criticism either, but, in the absence of anyone else speaking, I finally offer some quiet reflection on the campaign – and take up my work and quit the room at the resultant invitation to leave if I don't like it, delivered in the manner to which we are all now accustomed.

I begin three years of spinning in too many directions, rescued occasionally by flight from the country. During the first of these, to Britain as the guest of the British government, I fly to Vienna to observe the preparatory conference for the UN Half-Decade Conference in Copenhagen of the Commission on the Status of Women. The New Zealand delegate is former MP Colleen Dewe. When she is hospitalized it takes the cabinet three days to approve their only woman colleague in government as the alternative. I learn quickly, helped by the inevitable caucus kick of 'how would you know?', that I am clearly unsuitable to represent you and that they know more of the prospects of birthing, the plights of married women, and our 'discrimination' (we are not oppressed, I am told) than I will ever know.

But in my constituency Oparau and Ngutinui need upgraded telephone services, Cambridge needs a bypass, the Te Awamutu MOT licensing station needs more staff, Mangakino needs a doctor, they are still clear-felling the Pureora Forest ...

There is another abortion debate.

I accept the challenge of chairing the Public Expenditure Committee and cannot believe the furore when I suggest we visit some departmental offices (what is there to hide? how could it hurt?). We compromise: the State Services Commission suggests whom we might visit.

A storm breaks when I ask for all the management audits conducted on departments to date, alerted to their existence by a minister who had inordinate difficulty getting his hands on a copy of the audit of his own department. 'The assurance of confidentiality is vital to the continuation of the program of audits,' I am told.

We compromise again and the State Services Commission gives us a précis of the recommendations on each. Dissatisfied with management systems in the Ministry of Works and Development, and urged onwards by an Auditor General's report, we decide on a division-by-division subcommittee examination of that department, starting with the water and soil division. The dam bursts. We compromise and examine the architects.

I am invited to a United Nations Institute for Training and Research (UNITAR) seminar in Oslo on 'Creative Women in Changing Societies' as the Oceania representative – Germaine Greer cannot go. I am excited, surprised, delighted to be there, and very humbled. These women are here as creatures of their essence: I am here because of what I do with my status.

As my candidacy for the 1981 general election is confirmed, and the Labour candidate for Eastern Maori helps the editor of the Waikato Times in his quest to sell, with headline assertions that the government's policies on women are influenced by barren lesbians, I am rescued from a downward-spiralling fatigue with an offer of a teaching fellowship at Harvard University for four months. This is a constructive and cathartic period, to prepare for the horror of the 1981 Springbok tour. (For 56 days in July, August, and September 1981, New Zealanders were divided against each other in support of or in opposition to the tour of New Zealand by the South African apartheid regime rugby team. More than 150,000 people took part in over 2000 demonstrations in 28 centres, and 1,500 were charged with offences. The government of which I was part pretended it was against the tour, but did all it could to facilitate its continuation. It was a highly manipulative racist action and totally poll-driven. It led to a boycott by African nations of the Commonwealth Games in Brisbane Australia in 1982.)

On this subject there is much I know I will not tell you about just yet. I did a lot I cannot tell you about. There were gestures I might have made that I didn't make; but to this day I cannot think of anything constructive that might have changed the course of those events, that I did not do – any opportunity that I did not take. This gives me no comfort; nothing diminishes the guilt I still feel.

I read recently reports of a speech by Salman Rushdie, author of *Shame* and *Midnight's Children*, which summed up this period for our country. He said:

> We live in an age in which the people who control history, who control reality, are increasingly telling lies about it. Politicians have understood it. In order to control the future, it is necessary to control the past. And it is the people who control the memories of nations that control its destiny. When Mrs Gandhi says there was no forced sterilisation programme, then simply an act of memory becomes a political statement … So we find memory politicised in an age when controls tamper with history. So fiction become truth, while politicians tell us lies.

What will be recorded? Answer me this: did the government ever ask the New Zealand Rugby Football Union NZRFU to stop the tour? Or more to the point: did the government actually oppose the tour?

And I learned of another way in which I was seen by the men I worked with, neatly summarized by Doris Lessing in an interview about Zimbabwe in 1980:

> There are always a few mad people screaming 'For God's sake, look, this is what's going to happen!' They got put into concentration camps or ignored or treated as we were treated, a sort of humourless patronage: 'Oh, listen to them.' I mean, there are many different ways of dealing with minority opinions. It's often just as effective to treat people with indulgence as it is to put them in concentration camps, you know. If the object is to silence people there are many different ways of doing it.

The government wins the 1981 election with a majority of one. Most of my colleagues are fearful to be politicians. But what are they doing here if they have never contemplated the possibility that it may have to

be their solitary vote that changes the course of something? Isn't anything that important to them? Oh, I know only too well how one
wishes it was somebody else in that position exercising 'power' you
don't seek or want to have. It occurs to me that wars may even have
been averted if one or two more men had been prepared to do their job
rather than secure a political future.

There is another abortion debate, and now there are eight women in
Parliament who work together. I have been joined on the government
side now by Ruth, who unburdens me, and is, a skilful woman warrior.
She confesses her realization that my reports of the battlefield, which
she has heard with some scepticism, were always understated.

We watch our six sisters across the House, feeling with them as they
quietly leave the chamber when their Palmerston North colleague
launches an attack on the domestic protection legislation; as their colleague from Porirua downs all forms of childcare facilities. (You will
not find these speeches in Hansard: members learned a long time ago
to save their most pernicious remarks for the unreported committee
stages of legislation and estimates.) And I wonder how much longer
the women opposite will be prepared to have their independence,
good sense – certainly their feminist consciousness – shackled by the
ludicrous caucus rule that states: 'If elected, I will vote on all questions
in accordance with the decisions of the caucus of the Parliamentary
Labour Party.' We will cheer mightily the day they say 'to hell with it!'
and don't look for a conscience-vote cop-out.

I want to tell you that male parliamentarians are not unfeeling: I have
seen them weep during debates on abortion and adoption, and with horror in recognition of the reality and depth of domestic violence. They
weep in greater numbers, however, in saying farewell to Parliament. You
will not know this: such incidents are not news, and 'weakness' on the
part of the patriarchs must not be revealed to you. My electorate executive don't like it if I am reported to have wept; or to have acted on my
conscience in the abortion debates; or to have carried out party policy to
oppose the racist Springbok tour; or to have asked for constructive
implementation of our policies on nuclear arms: they must suffer the
tedious and arrogant letters of other National Party electorate executives
'disapproving of' or 'condemning' the Member of Parliament for Waipa.

I wonder how many such letters are sent to the electorate executives
of alcoholics or adulterers – but I forget – that's 'normal' behaviour and
we all understand that doesn't cost votes. It's just thinking and feeling
and researching and honesty that cause so much trouble.

There have always been moments of comfort – supportive words on the street, kind letters, some real people who work in Parliament Buildings and, having no games to play, become touchstones for sanity: librarians, messengers, secretary-typists, catering staff. There are those who bring flowers and those who are, unasked for and so welcome, at my door when I need them. There have been, too, colleagues who would bring me water when my voice broke, handkerchiefs when I wept, who would shift from their allocated seats in the House to sit close to me and quietly talk me through the speeches I found most difficult to deliver, whose quiet simple notes and reassuring phone calls I have cared for and needed.

There have been few moments of open laughter, few events I found good-naturedly funny. There is always wry humour (where if you didn't laugh you'd cry), such as reading an interview with Helen Caldicott – Australian physician and outspoken anti-nuclear advocate – in the *Listener* of 21 May 1983, where she speaks of missile sizes and phallic envy, and recalling a recent Disarmament and Arms Control Select Committee meeting where a colleague, armed with a United States Information Service publication, points to the central spread featuring a Soviet submarine, and is utterly consumed with its size and its weight – 'Look at it, look at how big it is!' Who cares? I wonder, when the Trident can carry more nuclear-headed missiles and fire them with more accuracy. (By the way, have you noticed the shape of every war memorial – in fact, all memorials to famous men? I don't suppose they even notice how perversely obsessed with that shape their world is.)

Then there is the omnipresent 'boys' brand of humour, delivered over the tables at Bellamy's, now drawn together in one long line in the Members Only dining room, so that they can still all pretend they're prefects at boys' boarding school and act in much the same way. Lunch can be a gross experience.

MP No. 1: How can you legislate against rape in marriage? It couldn't be implemented.

MP No. 2: That's not the point – why should you be able to rape your wife in the bedroom but not beat her up in the kitchen?

MP No. 3: Then beat her up in the bedroom and rape her in the kitchen!

Honourable Members: Ha ha ha.

On such occasions I feel invisible – and ill. Our invisibility runs to every policy area, and is of far greater depth and significance than our utterly disproportionate representation everywhere (except in parenting, of course).

I have lodged more than one thousand questions to ministers in the House in nine years: most bear no fruit.

The Minister of Social Welfare replies: 'There is no known figure which can provide an estimate of the number of children in unsupervised day-care situations on an average weekday.'

The Minister of State Services replies: 'There are approximately 2000 cleaners and 700 tea attendants employed as short-hours wage-workers. It is thought that those employees are predominantly female. No precise details are available.'

The Minister of Statistics replies:

> The specific exclusions [from the New Zealand System of National Accounts] are those activities taking place within the household sector whose products are seldom or never marketed, e.g., services of housewives and household maintenance ...
>
> [These non-market activities] are relatively unimportant in a developed economy.

There will be those who will say this is a bitter letter. They will be the same people who have been confused by a lack of personal ambition in office. You will know otherwise: from the beginning the issues have been paramount – and utterly simple. I write to report to you, and you will know I have hardly scratched the surface.

Perhaps one day I will be free to write again, but for now there are women to be appointed to statutory boards and commissions, rural maternity hospitals to keep open, rape laws to be changed, voluntary and (unpaid) housework to be included in the census, a select committee report on disarmament and arms control to table, some (any?) progress to make on childcare ...

I don't believe we shall ever be finished.

In sisterhood, and with heartfelt thanks,
Marilyn

I did not expect my male colleagues to pay a great deal of attention to this letter. Yet three weeks after its publication, the prime minister quoted (reasonably accurately) large chunks of it as he abused me in the Government Whips Office, the night he decided on a snap election in 1984. Between his commentaries he

*would bark at his Chief Whip (and recent Commonwealth Secretary General)
Don McKinnon 'We don't behave like that do we Don?' and McKinnon would
dutifully respond 'No Prime Minister.'*

4 The 'Pacific' Region

*In January 2006 I received a package in the mail from France. It contained a
small book* Voix Rebelles du Monde *edited by the French NGO ATTAC.
The book contained texts on twenty-six different personalities who Susan
George – former vice-president of ATTAC – described as being people 'who
have tried to live honourably in the circumstances of the place and time in
which they have found themselves'. I knew many of these names, and I
was enormously honoured to find mine among them. But then ATTAC asked
each of us to contribute to their next publication. The question was: 'From
the viewpoint of your continent, your region, your country, with its own
characteristic problems, how do you see the world in 2015?' I come from the
South Pacific, but in my lifetime I have tired of people from New Zealand and
Australia being deemed to 'represent' the Pacific. What this also means though,
is that most places I go, no one knows anything about the South Pacific. So I
chose to use my space to write about the political economy of this region.*

I live in Aotearoa/New Zealand, and my life has been a reaction to and
reflection of the issues of my country and the South Pacific region, and
the Antarctic. Yet most of my northern hemisphere friends, who know
of Australia and have read of 'getaway' south-sea-island holidays such
as those in New Caledonia, have never heard of many of the states and
territories that I think of as my neighbours: the Cook Islands, Fiji,
French Polynesia, Guam, Kiribati, Marshall Islands, Federated States of
Micronesia (FSM), Nuie, New Caledonia, Palau, Papua New Guinea,
Pitcairn Island, Samoa, American Samoa, Solomon Islands, Tokelau,
Tonga, Tuvalu, Vanuatu, and the Wallis and Futuna Islands.

When I look south to the Antarctic continent. I think immediately of
ozone depletion and the increasing hole in the ozone layer, affecting
food chains and increasing risks of skin cancers for all people and ani-
mal species. The escalating numbers of massive icebergs breaking free
from this continent demonstrate the steadily rising temperatures
warming the Antarctic region. Glaciers in the West Antarctic are now

losing 60 per cent more ice into the Amundsen Sea than they accumulate from inland snowfall, all part of the outcomes in the chain reaction to global warming.

When I look south, I am reminded of the hunting and killing of whales by the Japanese in the great Southern Ocean. I remember that the Antarctic Treaty of 1959 effectively created the world's first nuclear and military free region. While coal, hydrocarbons, iron ore, platinum, copper, chromium, nickel, and gold are among the minerals found thus far on the continent, the 1991 Protocol on Environmental Protection to the Antarctic Treaty currently prevents a struggle for resources. In 1998 a compromise agreement was reached to add a fifty-year ban on mining until the year 2048, further limiting economic development and exploitation. By 2015, I expect to see countries with no relationship at all to Antarctica, recruited to the Treaty Organisation to assist with votes to overturn this ban.

From where I stand, when I look north, I see the Pacific Ocean covering one-third of the earth's surface, with a small population of less than ten million people. Only 500 of its 7,500 islands are inhabited. The size and proximity of this ocean means that those of us who live here are aware that environmental developments in the South Pacific will have a significant global impact on the world's fisheries and on climate change. The use of our region as a nuclear testing ground, by the United Kingdom, the U.S. and France, still results in health and environmental issues for the population. Yet this abuse also gave rise to one of the Pacific's prouder moments, the declaration of the world's first populated Nuclear Free Zone.

Students of colonial history will recognize names of the former colonies of the United Kingdom and France among the countries of the South Pacific. The UK has largely withdrawn, closing many diplomatic posts in 2004–5, including those in Vanuatu, Tonga, and Kiribati. The French are expected to leave New Caledonia inside the next fifteen years, although there are strategic nickel resource claims to be negotiated, and the rights of the Kanaky people to be fully recognized. The United States does not have a significant presence in the South Pacific, apart from American Samoa and in rehabilitation efforts after cyclones, but sovereignty issues and indigenous claims for the results of nuclear testing are outstanding in the North.

To the north-west we have West Papua (which some of you may know as Irian Jaya. In 1962 talks between the Dutch, the U.S., and Indonesia agreed to put West Papua under UN administration pending a poll on independence. This was never held. In 1969 Indonesia took over and changed the name to Irian Jaya.) This is an island of genocide, where Indonesia continues a tyrannical rule. When the Netherlands sought to withdraw, the U.S. opposed independence. One thousand men were lined up in place of a plebiscite and threatened with death if they did not agree to occupation by the Indonesians. They agreed. The occupation continues. In March 2006, Australia gave refugee status to forty-two West Papuans who arrived in a traditional canoe protesting the genocide. In context you should understand that it was almost impossible under the Howard government (1966–2007) to qualify as a refugee in Australia, so to do so your case had to be pretty clear-cut.

There are a couple of things that are special about the situation in West Papua. One is that the genocide has particularly targeted the older people: tribal leaders who were the guardians and teachers of language, culture, dance, stories, and song. The Indonesian military and their recruits have understood that these treasures were more powerful than young men with guns, and have systematically 'culled' with this in mind. Human rights groups suggest that around 100,000 Papuans have been killed by Indonesia; the armed forces have bombed, napalmed, and strafed tribal villages and tortured and murdered the people.

The other feature of dealing with the Indonesians that is important to understand is what the programs of 'transmigration' have meant. For decades, funded by the Asian Development Bank (ADB) and the Japanese International Cooperation Agency (JICA) amongst others, these schemes have forcibly rounded up people from Java, in particular, and transhipped them off to Timor, West Papua, or Aceh. The government has said this is to relieve overpopulation on Java, but the schemes have been politically motivated to attempt to get sufficient Javanese in these areas so that when a plebiscite on independence is held, the majority will vote to remain as part of Indonesia. But this approach didn't work in East Timor, largely because the transmigrated men usually left as soon as they could, and projects for agriculture or income generation were cynically meagre and badly managed. Timor Leste was invaded by Indonesia in 1975, as the Portuguese colonizers began to withdraw. Timor was occupied with violence and brutal murderous tactics until 1999, when the United Nations – supported referenda delivered an overwhelming vote for independence. Pro-Indonesian militia remained and continued the violence until peacekeepers and a UN transitional authority were established. Once the independence day celebrations were held in 2002, the international community withdrew their projects, programs,

and people and moved on to the next 'trouble' spot, severely undermining the capacity and sustainability of the non-government organizations,
whose on going activities were absolutely vital at that point in the new
state's development.

Early in 2006, to the east of West Papua, Dili, the capital of East
Timor, was in flames, and another international peacekeeping force
was hastily assembled. Timor has enormous gas and oil reserves, yet it
is the lowest-ranked country on the United Nations human development index.

These two sad histories and the current violence introduce both Portugal and the Netherlands into the list of regional colonizers, and help
to explain why the European Union (EU) has recently promoted a
Pacific Strategy.

In Papua New Guinea reports indicate that 2 per cent of the adult
population (i.e., about 100,000) are likely to be infected with the HIV/
AIDS virus. The world's first refugees officially evacuated because of
climate change have come from the Carteret Atolls in Papua New
Guinea. Ten families at a time were moved to Bougainville over 2006–7.
The six Carteret Atolls will be submerged by 2015. The Carterets will
join many other Pacific Islands that are on the point of being uninhabit-
able, including Tuvalu, much of Kiribati, and the Marshall Islands. A
Canadian multinational company, Nautilus Minerals Inc., has gained a
license to mine gold off the coast of Papua New Guinea. The mining
will target huge mineral rich deposits around sea-bottom volcanic gey-
sers. Nautilus is also licensed to prospect in the national waters of
Tonga, Fiji, and the Solomon Islands.

The past decades have been far from peaceful in this 'Pacific' region.
The first coup in Fiji occurred in 1987, with an overthrow of the elected
government of Timoci Bavadra. Bavadra's party was generally supported by the Indo Fijian community, which was 49 per cent of the
population, compared to 46 per cent of the indigenous Fijian population. Originally indentured labourers, the Indo Fijian community occupied many of the professional and business positions in the economy.
This coup led to a new constitution, in which the offices of the president and the prime minister, two thirds of the Senate, the majority of
the House of Representatives, and 50 per cent of the judiciary, were
reserved for ethnic Fijians. This racist constitution was subsequently
revised in 1997, but because so many Indo Fijian people had emi-
grated, indigenous Fijians were the largest group in the population
after 1994.

After the parliamentary elections of May 1999, a people's coalition took power, bringing the first Indo-Fijian prime minister, Mahendra Chaudhary, into office. This time the coup leaders were civilians who were no longer profiting from government contracts. They took over the Parliament and held members of the governing cabinet and parties at gunpoint for over fifty days. The 1999 election had also resulted in eleven women winning seats in Parliament, and most were in the governing party. Fifteen years later, when I met and talked to the women held, they were still traumatized by this experience.

The Solomon Islands have been a mess for some years. Here, 'militants teamed up with corrupt politicians, police officers, and public servants to commit crimes and extort millions of dollars from the Government in the guise of the local custom of compensation.'[22] Between 1996 and 2001, exports declined 60 per cent. By mid-2003, the country's debt was registered at AUS$352 million, more than three times the country's annual budget. The governor of the Central Bank, Rick Hou, issued a statement reporting that since 1999 the government had defaulted on all interest as well as some principal payments, and it had failed to bring spending under control. The Central Bank described 'a fall in incomes, increased unemployment and widespread poverty and a poor delivery of social services, particularly in the education and health sectors.'[23] Government employees were regularly either paid late or not paid at all.

As a result, the situation in Honiara was little short of a civil war. A team of brave women worked together to visit the dugout lines of warring parties in the trenches, and began the move for peace. The peace talks, hosted by the Australian government, were held on board a naval frigate anchored off the coast. No women were invited to the talks. A Pacific Regional Assistance Mission to the Solomon Islands (RAMSI) moved in to help restore order and to get the government working again.

But their presence did nothing to stop major violence following the elections in mid-April 2006, fuelled by the chequebook diplomacy warfare being waged in the Solomons by China and Taiwan. Mobs rampaged through Honiara and burned down the historic Chinatown

---

22 Tarcisius Tara Kabutaulaka, 'Australian Foreign Policy and the RAMSI Intervention in the Solomon Islands,' *Contemporary Pacific* 17, no. 2 (2005), n.p.
23 Ibid., n.p.

district, incensed by the appointment of a new prime minister they regarded as being in the pocket of the Taiwanese. Hundreds of millions of dollars in kickbacks had taken place in recognition of Taiwan rather than the Peoples Republic of China. Taiwanese officials were known to have briefcases full of dollars which they dished out to government leaders. In 2000 the Government of the Solomons asked the Government of Taiwan for U.S.$150 million to preserve diplomatic relationships.

An audit conducted in 2006 by Australian officials found that at least AUS$18 million received from Taiwanese, Chinese, and South Koreans, in return for forestry and fishing concessions, had gone missing from the Solomon Island's government's national coffers in just two years.

The New Colonizers

The tussle between Taiwan and Mainland China has led to instability in Vanuatu, Papua New Guinea, Kiribati, Tuvalu, and Nauru. So far, since establishing formal relations with Fiji and Samoa in 1975, China has Papua New Guinea, the Cook Islands, Vanuatu, the Federated States of Micronesia, and Tonga onside. Taiwan has 'bought' Kiribati and Nauru from Beijing, and also has the Marshall Islands, Palau, the Solomon Islands, and Tuvalu in its pocket.

The activities of the Chinese are of special importance. They have built a parliamentary complex in Vanuatu, government offices in Samoa, a courthouse and police headquarters in the Cook Islands, a sports stadium for the 2003 South Pacific Games in Fiji, and supplied the VIP car fleets for states hosting the Pacific Islands Forum. They are not 'donors' in the ordinary way. Typically, they will bring the entire workforce from Mainland China, build a perimeter fence around the housing, bring in their own chefs, their own food, work in shifts for twenty-four hours a days for six days a week, complying with great reluctance with the need for there to be a day of rest on Sunday to recognize the Christian church's expectations in most Pacific states.

Chinese projects fail to comply with best-practise building standards. Several cartoons in the Cook Islands' dailies showed a courthouse that had no access for elderly or disabled persons. Even I observed that the glass used in the windows of the courthouse is thinner than it should be and, therefore, likely to blow out in the next cyclone. All internal signs are in the Chinese language.

In early April 2006, Chinese premier Wen Jia Bao held a meeting in Fiji for the First China Pacific Island Countries Economic Development

and Cooperation Forum. Wen's Fijian visit was the first by a Chinese
premier to the region and was an indicator of how seriously his nation
plays the game. (When the prime minister of the Cook Islands, population 20,000, Dr Robert Woonton, was greeted in Beijing in 2004, he was
met at the Great Hall of the People, had a nineteen-gun salute, and the
flags of his country circled Tiananmen Square.) Wen delivered loans
totalling ¥3 billion, removed import tariffs, cancelled debt for the poorest, promised to provide free malaria medicines to countries,[24] and
added Papua New Guinea, Samoa, and the Federated States of Micronesia to the list of destinations Chinese tourists were allowed to visit.
All countries that recognized Taiwan were excluded from these measures. The Foreign Affairs Department in Australia has commented:
'We see chequebook diplomacy as directly undermining the efforts (to
improve living standards, good government and political stability)
that we have made over many years.'[25] It will be very interesting to
watch Australia watching China, as Australia has just agreed to the
sale of billions of dollars of uranium to China, and Beijing has promised a free trade agreement with Australia within two years.

Japan remains one of the Pacific's top three aid donors. At a meeting
of Pacific leaders in Tokyo in late May 2006, the Japanese government
promised fresh aid of about U.S.$630 million over three years to the
Pacific region. The money was pledged in exchange for Pacific support
for Japan's bid to win a permanent seat on the UN Security Council,
and to gain the votes of Pacific members of the international whaling
forum to enable Japanese killing of whales. It was also seen as a bid to
increase Japanese influence in the region. As a result, Kiribati, Tuvalu,
the Solomon Islands, Palau, and the Marshall Islands (the Taiwan
camp of countries) supported a vote for a pro-whaling agenda at the
2006 meeting of the International Whaling Commission.

In May 2006, the European Union launched a formal Pacific strategy
that the twenty-five-member-state Union has committed to. The key
strategic goals were building stronger political relations on interests of
common concern such as global political security, trade and development, focusing development cooperation on areas of important Pacific
need such as sustainable natural resource management, and increasing

---

24 Recent reports in the *Guardian Weekly* are that Chinese malarial medicines are causing
     chaos in Africa because they don't work.
25 Unpublished briefing papers.

aid efficiency, including better cooperation between donors. The European Union injected about U.S.$4 billion into Pacific aid between 1975 and 2005, and a new five-year funding package began in 2008. The 2004 figures showed, that when combined with the additional donations from member states, the European Union was the second biggest financial contributor to the Pacific after Australia, which injects over AUS$700 million a year.

New Zealand spent NZD$173 million in the 2005–6 financial year in aid to the Pacific, more than half its total aid budget. A quick brush over multi- and bilateral programs sees engagement in poverty assessments, education, revenue collection and government financial systems improvement, customs, statistics, quarantine, services to private enterprises, insurance, micro-credit investment and regulatory environments, policing, tourism, health, trade, governance, environment, justice, human rights and security – and that's just the start.

Since 1981, Australia and New Zealand have offered non-reciprocal duty-free and unrestricted or concessional access to all products originating from islands belonging to the South Pacific Forum. The generally poor economic performance is linked to a lack of opportunities for diversification and industrialization as well as relative isolation from markets. There is a lack of interest on the part of private investors. The net private capital and total capital flow in the Pacific Islands remains at less than 50 per cent of the total with official development assistance filling in the remaining part. Remittances from migrant workers have tripled to the equivalent of NZD$558 million in the past ten years, with 42 per cent of Tonga's gross domestic product and 26 per cent of Samoa's GDP coming from this single channel. Western Union, and the region's two largest commercial banks, Westpac and the ANZ, have been extracting between 15 and 20 per cent of remittances sent from Australia and New Zealand on every transmission.

Christian churches have to be included in any list of old and new colonizers in the Pacific. Pacific cultures were colonized by Christianity in the nineteenth century. Today, remittances to the Pacific countries from some Pacific Islanders abroad are frequently paid directly to church-building funds as villages compete to build larger churches than their neighbours. Having the biggest church is now the 'big man' indicator. In much of the Pacific, where land is owned communally and cannot be sold to foreigners, churches have exploited this situation. On the ride from the airport in Kiribati into Tarawa one passes and observes church after church after church, representing both the old and the new fundamentalist Christian types. The churches are extremely sexist. Many, for example, those in the Solomon Islands, will not allow women to train for ordination. Churches have been a major problem in human rights advocacy work to condemn domestic violence, as they frequently use Old Testament justifications around this issue. Some are very homophobic, and in general have not been useful in the education activities around HIV/AIDS. Yet the exceptional, courageous Pacific women who emerge as peacemakers and leaders are often committed Christians.

My large neighbour, Australia, is seen as the regional policeman, operating in the Pacific in the male style of a male-dominated region.

A Male-Dominated Region

In terms of propensity to use bribes, moves by Transparency International to establish an international corruption index show China leading over South Korea (in fishing and forestry in the region, for example), Taiwan, then Italy and Malaysia followed by Japan. We are pretty surrounded in this region by the best in the business. The bribes buy the votes of the male politicians, and support the election campaigns of those politicians.

So it's not surprising that political representation from women in the Pacific is second only to the Gulf region as the worst in the world, and if the figures for the New Zealand (32 per cent) and Australian Parliaments (24 per cent and Senate 35 per cent) are removed, the figures are worse than the parliamentary representation of women in the Arab region. The Pacific representation in Parliament for women/men is as follows: Fiji, 8/71; Kiribati, 2/42; Samoa, 2/49; Vanuatu, 2/52; Tonga, 1/30; the Marshall Islands, 1/33; Papua New Guinea, 1/109; there are no women representatives in the Parliaments of Micronesia, Nauru, Palau, Tuvalu, and the Solomon Islands[26] (four out of the six in the Taiwanese camp). The nature of democracy is such that Pacific politicians change sides to change the nature of government, generally based on who is paying the most.

When the UNIFEM Survey asked women Pacific politicians whether they were expected to find money to buy the support of key figures, only three replied in the affirmative. But 61 per cent expected to

---

26 See www.ipu.org/wmn-e/classif.htm.

finance community festivities. Some of these expectations included paying for coffins; malang donations to bride prices; covering the cost of guides, carriers, cooks, school fees, food, alcohol, community celebration, and donating to churches. Forty-four per cent noted that the church expected donations during the campaign process. Almost a quarter, (22 per cent) were expected to buy alcohol for constituents during a campaign.

Women in the Pacific survey were reluctant to enter politics because of the societal perception that politics was a male domain. They were deterred by the prevalent or threatened violence in elections; the nepotism, monetarism, and corruption of politics; the intimidation of voters; the character assassination; and the sexual harassment of women politicians. The prevailing male-dominated political environment of confrontation, harsh competition, closed male networks, need for financial resources for election expenses, and excessively long hours of work, constituted additional barriers to women's participation in politics.

In the many parts of the Pacific, mainstream market economics, (the imposed notion of) nation states, churches and traditional protection systems have broken down. Women are increasingly vulnerable to the criminality and levels of violence in communities, supported by the spread of small arms. Violence is endemic. I was spending some time with a woman politician in the islands recently, and she was asking me for alternative strategies to highlight the rates of domestic violence. I suggested that the staff at the admissions desk in the public hospital be asked to begin a register and to automatically call the police when a domestic violence victim presents for care. She looked at me in a strange way and didn't respond. I found out, subsequently, that her own name would be on the list several times a year. The more common response to cases of domestic violence in the Pacific is the phrase 'She has had a bad fish day.' Before racing off to measure toxicity levels, which you are tempted to do because there do seem to be a lot of bad fish about, you need to understand that 'she ate some bad fish' is a metaphor, and she will have recovered when the bruises are not so obvious.

Much of the political economy of the Pacific is redolent with corruption, violence, and hypocrisy. It is an extraordinary challenge to feminist activists.

As you can see, I continue to live in a region where the national income accounting framework doesn't have much to say about well-being. In many countries, the statistics office is one man driving a desk in the planning or finance ministry, waiting for the next multilateral project to conduct the next required Census, or labour market survey, or at this point, the money from the Asian Development Bank to monitor the Millennium Development goals.

Yet substantial numbers of Pacific island people live healthy lives in a subsistence and barter economy. For much of the Pacific, traditional communal ownership of land continues to sustain families as it has for centuries. Generally, the word 'poverty' is deemed inappropriate and the word 'hardship' is preferred to describe a lack of access to basic needs, unequal access to basic services – especially to health and educational services, a lack of opportunity for training, poverty of opportunity, vulnerability to poverty and being 'in need.' This kind of poverty results in youth unemployment, internal disorder, internal migration, external migration, and loss of key personnel from critical sectors, an erosion of the ability to deliver services, and a lack of connectivity between local and central government. With the globalization of services, the Pacific becomes a recruiting ground for health and education professionals, and poverty of skilled human resources becomes a major problem. In many cases, it is hard for a country to retain just one competent doctor.

While data for the Pacific Island countries is incomplete, what is available suggests that the incidence of 'traditional poverty' is rising, along with a prevalence of underweight children and an increasing number of malnourished children. In addition to estimates of 100,000 HIV/AIDS cases in Papua New Guinea, Fiji, and Tuvalu also have high numbers of reported cases. Numbers are also increasing in other parts of the Pacific. Stretched health care systems mean that the burden imposed by just a few cases of HIV/AIDS is significant. I expect, in a very seafaring part of the world, that the numbers are far more extensive than is ever acknowledged. But on my visit to the Solomon Islands in 2005, the private secretary of the Ministry of Health, who is himself a medical doctor, advised me that there was no HIV in the Solomon Islands. (It reminded me of the delegate from the USSR, who insisted, at the Mid Decade Conference for Women in Copenhagen in 1980, that there was no wife beating in the Soviet Union. This had to be footnoted in the document.)

The Environmental Exploitation

Most of the 'growth' recorded in the guestimates of the GDP statistics of Pacific island states will be driven by environmental exploitation.

Minerals are exported from Papua New Guinea, New Caledonia, and Nauru. One of the characteristic of mines in Papua New Guinea is that the tailings dams are unreliable because of the region's unstable geology. Tailings are, therefore, discharged into river systems. In a number of countries, coral from the reefs is mined for road construction.

In the Solomon Islands, the rate of logging for the past ten years has been unsustainable. At current rates of exploitation, all accessible forests will have been logged within the next five years. In Papua New Guinea, forests administration is notoriously corrupt and forestry operations have been badly managed. Logging is often carried out in an unregulated manner, precluding forest recovery. In Vanuatu, logging escalated at such an unsustainable rate that in the early 1990s the government established a ban on log exports and exports are now exclusively in the form of sawn timber.[27]

Marine resource exports are focused on tuna, which generate the largest flow of receipts and constitute a major or even the main source of government revenues in small atoll states. The bulk of the tuna catches are by foreign fleets that ship them to the canneries of southeast Asia or American Samoa, or in the case of longline fisheries, directly to the markets in Japan. As a result of over-exploitation, there is a major depreciation in stocks of bigeye tuna.

Renewable resources are also the direct source of subsistence for large proportions of the rural populations of these three countries. In the subsistence economy, there is a reliance on inshore fish stocks for basic health, but the export of live fish and the aquarium trade are depleting inshore fish stocks. The inshore fish stocks are the key nutritional component to island diets. I remember visiting Kiribati in the early 1980s. When I went to the primary school, there was a clearly visible and distinguished change in the physical size of students in the younger classes. There was no secret about the explanation. These children had been born after independence, after the establishment of the first naval school for Kiribati men that trained them to work on the international fishing vessels coming to exploit the 200-mile Economic Exclusion Zone (EEZ). Their absence meant that there was an immediate change in the amount of inshore

---

27 Colin Hunt, 'Economic Globalisation Impacts on Pacific Island Environments and Implications,' in C. Tisdell and R.K. Sen, eds., *Economic Globalisation: Social Conflict Labour and Environmental Issues* (Cheltenham, UK: Edward Elgar, 2003).

subsistence fishing carried out, and a diminution in the protein in children's diets. The consequence was an outbreak of rickets, which was clearly noticeable.

This is a region that was thought of for so long as being resource poor. One consequence of this neglect has been the survival of rich cultures of stories, dance, song, ritual, navigation, and a range of skills for survival after cyclones – none of which is visible in any of the state's systems of measuring wealth, income, or well-being. It's also a region where it was the twenty-first century before many Pacific island nations were finally assisted so that they had their own curricula in primary schools: their own language, geography, history, arts, and literature.

Now, many of you might have thought that the end of forestry resources and overfishing might have brought an end to the rape and pillage of the environmental resources of the region. Stand by for more. Australian companies are chasing nickel and gold in the Solomon Islands. In the waters off the Cook Islands, for example, there are abundant reserves of manganese modules and other rare minerals such as zirconium, nicobiura, and yttrium, which are important in super conductivity. Technology advances for seabed harvesting 5 kilometres below the surface have been developed by the Japanese. The Norwegians and the Chinese have also been having discussions with the Cook Islands about the manganese. It is an enormous field, and raises the likelihood of deposits in much of the region. Nauru is boasting that it has offshore uranium deposits.

What if there are mineral deposits in offshore Tuvalu or Kiribati? Whose will they be? There is a strong possibility that these nation states will no longer be there by 2015. No one seems to want to talk about the rights of current nationals to the wealth of Tuvalu or Kiribati when global warming has forced the complete abandonment of the nation state. Who will have the rights to the 200-mile EEZ for example, or to any mineral deposits on the seabed?

Towards 2015

One of the prospects for 2015 is that parts or the whole of these South Pacific countries will simply be strips of coral for Western or Chinese holidaymakers.

Stephen Hoadley has pointed to ethnic tension and crime in Papua New Guinea, near bankruptcy in Nauru, police and outer island discontent in Vanuatu, ethnic discrimination and political tension in Fiji, suppression of the press and democracy in Tonga, and Kanak independence aims in New Caledonia as potential future sources of discord in the region.[28]

Discussions of the present and future of the Pacific island nations frequently uses the failed state discourse. But some of these island nations have never been 'states' in the Fukuyama sense. T.T. Kabutaulaka argues that the state in the Solomon Islands has always shared and competed for control with other entities, including churches, non-government organizations, traditional political organizations and leaders, and special interest groups such as women's and youth organizations.[29] The state has often played a secondary role, but the nature of international law and agreements has meant that the state has depended on harnessing natural resources for its activities from lands and near-shore areas, which are owned by customary owners. Conservative think tanks like the Australian Strategic Policy Institute influenced the Howard government's foreign policies and urged policies such as individual land ownership titles. Solomon Islands commentators do not see the nature of ownership but the nature of leadership as the problem. Rick Hou, governor of the Central Bank, has reported that the country's economic problems could be attributed to the rottenness of leadership.

There's no question about a prevailing rottenness in an overwhelmingly male leadership, although the Tongan princess does her best to even the scales. It's all just too simplistic to seek to impose yet another cliché-ridden Western male solution here. For perfectly sound reasons, the Pacific still has significant barter as a form of trade and significant social capital for the survival of its skills, language, and culture. Many indicators of well-being fall outside the Western economic paradigm of values. These can also be in conflict with the nature of what is seen as the key principles undermining good states as opposed to failed states. Community ownership of land works perfectly well in many areas. The trouble begins when the outside exploiter enters the game and uses bribes to secure an individual title.

In 2015, the Pacific will look much the same, but more so. I'd love to be able to dream that this might all be different, that this expectation is

---

28 Centre for Strategic Studies, 'Pacific Island Security Management by New Zealand and Australia: Towards a New Paradigm' (Victoria University of Wellington, 2005), www.vuw.ac.nz/css/docs/Working Papers.
29 Kabutaulaka, 'Australian Foreign Policy and RAMSI Intervention in the Solomon Islands.'

just the imposition of a palagi (white) woman from outside the culture. But I don't think that will be the case.

Any possibility of change will be completely dependent on women. If gender equality was a focus, there would be opportunity for a transformation, where the practise of Pacific politics reflected Pacific values.

Pacific women are very threatening to men in the Pacific. The men come up with all the reasons we have been hearing since the first UN women's conference in 1975, about how destabilizing to their culture and way of life these Western feminist ideas are, as if these are novel words and as if we haven't heard them before from their brothers in every region. They stem from two fears: one, that they will be exposed and found out as the corrupt players they are, and two, that they think that women in power might be as abusive and retaliatory as the men have been. They can only think this because they have paid so little attention to what women have been thinking, saying, and doing all these years.

The final goal in the Pacific plan is that of security, calling for 'improved political and social conditions for stability and safety.' When I read through the names of the women from the Pacific region who were among those 1,000 peace women nominated for the 2005 Nobel Prize, they are the women who led the daily prayer vigils for the fifty-six days of the 2000 Fiji coup, the women who endured the civil war and blockade in Bougainville, who led the opposition to the Australian copper mine on the island, and who made a major contribution to the peacebuilding efforts. Don MacKinnon, Commonwealth Secretary General, told me when speaking of Bougainville, that 'the women made the peace.' There are women running 'centres for women and children' in Tonga (a euphemism because they cannot be called domestic violence refuges). There are women who stood between the warring factions in the Solomon Islands, none of whom were included in the peace talks held on an Australian frigate. There are women who have campaigned in the region all their lives against nuclear weapons, for indigenous peoples and indigenous rights, against nuclear waste dumps and nuclear testing. Women are AIDS/HIV activists, and activists for peace, social justice, conflict resolution, ecological justice, democracy, alternative energy, and the participation of women and girls in civil society.

Another Pacific region, a feminized Pacific, is possible, and that is what I dream of and work for.

Women of Influence

1 Crusader Bella

May 1985

I first met Bella Abzug in 1980 in Copenhagen, at the UN Mid-Decade Conference on Women. She was attending the NGO conference, advising the official U.S. delegation, from which she had been inexcusably excluded, and was 'stringing' as the interviewer at the conference for public service television stations in the United States.

Bella was born in July 1920, one month before women won the right to vote in the United States federal elections. After her years at Hunter College (the senior college of the City University of New York), she was turned down by Harvard Law School, which did not admit women, and she won a scholarship to Columbia University Law School in New York, specializing in labour and civil liberties law. Her early clients were Hollywood actors targeted by the McCarthy witch-hunts of the 1950s. She also took on the case of Willie McGee, a black man from Mississippi, who had had a long-term consensual relationship with a white woman. He was sentenced to death on a trumped-up rape charge. As McGee's defender, Bella was denied any hotel room, and spent the nights of his trial sleeping in a bus station. McGee was ultimately executed, and Bella was a campaigner against capital punishment for life.

In 1970, she was elected as one of only nine women in the 435-seat House of Representatives. Her first official act was to introduce a resolution calling on President Nixon to withdraw all U.S. forces from the Vietnam War. Bella ran unsuccessfully for the Senate in 1976, and did not win a campaign for public office after that time.

I was to meet her and work with her many times over the next decades, and enjoy her intelligence, her wit, and her politics. One such meeting was in Houston in 1985 at the Wise Women's Council, which was in the nature of an unofficial preparation for the UN Women's Conference to be held in Nairobi, Kenya, later that year. We had been brought together by an activist philanthropist, Gen Vaughan, who was to finance the peace tent at the NGO conference in Nairobi. I was always in awe of Bella's rhetoric: she was never 'casual' in her speech. Even among friends – as we all were at that time – her ideas emerged so measured and precise as if a galley of speechwriters had been on the job for

days. One day while she was talking at the conference, I took some notes
and wrote the following portrait:

> Peace is a condition in which dominant institutions, hierarchies, and rela-
> tionships are stripped of all tools and weapons of force and violence
> through a process which alters fundamental orientation and history by
> requiring equal decision-making by men and women with the goal of
> achieving political, economic, social, and personal perspectives, funda-
> mentally committed and resolving all needs, differences, and disputes by
> standards of equity and pacific resolve.

Bella, now in her sixties, is unlike most American political figures. She
has been consistent in style throughout her life and is continually wid-
ening and deepening her radicalism.

As a teenager, she was student president of Hunter College, involved
in the support of staff under investigation for anti-American activities.
She completed Law school, and old film sequences show her as one of
the council for the Rosenbergs. She was, and is, an attorney who took all
the wrong cases for the right reasons – the early race discrimination
cases, the early freedom of expression cases.

Bella was co-founder of the Coalition of Labour Women's Unions
and Women U.S.A. She was one of the founders of Women Strike for
Peace, of the National Women's Political Caucus, of the Congressional
Women's Caucus, and has been involved in the establishment of nearly
every major credible peace organization in the United States.

> The women's movement and the civil rights movement were reborn in
> response to the violence of the Vietnam War and the oppression we have
> in common. The feminist movement in the United States has been a major
> force in fighting against the social and economic problems affecting
> women of colour. There has been a great amount of consciousness on the
> part of feminist activists in America – they are well aware that none are
> equal unless all are. But we have not done enough towards having a
> greater discussion of the newer and deeper problems of colour.

Bella became a member of Congress in the early 1960s. She never fal-
tered in the practice of her politics – whether exposing the lies of the
war (and she did that) or marching in the streets for abortion rights or
the equal rights amendment. Her Mae West/Sophie Tucker voice
brought real hope. Former congressman and Senator John Culver told

me of the mornings that a certain number of signatures would have to be collected for a resolution, and members would arrive late. 'For God's sake ... where the hell have you been?' she'd say. 'Don't you realize one day there might be a revolution in the morning?'

She was voted the most effective member of Congress by her peers. She does not suffer fools gladly. She has no patience for self-defeating tactics however glamorous or seductive, and no patience with the self-conscious purism that is elitist. She respects power and the skills required to maintain it, and she has an enormous sense of humour, subtle but fair.

For the Houston Women's Convention in 1977 she received assurances of $5 million, without tags, from the administration to ensure its success. Because of her insistence, there was more minority participation than in any other gathering so far held in the United States. I remember that great line when she received the torch to open the convention: 'Some of us run with a torch and some of us run for office, but none of us run for cover.'

Former U.S. president Jimmy Carter appointed Bella co-chair of the National Panel of Women. She wanted the panel to be consulted on the budget, and she attacked the social cut-backs and the military budget. Cornered, Carter responded, 'These aren't women's issues,' and requested her resignation. Within twenty-four hours, all of the appointees on the panel resigned and were replaced by a presidential advisory group.

Now we sit together enjoying a Texan spring morning, only a few miles from NASA. The hat is on, the body is forward on the chair, the hands move with the ideas, the eyes are bright, and she sounds as if she is saying it all for the first time.

Women have never been inside the places of power, even after the suffrage movement, although they made a major impact in spite of that. For instance, they played a major role in securing the only major nuclear treaty ever to have been signed.

We have to show there are alternate ways of dealing with situations and alternate solutions to problems. We need to change stereotypical concepts. We must lead a crusade insisting that our voices be heard in all the major discussions on national security. To get other women to join us, we must have a platform revealing our ideas. And we must have it within our own government. We must create a National Security Council and a shadow cabinet to be side by side with them in comments, ideas ... in all

places where they meet to discuss war and peace. We must appear bearing a vehicle of hope and optimism. It would be a direct challenge.

There would be teams of spokeswomen, so that conceptually we would
break out of the bind of male power structures and patterns.

We must show the people that there are alternatives. We must let everyone know that we're going to fight for the leadership of this world.

Right on, Bella. But oh, what a tragedy it was for this world, and for
your country, that you were no longer in office there.

*Bella visited New Zealand in 1988 to participate in the filming of a television
series 'The Women's Summit' and to be a tourist. I have memories of her
swimming in the Pacific at Te Arai in late April, hanging laundry out on a
line in the fresh air for the first time, being besieged by goats as she carried the
'nut' bucket to them for treats.*

*In 1990, Bella was one of the founders of the Women's Environment and
Development Organization (WEDO). Once WEDO was registered as an
'official' NGO with the UN, Bella initiated the Women's Caucus. This drew
together women from all the disparate NGO groups to analyse documents,
propose gender sensitive policies and language, lobby for them, and at times to
transform them into a Women's Agenda for the Conference. Beginning with
just small meetings, this has grown to be a major part of the UN NGO presence, and is taken so seriously that official member states of the UN are frequently in attendance.*

*With a pacemaker, having survived a breast cancer operation, and with a
number of other ailments, Bella became a strong and loud activist for people
with disabilities as she continued her other work. Bella made her last speech at
the UN in New York on 3 March 1998, and entered hospital for heart surgery
the next day. She died there on 31 March 1998.*

2 Woman of the People

October 1985

*I met Maria de Lourdes Pintasilgo in Oslo in 1980. I clearly remember two
conceptual leaps I made in my knowledge listening to her. English was*

supposed to be my first language. But Maria spoke of 'pre-literate' women. 'I don't use the word "illiterate,"' she said, 'all women would read if they were given the chance.' And when we discussed the dynamics of power, I learned that power in and of itself was not the problem: power over was the problem, not power with or power to or power for. I haven't forgotten these treasures, and many more that I have learned from her since.

From all over the country, Portuguese people from all walks of life went to Lisbon on 27 July 1985. They went by plane, car, bus, and donkey cart. They went to hear a candidate launch a presidential election campaign.

Parliamentary elections were held in Portugal on 6 October. Presidential elections will be held in early January. The Portuguese constitution says the president can be a non-party candidate and can appoint the prime minister of his or her choice. Maria de Lourdes Pintasilgo will be the first presidential candidate without party backing, running against candidates from the Social Democrats, the Communist Party, the Christian Democrats, the Socialists, and the Democratic-Renovator Party.

The Portuguese external debt is currently U.S.$15,300 million, while the internal budget deficit is U.S.$2,000 million. The unemployment rate is 11 per cent, the inflation rate 29 per cent. The wages of more than 150,000 workers have not been paid for some months. Real wages have fallen by 20 per cent in the past two years.

Recently, newspapers have reported the collapse of coalitions in the current government. The party system is increasingly discredited, and instability is such that while the Communist and Socialist Parties vociferously oppose the independent candidacy, the army is standing back from the election hoping there will be no victory, no coalition, and a collapse during which it might re-establish supremacy.

Newspapers note this independent candidate has no known power base, 'only the people.' Polls in February recorded Mario Soares at 8 per cent; Freitas do Amaral at 11 per cent; and Maria de Lourdes Pintasilgo at 27 per cent. She doesn't have extraordinary rhetoric, just honesty, compassion, vision, and enormous common sense. On 27 July, Pintasilgo made these points to those at her campaign launch:

The future president should be independent.

The presidential office cannot be used for special benefits.

I shall never accept the parties' support in exchange for political favours.

Our country doesn't have to spend the rest of its life knocking at others' doors. (Neither the Socialists nor the Christian Democrats have any problem in becoming a U.S. satellite.)

Politics today is an art, science, and technique.

Politics cannot be a game of words between parties.

Portuguese politics have too many words and no action.

How can a country progress without a development plan?

There has been a lack of political will in the execution of the government programs.

The political system hasn't exhausted its possibilities.

The power doesn't exist for itself.

The next revision of the constitution should include a referendum.

To regionalize is to recognize that the reality of a country is multicentred.

My political attitude springs forth from the fact that I am a Christian.

The dedication to my neighbour (born from faith) is inseparable from intervention in social life.

You cannot govern if you remain in your office and don't listen to the people concerned.

These are not the empty words of someone who does not know what she is talking about. Born in 1930, Maria de Lourdes Pintasilgo graduated in chemical engineering and became a researcher at the Commission of Nuclear Energy. From 1954 to 1960, she was the project director for the Research and Development Department of the biggest industrial company in Portugal. From 1960 to 1969, she was coordinator of training and research programs, as well as pilot projects, in the fields of development and sociocultural action in Portugal and abroad, in the context of the international women's movement known as 'The Grail.' From 1970 to 1974, she was the chair of the Portuguese Interministerial Commission for Social Policy Concerning Women, and then became Secretary of State for Social Welfare until 1976.

De Lourdes was recalled from her post as Portuguese ambassador to UNESCO, where she served from 1976 to 1979, to become interim prime minister of the fifth constitutional government in 1979. She did not run for office in the elections that followed and has since served as adviser to the president.

In 1983, de Lourdes was invited to join the Interaction Council – an organization of former Western leaders of national states. Most former leaders are asked to join, and her colleagues included Edward Heath, Olaf Palme, Willy Brandt, and Malcolm Fraser.

I wanted you to know about Maria de Lourdes Pintasilgo and about that forthcoming election. I first met her in Oslo in 1980. At that and every subsequent meeting she has added profoundly to my knowledge and understanding of politics. I consider her one of the most extraordinary people I have met and a truly radical feminist. I wanted to tell you I thought her election to office might be one of the sanest, hopeful, and celebratory political events this planet could witness. Then I thought, you'll just think I've gone too far again. So I was overjoyed to find that a Portuguese compatriot of the candidate, Artur Portela, journalist and intellectual, had already done this.

He said:

It is true that there is newness in being a woman candidate in a state which has been for 800 years politically male ... But the content of the eventual candidacy of Maria de Lourdes Pintasilgo is something else. As is her image. As is her call. Maybe there will be the humanization of politics, the democratization of democracy ... Maybe there will be the rediscovery, in the old social and cultural Portuguese fabrics, of energies which are new or even anonymous in civic life ... MLP is a political, moral and cultural personality by herself. She has proved it. In what she has done. In what she has attempted. In the way she has exercised political power ...

It may be utopia at the reach of our hands, it may be the breadth not only trans-European but transcontinental, truly planetary ... It is very likely that there will be, in this candidacy, a unique meeting of simplicity and grandeur, of [the great modern poet] Pessoa's village and the whole world ...

Maria de Lourdes Pintasilgo won the primary election, and then the United States pumped U.S.$18 million into an Educational Trust Fund, and indirectly into the Soares campaign, and he emerged the victor. She continued as deputy chair of the Interaction Council, and spent several years as the chair of the UN University Wider Board. In 1993, she accepted the invitation to chair the Independent Commission on Population and Quality of Life. Its report was published as 'Caring for the Future – A Radical Agenda for Positive Change.'

In the preface, Pintasilgo wrote:

The common way of understanding linkages by adding two complementary terms – population and development, population and poverty – was scientifically limited and unsatisfying. The way out was for us to attempt to establish more concrete and partial correlations among all the elements that emerge in what is called population dynamics, to look from new angles at their interface, and to determine in each case 'the point of entry' into the matter.

This approach did not prove easy. I was going to discover how the mentality of specialisation remains widespread, and how it functions as a dike against new thinking, new ways of acting. Interdisciplinary knowledge, an inter-sectoral grasp of problems, integrated policies for action: these asked for a quantum leap forward.

Instead of the usual reliance on secondary research and the opinions of 'experts,' the Commission decided to conduct public hearings in each of seven regions. The 'people's voices' were to become the driving force for the Commission. Pintasilgo wrote:

Two practical lessons came from the hearings. The first was the level of integration at which policies and services made sense for both individuals and communities. Even in the most destitute areas, people do not wait for isolated, discrete actions to occur. They want to see together what they experience as a whole, whether stepping stone or impedance to a better quality of life.

The second was a warning signal. In all regions the Commission sensed a revolt against institutions that had come equipped with their own recipe for reducing the rates of population growth, and yet often failed to see the overall, interdependent conditions in which people lived.

Maria de Lourdes Pintasilgo also broke so many stereotypes: the stereotype of the scientist who is clinically detached, objective, concerned with validity and reliability was banished here. A devout Catholic, she was a supporter of women's reproductive freedom, and the 'rediscovery of a much broader expression of human sexuality.' She was comfortable running for office bearing the 'feminist' label. And she was the leader of a nation state, who never doubted for a moment that the people knew best.

Maria de Lourdes Pintasilgo died suddenly in 2004. In her lifetime she had been a general director, an ambassador, a Secretary of State, a minister, a Member of the European Parliament, and a prime minister. She had been

*called on to chair more fora of 'wise people' than anyone else I know. Her writ-
ing brought a feminist perspective to issues from economics to religion. She
was especially concerned that there be a dialogue about social rights and
equality in a participatory citizenship. When calling for the equal representation of women and men in elected office, she said: 'Parity democracy is not
simply one aspect of equality. It goes beyond this issue by offering women and
men a unique opportunity to face up to the question of identity as a key aspect
of the organization of society. It represents a newly emerging stage of democracy.' Maria de Lourdes Pintasilgo was the wisest woman I have ever met.*

3 An Advocate for African Women and Girls

June 1988

In 1988 when I was involved with the television series A Women's Summit,
*we were trying desperately to contact Phoebe Asiyo, Kenyan Member of Par-
liament, but without success. I turned to Chris Laidlaw, who was at the time
New Zealand's ambassador to Zimbabwe, to ask for help in getting in touch
with Ms Asiyo. I explained the concept for the television series, and he immediately suggested that we should be in touch with Gertrude Mongella from
Tanzania. And thus we met for the first time in Auckland. She told her story
in a quiet, lilting voice.*

I am Gertrude Mongella from Tanzania. I am married and I have three
sons, aged 18, 16, and 13. I was born on an island in Lake Victoria with a
population of about 170,000. I grew up there and went to primary school.
I was the second of four children. My father was a carpenter and participated a lot in the foundation of the political party. [Tanzania is a single-
party state.]

I was married in my second year of university, and had my first son in
the third year, so I was a wife, mother, and student. When I finished college, I started teacher-training. One day, after independence, there was a
meeting in the staffroom to form a branch of the party. I looked around
the room and thought that no one there was qualified to lead, so I stood
for the chair and won. In this way I started getting to know the experienced politicians in my district.

In 1975 some women leaders rang to ask if I would stand for the East African Legislative Assembly. This [body] comprised Tanzania, Kenya, and Uganda. My husband, who is now director of the national archives for Tanzania, encouraged my political participation. 'If you don't show the way, other women won't try,' he said. So ... I said yes, never expecting to go anywhere. But the party screened the names and I found myself a candidate. No one knew me. I was young and breastfeeding my third child. But I won, and had to go to the assembly in Nairobi.

In 1977 the East African Community broke up, but the party started to have confidence in me and I was appointed to the central committee of the party. In 1980 I was elected to the Tanzanian National Assembly, and two years later I was elected to the national executive of the party. There I proposed we adopt positive discrimination – a quota system so that we had a minimum number of seats for women. If we got more that would be good. Currently, we have 20 out of 200.

In 1987 I proposed the same principle of quotas for party elections, right down to branch level. Each branch had three delegates, but the old men were taking care of themselves and breeding discontent. So now, of the three delegates, one is a man, one is a woman, and one is from the youth section. Meanwhile, in 1982, I was appointed Minister of Women's Affairs and Regional Development, and later Youth and Culture. When I became Minister of Lands, Natural Resources, and Tourism, I banned the ivory trade. This was not easy. It's a corrupt international system.

When I entered politics, I had thought, You will behave like a lady. Men never forgive you if you don't behave like that. But I learned to be prepared to earn enemies or I'd be compromised. Before, most of the women who were in politics were divorcees, so it looked as if only women who had 'failed' went into politics. Don't forget the environment in which we women are operating. Men don't want to see intelligent women in politics, but I do think it's the less intelligent men who fight you.

There are now five out of the twenty-two cabinet ministers who are women. I am on the central committee of the party for my second term, but I am the only woman member out of fifteen.

I do relate to other women. We are used to being treated poorly, used to being submissive. In politics one can sometimes make enemies with other women: there can be divisions, if we are not careful, between educated and uneducated women. But I love to work with rural women. Their appreciation is so much more. The poor and the powerless need us more than anyone else.

The priorities I am working on are housing and immunization. Good vaccination programs are slow, but we'll target all children under five by the end of this year.

Sometimes I think that in Tanzania nothing concrete is done by men. The average Tanzanian woman walks approximately 7,000 kilometres a year carrying water. These women gather firewood, they have babies. If all of this was computed in something like horsepower, someone would do something about it. Do you think anyone here could help us?

In the days that followed our introduction, I watched and listened to Gertrude Mongella from Tanzania – at the *powhiri* (welcome) of the Maori Women's Welfare League, and during the production of a television series in which she participated. She met with ministers in Wellington, spoke with Tanzanian students, visited Rotorua, and had a full program of activities at secondary schools and polytechnics in Auckland. A gracious woman of quick intellect and a joyous sense of humour, she made many friends here. And women apparently divided by oceans, national boundaries, race, culture, religion, wealth, sexual preference, and age recognized in those meetings the language, experience, and wisdom that unites us all.

The meeting with Bella Abzug in New Zealand led to Gertrude Mongella's participation in WEDO. Her increasing political status on the world stage culminated in her appointment as UN Secretary General for the Beijing Women's Conference in 1995. She has also been Tanzania's ambassador to India and a UN Special Envoy on Women and Development. She has been an active member of the Global Board of Directors of The Hunger Project and a member of the OAU African Women's Committee on Peace and Development.

In 2000 she was the keynote speaker at the African Regional Conference on Women.

The Sixth Regional conference is an opportunity to candidly answer some basic questions on the advancement of the African women. Since we left Beijing: How much action has been taken to ensure that women and girl children enjoy their human rights? How many women have crossed the poverty line? To what extent have the obstacles been removed for the women to fully participate in public life and decision-making at all levels? To what extent has the level of violence against women dropped in our societies? How many new schools and health facilities have been put in place for the accessibility of the majority of women? How many women have managed to get an extra hour of sleep from the fourteen-hour working day?

In Dakar and Beijing the African women reminded the world of the need for peace. We all said loud and clear 'Enough is enough, Now!' How many women have died, have been raped, and have been displaced in those five years of old and new wars and armed conflicts? Have our voices on peace been louder than the sounds of a gun?

We cannot claim to have come close to the completion of our mission.

In 2007 I met Gertrude again in Uganda, when we were both at the meeting of the Commonwealth Ministers of Women's Affairs. She was the constituency MP for Ukerewe in the Tanzanian Parliament. She became a member and the president of the Pan African Parliament in 2004. She retained a great sense of humour. She was a passionate advocate for women and girls. It was wonderful for me to see how highly thought of she was by the African women at the conference.

1 Way 2 C the World

1 Thailand

My first visit to Bangkok was a stopover. I was twenty years old, and I stayed at the YMCA. It was my first 'overseas experience.' A graduate in political science, I maintained a galling ignorance of Thai politics – in fact, of most Asian politics. I was simultaneously challenged and terrified at being alone in this seething mass of people, and aghast – as only a Kiwi abroad for the first time can be – at the vast military presence. At one intersection, a young motorcyclist didn't stop for an army vehicle crossing against the current of traffic. I can still see the uniformed men hitting his already bleeding head with truncheons and literally kicking his body off the road.

I remember the compulsory trip to the golden Buddha. I remember the floating market, the panic of bargaining for the first time. The National Geographic images of the exquisite handicrafts and the houses on stilts rapidly lost their romanticism once I could smell my surroundings and actually survey the land that lay beyond the selected containment of a camera lens.

My second visit in 1978 was completely different. As a Member of Parliament, I was chauffeur-driven and air-conditioned, moving from one series of meetings to another, along with the expected stop at the Thompson silk shop. My strongest memory from this visit was a piece of art on the wall of a member of the New Zealand Embassy diplomatic staff. It was Laotian. The traditional image would have been of bright stars in the sky, of elephants walking under these in a line with their tails and trunks entwined one behind the other. In the foreground would have been women and children, smiling widely and holding their arms and hands out in front of them, as if to embrace and give thanks to the elephants and stars.

The traditional image had been adapted. The stars had become bombs. The elephants' trunks rose in front of them trumpeting towards the bombs and their tails rose at a similar angle. The faces of the women and children were contorted to resemble Edvard Munch's *The Scream*, and their arms rose above their heads in a futile gesture of protection.

Now I am on my third visit to Bangkok, staying with friends, and walking and observing and listening. From my window I watch women involved in heavy work on a building site. They are brought here from the country, and work twelve hours a day, seven days a week. They seem to live under corrugated iron lean-tos on the construction site, without water. It's 34°C and I can manage about fifty metres before breaking into a sweat. But these women wear wide-brimmed straw hats on top of a long scarf around their heads enveloping all but their faces. Their arms and legs are totally covered. I learn to expect to find young Thai women dressed in this way for any outdoor labour. The apartment where I stay has a live-in maid, also from the country, who also works a twelve-hour day. This maid is considered lucky, as she is only a maid, and owes her 'farang' (foreign) boss no sexual favours.

The women I see on the streets make and sell food of all description, thread flowers into garlands, recycle waste paper into paper bags, sell newspapers and flowers to car passengers in traffic jams, sweep the streets, and carry heavy loads on bamboo poles bending across their shoulders.

There are a number of very powerful women in the commercial and business world in Thailand. Often, this power is passed from father to daughter. A dowry (khongman) is given by the man to the woman on the day of engagement, and becomes her property upon marriage. Property bought by either spouse after marriage is considered common property, and both spouses have equal rights over it unless an agreement is otherwise signed by both before marriage. Property owned individually before marriage is considered separate property and can be disposed of without the consent of the spouse. Daughters and sons share inheritances equally, and a woman may will her property to a daughter or son without her husband's consent.

Thai women who marry foreigners cannot own land and generally lose inheritance rights. Thai men who marry foreigners do not endure the same treatment, but their spouse cannot own land. The children of Thai women and foreign men cannot claim Thai citizenship. In a way which is both distressing and totally understandable, a growing number of Thai women, particularly those who are bar girls or prostitutes, see bearing the child of a foreigner as a passport out of Thailand to the country of residence of the father. Under the criminal code, abortion is legal only in cases where pregnancy and childbirth pose a severe threat to the woman's life or health, or if the pregnancy resulted from rape. Illegal abortions are punishable by a fine or up to three years' imprisonment for the woman, along with a fine and up to five years' imprisonment for the practitioner or anyone who aids the woman. A proposed bill to liberalize abortion passed the Lower House of Parliament in 1982, but was stalled by legislators in the Upper House. Since then, the incidence of illegal abortions has been steadily increasing. Each year, an estimated one million women seek illegal abortions, and approximately 10,000 of them die from the procedures.

I don't cope well with the work situation of vast numbers of the women in Bangkok. These are bar girls and prostitutes, performing in live sex shows, or chosen as partners in tea houses, or lined up in glass cages, each one numbered, to be bought by one of the masses of male clientele. The latter consist of the armed forces of Singapore, the U.S., or New Zealand, or the airplane loads of sex tourists who flock here from around the world.

Some of these women are young girls, sold into whorehouse slavery. Many will be relatively wealthy, with families of their own. They want another job, but as textile workers, shop assistants, or domestic servants, they cannot earn anything resembling their current income as sex workers. In the countryside, the women are peasant farmers working on leased land, or are otherwise employed by the owner, usually Bangkok resident. To be a prostitute in Bangkok, I was told, is the best of the alternatives available.

It is illegal under the criminal code to work as a prostitute or to live off the earnings of a prostitute, punishable by fine or imprisonment. But the practice became institutionalized during the Vietnam War, when U.S. troops were stationed there. And when they left, tourism took over. A 1981 report estimated that 300,000 women and children worked in approximately 1,157 places offering sex services in Bangkok alone, earning an average of $40 per month, while sex-tour guides and hotel/bar (brothel) owners kept the profits.

It took me four days to work up the strength to visit the prostitution area of Bangkok at night. I was accompanied by a friend, a black American male, who at times in his diplomatic career had been seconded to the UN Commission on the Status of Women. I had warned him that I couldn't take very much of this side of the tourist trade.

We began by visiting a handful of the 'soft' shows, where twelve- to sixteen-year-old girls dance in numbered swimming costumes on catwalks. They live, eat, and sleep in these places. They know nothing else. The men swing their Gucci bags or kick their sandaled feet and drink their alcohol, fawned over by girl children whose social status in the country of these men would be so low that they wouldn't be spoken to. (The American immigration question is how these pre-literate peasant girls who know only enslaved prostitution will survive when they enter, with their half-American child, the country of paternity. And, soon of course, many more countries – and wives – will confront the results of the grotesque abuse of womankind in this city.) These are the child prostitutes.

Oh yes, the boys have a club, too, but the boys have more chances to get out, more choices about life, and are far more expensive for the night. We visit one of these bars. It is the cleanest, most spacious, and most up market of anything I saw that night, though I'm sure they are not all like this one.

We move to a loud, dark, crowded establishment boasting a Western menu, full of European men and a surprising number of European women. The 'performers' are Thai, in a series of live sex shows. What any woman could ever enjoy about watching this is beyond me, so we didn't last long there.

The last stop was the open space of the 'Cattle Market,' where prostitutes of all ages, and with insufficient earnings for the night, go to wait for the ugliest of men who have been unable to attract a girl for the night. Observing this desperate spectacle, my emotions were those of intense and overwhelming grief. I finally succumbed to the tears I had been fighting all night.

David had become increasingly quiet through the night. I knew that he had often shown male friends around the bars of Bangkok in the past. In the early morning, as we sat quietly in the apartment, he said, 'I've never seen it all like that before.' For a start, no one else has ever asked as the first question: 'How old are these children?' He said he imagined I would be feeling about the way he would if he were invited to a slave auction of black men in chains. 'These are your people in chains,' he said. 'I will never do that again.' That there was an end to that form of enslavement was my only comfort for the evening.

The day that I was to leave, the *Bangkok Post* carried a devastating enslavement story. There had been a fire in a brothel. In the ruins of the building were found the skeletons of the young girls who had worked there. They were chained to their beds.

Since 1984, Thai women activists have successfully campaigned for signifi-cant changes in the law. The new constitution of 1997 included six articles related to gender equality. The then prime minister Thaksin introduced a scheme to give all of Thailand's 77,000 villages a grant of U.S.$27,000, and *insisted that the village committee for making decisions on how the grant would be spent must be half men and half women.*

In December 1996, the government enacted the Prevention and Suppression of Prostitution Act, *which protects prostitutes under 18 years of age, while meting out severe punishment to customers, procurers, and brothel keepers. Parents who sold their daughters were also to face a penalty. It appears that this has simply pushed some of the procurers across the border to traffic in girls from Burma and Cambodia. New measures were introduced in November 1997 for the prevention and suppression of trafficking in women and children.*

The abortion law is still very limited. There are about 300,000 to 800,000 illegal abortions each year. A national study reported that the incidence of illegal and unsafe abortions is highest among female farmers.

I have returned to Thailand on numerous occasions since 1984, but never yet as a tourist. My only visits to Bangkok have been for briefings for regional assignments, or for 'Expert Roundtables.' These are long days and nights in hotel rooms or conference venues, where only the traffic experience of moving from one to the other distinguishes where you are in the world.

In the last decade I have only passed through Bangkok's airport on my way to Khon Kaen, Thailand's third largest industrial city, where New Zealand built the Mekong Institute. I have joined others here to teach modules to bureaucrats from Yunnan Province, Myanmar, Vietnam, Cambodia, Laos, and Thailand as part of New Zealand's 'development' initiatives in the region. I have greatly enjoyed this activity.

2 Burma

October 1984

The maximum stay allowed to foreigners was six days. The visa and arrival at the airport in Rangoon involved endless paperwork. I was amused at this. I couldn't see how so much paper could be efficient. I felt the same when I arrived to register at the Strand Hotel, which, along with the railway station, made me feel as if I was in a carbon copy of the British Empire's Ministry of Works. It was as if the buildings of a certain era in Wellington – or any other colonial city in New Zealand – had been transported.

I did not have time to unpack my toothbrush before there was a knock at the door and I was escorted downstairs. I had not filled in the back page of a form at the airport. They had found me already. I got the message, and wiped the patronizing smile off my face.

I had already decided I couldn't afford the tourist flights to Mandalay or Pagan. I was pretty confused about just what was going on here. I had been asked by a friend of the maid in Bangkok to carry a parcel to her family in Rangoon. I'd seen the whole contents of the parcel: some very ordinary plastic household goods, a few toys, and some children's clothes. She had told me that 'imports were banned.' For ordinary folks they were, and so I was carrying treasures. Some of these would be used, while others would finish up on the pavement being sold alongside so many other strange bits and pieces that had found their way across the border.

I had religiously obeyed the rules that severely restricted the foreign currency I could carry into the country. I was a great disappointment to the folks hanging out around the side of the Strand who urged me to go to the diplomatic store and buy cigarettes for them. Since I wasn't about to break a traveller's cheque for a wheelbarrow-load of kyat in change, I disappointed them. I would have got about twenty kyat for a U.S. dollar on the black market; I would get eight kyat in the store.

Strolling about in the daytime was quite pleasant. Apart from the guys around the side of the Strand, everyone just left you alone. I wandered along past charming city tea shops, to the golden pagoda Shwe Dagon, the air around the temple heavy with a blend of frangipani and incense. [Frangipani have prolific flowers with a deep exotic fragrance at night, though they have no nectar.] I had an avocado smoothie, and I wondered what to do next. I asked the guys at the hotel if there was a memorial to U Thant anywhere. [U Thant was a Burmese diplomat and the third UN Secretary General from 1961 to 1971. He died in 1974, but the military junta refused a state funeral. This led to riots and his coffin was snatched by students. The protests were crushed by the Burmese military regime, and U Thant was buried at the foot of Schwedagon Pesoda.] Some of them walked away immediately. None of them looked me in the eye to reply. I wandered away, and soon a young man fell in step beside me and asked if I would like to hire a car for a sightseeing tour. I understood now. So off we went: this bright postgraduate in political science made his living as an informal tourist guide. He showed me U Thant's former home, and explained that driving in his car with me now was the only safe way to talk about his country. When we walked at Inla Lake, we spoke only of where I might travel in the remaining days on my visa – tourist to guide chatter. Inside the car, I cross-examined him as we drove, frustrated with my ignorance. What explanation does the government have for prohibiting imports? Who is the government? Does all the overseas currency purchased on the black market go to the leaders of the three private armies in 'uncontrolled' areas, or is it more likely to end up in the hands of the Burmese military? What roles do the superpowers play in Burmese politics? Why is U Thant discredited here? Finally he said to me, 'You cannot talk about these things to anyone else in this country, and especially in any open area. You cannot trust anyone. No one will tell you the truth about Burmese politics. To do so, you would be a traitor.'

My guide had suggested that I take a few days to visit the Shan State, and Lake Inle in particular. I had read my guidebook. I was supposed to have a permit to go into the Shan State. There were at least three private armies just in that area, and the Shan was the greatest opium-growing area. But he wanted me to 'see something beautiful in this country, not to remember just tyranny.' He had a friend who was leaving early in the morning to take a utility truck to Kalaw, and I could go with him. I could catch a train back, he said.

So off I went, along what oft-times resembled the steep, winding roads or Skippers in the South Island, frequently sighting the wreckage of the large old army trucks that had hurtled off the edge the narrow road with their full loads of produce, animals, and people. On arrival at Kalaw, they took me to the 'Guest House,' an old British Hill Station residence, 'where the British High Commissioner used to come and stay.' The overgrown tennis court was a testament to the old days. The plumbing had completely broken down – there was no running water for anything. At night I was given a candle, so that I might more clearly see the lizards running across my walls and the bat life in the bedroom. For several days I lived on a diet consisting solely of bananas, mint tea, and boiled rice. Yet the Shan is the food bowl of Burma. All around Kalaw the staples of rice, bananas, and tea grew in fine symmetrical rows, along with cabbages, chillies, mustard, chokos, and avocados. I even saw cherries and pears.

I spent the day wandering around the town with my camera. I observed the hill tribe women who had been down at the Kalaw market. I wanted to get photos of the high school students in their 'British uniforms' as they left school. An older man came to sit and talk with me. He had excellent English and was very confident. He told me he also spoke excellent Japanese. He worked for the British army in the Second World War until the Japanese advanced; then he worked for them until they were in retreat. I was simultaneously on guard, and delightfully innocent. I was very pleased to spy some other young Europeans, who turned out to be Canadians. They were off to Lake Inle the next day, and asked if I would like to tag along.

We spent a long day on the lake. The villages were built on stilts over the water. Silt and water hyacinth provided the foundation for onions, tomatoes, cress, and potatoes, which had been grown hydroponically for centuries. The Intha people there had adopted the eccentric method of rowing their sampans with one leg. This left their hands free to drop their tall, conical nets on top of fish which they could spot in the lake. The water was crystal blue, and made the efforts of the worst photographer look spectacular. We visited a temple, stopped to look at weaving, and picked up some Shan shoulder bags. My graduate friend would be pleased, I thought: we were thoroughly tourists.

It was the same the following day, when we were guided for four hours to a village of the Palaung tribe. En route, the houses I saw were mostly made of thatch. Often the living quarters were elevated above the pens housing Brahmin cattle, pigs, goats, or poultry. The average size of a dwelling for a very extended family seemed to be about twenty square metres. The beds were mats on the floor, or slightly raised tightly woven bases on simple frames. Most members of the family left their home at dawn. There was firewood to gather, tea to pick, goats and cattle to watch (with the ever-present bells indicating location), rice to pound, nuts to rake and dry, fabric to weave, fields to work with yoked oxen and wooden ploughs, areas to clear with small hand-scythes, and always heavy loads to carry. Once a week, perhaps more frequently, a huge basket (which usually took two people to lift into position) was carried for several hours on the women's heads, over the mountain slopes to market, and filled with dried salted fish and other commodities for the family or village on the return trip. The family might spend an average of three of four kyats (U.S.$0.50) a day.

Some days, when the teacher made the walk in from the nearest town, there was school, but without pens or paper. The girls were unlikely to attend; if they had younger brothers or sisters they were, at seven and eight, already the caring nurturers, otherwise they were at work in the fields. At very young ages, and for varying lengths of time, the children could be Buddhist monks or nuns.

The houses were bare but very clean. The water, unfortunately, was not, and this inhibited primary health care work. Many people were without access to basic medical care, although the Red Cross symbol was often observed above empty buildings. Some 'aid' programs worked: the United Nations Development Programme's pine reforestation scheme was observably effective. Others were a too-frequent disaster: In a burst of enthusiasm, the German ambassador had decided to bring electricity to a hill village. The generator was delivered by helicopter. It ran on diesel, which the village could not buy. Even if it could be bought, the only way to get the diesel there was to carry it in on your back.

If the family lives close to a town, and particularly near a road or railway line, they might be involved in the constant preparation of food – boiled eggs, rice, chicken, vegetable samosas, to sell to travellers – twenty-four hours a day. When my train drew into stations at 3:00 a.m. on the trip back to Rangoon, half the vendors selling such things and offering cups of mint tea through the window were under the age of ten.

As a tourist, I reflected that everywhere the people were imbued with an enormous capacity for hard work, great patience, a will to survive in conditions few New Zealanders would ever tolerate, and a great kindness. But I also knew that I left Burma with no idea at all about the real horrors still taking place there.

The State Law and Order Restoration Council (SLORC) renamed Burma Myanmar, after the constitution was suspended in 1988 in a bloody military coup in which at least 10,000 were killed. When elections did take place in 1990, the National League for Democracy and its leader, Aung San Suu Kyi, won 82 per cent of the parliamentary seats. Even so, the SLORC refused to give up control of the country. Their rule is characterized by gross human rights abuses, rampant use of forced labour, arbitrary executions, systematic rape, forced portering, imprisonment of thousands of political prisoners, and denial of the most basic forms of freedom of expression and association. There are over 110,000 refugees in camps along the Thai border, and thousands more in Thailand who are unable or unwilling to stay in the refugee camps. Young Burmese girls are trafficked at an ever-increasing rate into sexual slavery in Thailand.

Whenever we go to teach at the Mekong Institute, there are always six participants from Myanmar. We know that at least one of them is always a spook. The other members of the team work out which one of them it is fairly quickly. I work

*it out by asking who plays golf. Sometimes when I teach there I use role-plays as
a strategy, and I always have an NGO group in my role-plays. I have had
women from Myanmar come to me later in tears, or to embrace me, exclaiming,
'I never thought I could say "human rights" out loud and be safe!'*

3 India

October 1984

I arrived in Bombay with just one contact, a friend of a friend who was
on the international executive of the YWCA. As soon as I made contact,
she had me out of my hotel and into the Y, where most of the other
women were permanent residents, working or studying in this vast city.

Anita was energetic and diversely political. In the immediate vicinity of the Y, she was organizing. A vacant lot had become a home for
several thousand. The sidewalks were impassable, and the road drains
were open sewers. I had to walk this block each day so that I could hit
the harbour's edge, which was the only way I could get my bearings
and read my map. Despite the heat, I had to carry a shawl so that I
could cover my nose and mouth, as I retched uncontrollably from the
sights and smells. It was the Muslim quarter, so I probably looked as if
I was attempting some degree of cultural appropriateness.

In this squat, women earned a pittance cooking chapattis all day. My
Western horror was that anyone could cook anything commercial
there. Anita's horror was at the extraordinary exploitation of pieceworkers, especially in the chapatti-making industry, where a company's cheap trick induced the women to become 'shareholders' in
that company. This meant they could not be organized into unions,
and that a boycott would hurt only the women, not the company.
Anita explained that these women, and so many other pieceworkers
she was attempting to organize, were so desperate for the pittance they
were paid that they did not complain. They understood how readily
dispensable they were as workers.

These squatters were relatively 'lucky' in other ways, Anita told me,
as they had been 'established' in this community for over two years,
and they were close to 'work' opportunities. We drove to the outskirts

of the city where the homes of thousands had been flattened and a wasteland temporarily stood for a great new development: I think it was for a new airport. Huge drainage culverts had been dropped, awaiting the next phase of the development. Hundreds of those who had been evicted had quickly established themselves back on the land, with a culvert as the family home.

Anita and I spent a lot of time talking about the processes of feminist politics. I'd asked her some of the tough questions that are inevitable on a visit to India. The evening before I had walked by (as had everyone else) an emaciated man in rags lying on the footpath in a hessian sack. He had an open wound in his calf and the maggots were crawling about it. How did this happen? Why did this happen? Her analyses involved class, religion, corruption, and colonization. We compared the agendas of the 'safe' women that governments might appoint to advisory committees, and the radicals such as she who integrated into NGOs where they had a certain freedom to use their initiative. She offered me the opportunity to see for myself how it was in Bombay, for she knew that the Maharastra State Women's Council was to meet later in the week. She said I should ask them the same questions.

So that is where I found myself on 31 October 1984, meeting with the members of the Maharastra State Women's Council at an open home for women in social distress. The rehabilitation centre offered free shelter, food, and medical care, conducted sewing, embroidery, and language classes, and ran a family counselling service.

Early in my discussion with these women, I explained how it was beyond my comprehension that a country with such a comparatively high growth rate, such a high comparative per capita GNP, with such enormous military spending, and in receipt of such enormous sums of 'aid' (the great proportion of it military), could have the vast numbers of people I had seen on the street in conditions that can only be described as subhuman. If there are forms of human existence that are more base, I cannot imagine what they are. I asked if there was the political will to change this.

I was told I had no conception of how it could change for 800 million people (that is quite true) and that it would take a century. I ventured to suggest that that was not the length of time the Chinese needed. 'Oh,' they replied, 'but we have a democracy, we have freedom of speech.' I had gone as far as I dared down this path, so we turned to the report on the centre.

The primary aim of the centre was reconciliation of the woman with her husband and family. One of the board members explained to me, 'The woman must learn to serve her husband and to serve her parents-in-law; her husband must not abuse her.' I was astounded, and repeated the words to her slowly, drawing attention to the distinction between the verbs. 'That is the way things are,' she said, 'a woman does not have to get married.' I didn't bother to pursue her argument with the response that that might be true in principle, but it was observably untrue in practice.

So I explained the operation of the domestic protection legislation, the habitation orders, the no-fault divorce, procedures of maintenance and custody, and the matrimonial property legislation in New Zealand. There was great interest and envy at all these things, but utter astonishment at my explanation of our proposed changes to the rape laws, and particularly the abolition of spousal immunity. Again they told me, the woman must serve her husband, and if not, then he will find another wife or see a prostitute. The bewildering series of oppressions enacted in India by colonial civil codes and religious laws leave the Indian woman with little protection, and the suicide rate among married women is of frightening proportions.

I had begun to say, as politely as possible, that to see the wife in that way was to afford her only the status of a legitimate prostitute, a piece of property, when news of Indira Gandhi's shooting reached us. We were told she had been shot several times, and All-India Radio would keep us informed. It was mid-morning, and the meeting broke up soon after the news of the shooting. The women left with their chauffeurs to get home to secure their residences in case of rioting. At least that is what the sole Christian woman on the council told me. She didn't have a chauffeur but her own car, and she wanted to know where I might like to be dropped.

By now we had a little more information. The prime minister had been shot by her Sikh bodyguards at point-blank range. They spoke of between seven and nine bullets having hit her. The radio said she had been rushed to hospital and was undergoing emergency surgery. I couldn't believe she had survived. So I asked to be dropped at any one of the large Western hotels – like a Sheraton or a Hilton – whatever was convenient. Almost all of these had teleprinter connections somewhere near their foyers, which just chattered away all day for those who could be bothered to read their emissions. As she dropped me off, my Christian companion said: 'The president and Rajiv Gandhi are both out of the country. They will have to keep her alive until they return.'

The first to confirm the death was the Soviet News Agency, Tass. Shortly after midday, the BBC also confirmed the prime minister's death. The 'free press and democratic' All-India Radio continued to report she was fighting for her life, and the street newspapers carried the same headline. The editions seemed to come out by the hour, still with a similar story. I tuned into my trusty short-wave radio. By 3:00 p.m. Moscow Radio had broadcast the news, and teleprinters at hotels now carried IPU and Reuter bulletins to the same effect. I began the long walk from the plush downtown along the harbour route to my Y. Even I could notice that there were not as many people about. Each new edition of a newspaper that reached a street corner bought a rush of readers, but it was a very subdued population.

When I reached the Y, many of the young women were praying for their prime minister. They believed she was alive, as 'they would tell us if she was dead.' I sat with them in the sitting room and waited. In the early evening, programming was interrupted and the death was confirmed to the Indian people. Clerics from Hindu, Muslim, Sikh, and Christian traditions led prayers. The statements from international leaders began. The tributes were of one accord: whatever her faults, Indira Gandhi had held together a country of diverse and extreme elements in a way no one had thought possible.

There were no riots, but the sustained grief that gripped this sitting room I sat in enveloped India. I left India the next day. The newspapers said the president and Rajiv Gandhi had both had to return from overseas, and that they had joined an emergency cabinet meeting at about 6:00 p.m. At that point, Indira Gandhi was able to die.

4 Ethiopia

November 1984

Ethiopia has a population of thirty-two million. Fifty per cent of them are under the age of twenty. More than six million of them are in dire need of food at this moment. One thousand of them die from starvation each week. The conservative estimate for the number of starving in the last six months is ten million, the majority of whom will be women and children.

Eleven African countries are suffering drought and receiving international aid; more are expected to be added to the list. None have the
population of Ethiopia, but neither do any of them receive the amount
of per capita aid going to Ethiopia. Somalia, Djibouti, Rwanda,
Burundi, Sudan, Chad, Niger, and the other countries are not of the
perceived 'strategic' importance of Ethiopia, bordering the Red Sea, a
short distance from Saudi Arabia.

My commercial airliner arrives in Addis Ababa within an hour of the
first of Bob Geldof's 'Feed the World' flights. [Geldof founded 'Band
Aid' in 1984 after watching a BBC news report on famine in Ethiopia. He
called on leading rock musicians to record 'Feed the World' and all profits were used to launch major aid flights to Ethiopia.] In the market the
next day I could have bought punctured oil containers bearing the
words 'Gift of the People of Canada.' This is the first market I have ever
encountered where no one wants me to take their photograph.

Nowhere else in Africa is the Soviet presence so visible. One arrives
in Addis Ababa to be welcomed by lavish decorations, still bright and
prominent from the celebrations in September 1984 of the tenth anniversary of the Popular Revolution and the installation of the Provi-
sional Military Administrative Council. Huge billboards of Marx and
Engels, vast concrete edifices of Lenin, 'peace' signs which feature
crossed machine guns, large coloured signs featuring Comrade Mengistu
Haile Meriam, chairman of the Workers Party of Ethiopia (formed for
the anniversary celebrations), and the ever-present call of 'Long Live
Proletarian Internationalism' are everywhere. All this illustrates the
truth of the rumour that, in the last year, in excess of U.S.$150 million
had been spent on this commemoration.

The government has had some cause to celebrate. The overthrow of
the old regime of Haile Selassie was the overthrow of feudal serfdom.
The building of domestic dwellings and rehousing programs in Addis
Ababa have been prolific and are still much in evidence. Ethiopia has
won international awards for its intensive literary campaigns. The
language, of course, is Amharic, spoken only in Ethiopia, with very
few books available, all of them heavily censored, and generally full
of rhetoric about 'capitalists,' 'imperialists,' and 'colonists.' My Ethiopian friends in exile have told me that all the other books were
burned when the homes of 'intellectuals' were ransacked. When these
people were arrested, the army didn't waste time with matters of
decorum. The 'intellectuals' were shot in the streets, which literally
ran with blood.

Each resident in Ethiopia, including *ferenghi* (foreigners), belongs to a *kebbele* (neighbourhood), which has a number and is affiliated with a district. Shortly before the revolutionary celebrations, every resident of Addis Ababa had to hand in their identification cards to receive new ones. Rumour has it that not enough new cards were printed. Daily, one may observe queues of patient people, many returning week after week, waiting to get an I.D. card. Without an I.D. card, there is no ration card. Without a ration card, there is no bread, oil, sugar, spaghetti, or flour.

I know that there is a regional office of the Economic Commission for Africa in Addis Ababa, and so there must be a 'women's desk' there. I wonder what they are working on at the moment. I also know I am quite ill. I find my way there. There is a women's desk – and a woman there. She can see I am sick. 'It's good you came here,' she says. 'The only doctors who will see you are Russian and they will want lots of U.S. dollars. But there is a New Zealand woman living here, married to an English engineer working for the EEC (European Economic Community).' She calls her, and Rosie from Rotorua arrives to rescue me.

For several days I have a high fever, and I am delirious at nights, but in the daytime, with discretion and at my insistence, we move around. Evidence of a great deal more of the Geldof deliveries can be seen at the market. As we walk through the market, a band of young boys gathers behind us to follow. They are not bothering us at all, but some adult males take up switch sticks and beat them back, apparently then expecting to be rewarded for relieving us of this nuisance. Rosie takes the sticks from them and snaps them in pieces.

I get some idea of where the whipping idea might come from the next day, when we take a circuitous drive so we can overlook one of the main roads into Addis Ababa. There is a never-ending, dusty, meandering line of skeletal people drifting into view. The army waits for them. 'They ask for their papers and ration cards,' Rosie says. We can see the soldiers turn some people around and begin to whip them back down the road. 'That's what happens when you don't have a card,' she says.

The daily lives of those who live in Addis Ababa are lives of bare survival and fear. Rosie's *manita* (maid), whom I pressed too hard for information, finally said 'Madam, people no speak. Sister no speak to brother, brother no speak to mother,' and clasping her hands to heart, she added, 'but in here we speak.'

Rosie takes me to the sole remaining 'project' for women in the capital. It's a small centre run by one Belgian nun. Women are at sewing machines making clothes from scraps and clean rags, or at looms weaving carpets with rough wool. The church in Europe has not sent much money for some time, but this sister cannot leave. 'Women beg for a place in the centre every day,' she says. 'Some sleep outside – some die outside.'

Before the revolution, daily life for Ethiopians was shaped by the feudal system of serfdom. The land reform was hailed as a vast improvement. *Selamia*, the publication of the Ethiopian Airlines, informs the visitor that 60 per cent of Ethiopia's land is arable, but only 10.4 per cent is presently cultivated. It says that 90 per cent of the population earn their living from the land, mainly as a subsistence farmers. The exports are coffee, oil seeds, pulses, vegetables, sugar, and foodstuffs for animals. The essay claims there is 'a thriving livestock sector exporting cattle on the hoof and hides and skins.' I don't think so. The land is nationalized, so that there is no title and no security of tenancy, and, as a result, there are no inputs into agriculture. Severe drought, poor soil, negative price policies for agricultural products, a decrease in demand for African agricultural products, and a poor allocation of resources for agricultural development all have taken a massive toll.

The situation is exacerbated beyond relief by the total invisibility of the real farmers and food producers, for it is in this part of the world that the concentration of women in agriculture is the highest. Following the last major Sahelian drought, the United States Agency for International Development (USAID) administrator's lack of understanding of the sexual division of control and resources seriously damaged the nomadic woman's economic and social position. Among both Fulani and Tuareg herders, one of the major concerns expressed was that the government's program to reconstitute herds lost in the drought was replacing cattle only for men. Women's stocks were not being replaced. This was crippling their social system. Animals were unavailable in dowry and bride wealth payments, which in turn meant that women had lost their independent property. This was apparently the unintentional result of a government program that issued a card to the 'head' of each family and replaced animals only to the family head.

In an effort to see if anything had been learned in the intervening period, I asked the director of the major agricultural multilateral agency involved in Ethiopia a question (shrouded in innocence): 'But who are the farmers here?' 'Oh, I don't know anything about that,' he replied, 'I only know about coffee' – confirming the fact that female labour is not seen as important in intensive agricultural systems which are equated with modern technology and which are oriented to the maximization of export productivity. This is reflected in the fact that the absolute number of female rural migrants to the city of Addis Ababa is greater than that of males.

Another major and disastrous effect: women are the gatherers and major users of water. Less than 10 per cent of the rural population of Africa has access to safe water within a reasonable distance, so women may spend up to six hours a day hauling water. This obviously detracts from their ability to engage in other activities, and for young girls, from their attendance at school. The poor quality of water and sanitation poses serious threats to life and health. Little improvement is expected in the situation of access to water before the end of the century. The issue is not a priority because it is 'women's work.'

A.W. Clausen, current president of the World Bank, says that there is a direct link between educating women and girls, fertility control, and infant and maternal mortality. But there is no time for education in these women's lives. Along with their other duties they must also gather and use firewood. Deforestation is now illegal in Ethiopia, and the price of increasingly scarce wood for fuel has risen tenfold in the last decade, now claiming up to 20 per cent of household incomes. Confined to survival and maintenance activities, these women continue to reproduce and add to population growth rates.

The African continent has had the highest annual population growth rate in the world in the last two decades. It has a young population, with 44 per cent under the age of fifteen. The world's lowest life expectancies and the highest rates of child mortality are also found in Africa. Ethiopia along with Upper Volta, Niger, Mali, and Guinea-Bissau have one of the highest crude death rates in the world.

How is it that the real drama of famine in Ethiopia and Africa has been ignored for so long? How is it that the city of the headquarters of the Organization for African Unity and the Economic Commission of Africa, with diplomatic representation from over seventy countries, could be silent for so long about such devastation? Western diplomatic representatives told me that warnings and protests to the Ethiopian government were met with the request not to meddle in domestic affairs. For over a year, while the government prepared for the tenth anniversary celebrations, all transportation priorities were given to the air, sea, and land movement of cement, signs, lighting, and military equipment needed for 12 September. There was a stranglehold on every project not connected with the celebrations. Aid project equipment for river diversion projects, hospital extensions, technical laboratories, and water supply contracts had no priority. Nor was priority given to the insufficient

quantities of grain supplied by the EEC. This was held up in backlogs at
the ports because of inefficient handling and the unavailability of any of
the nationalized transport system for distribution.

But the West has also played its part in this murderous political football. Aware that the last famine brought about the collapse of the total-
itarian regime of Haile Selassie, some hoped for another collapse in
this famine. The famine story broke just after Western governments,
led by the United States administration, found themselves 'unable to
guarantee the continued survival' of the International Fund for Agricultural Development, which has been prominent in assisting small-
scale agriculture in poorer countries, including Ethiopia, in just the
way that might make famine less likely in the future. The Reverend
Charles Elliot, former head of Christian Aid Charity, claims that the
United States and British hostility to the Marxist regime was based on
the hope that the famine would topple the government.

The dominant outside international presence since the withdrawal
of Cuban troops early in 1984 is indeed that of the Soviet Union, which
assists in the civil war in the north against opposition forces in Eritrea,
Tigre, Wollo, and Gondar – where three million victims of the drought
live in vast territories. Alternative relief agencies manage to get some
assistance to the north, often at night and in disguise. Crops and livestock in the north have been routinely bombed by Ethiopian and
Soviet fighter planes. The government of Ethiopia is now forcibly
removing more than 250,000 people from the north so that, they say,
they can be on less barren land. The leader of the Tigre Liberation
Front, however, claims that it is deliberate government policy to allow
people in the north to starve to death and to thwart the distribution of
food to the rebels.

Meanwhile, the Ethiopian government rejected the proposition of a
commission established by the British charity War on Want, headed by
Willi Brandt, to ensure that food aid reached areas where rebels were
active. Ethiopia said this was unacceptable, as it was set up without the
approval of the Ethiopian authorities. Under pressure, the government
finally allocated fifty army trucks to cope with the international relief
effort. But it took that government more than a month after the revolutionary celebrations to begin to allow relief missions to fly into Addis
Ababa, with the first arriving on 22 October.

It should be remembered that Ethiopia is the oldest independent sov-
ereign country in Africa, with a proud record of struggle against colo-
nialism. Ten years ago it experienced a violent upheaval and revolution.

Soon after this came the brutal suppression of a civilian uprising which started because the military had not moved to elections. The intellectual revolutionaries were systematically liquidated. All who expressed reservations about the creation of another regime of terror, who had helped the revolution take place but asserted that this was not the sort of regime they had fought for, were murdered.

At the symposium on 'Future Development Prospects for Africa Towards the Year 2000,' African governments, decision-makers, and scholars stated that 'the only way of avoiding the disasters ... is to foster a new political will, so that a new human-being orientated African development policy can evolve in which the continent can find its own identity and status instead of having them imposed on it.'

If such a political will is anywhere alive, or well, or living in Ethiopia, I saw no evidence of it. And the truths of the cause of this massive tragedy are even harder to find.

From Ethiopia I went to Portugal, where I had hoped to spend some time with Maria de Lourdes Pintasilgo, and to 'be a tourist.' I spent the whole time in the British Hospital in Lisbon with infections in my chest, stomach, and bowel, on a drip, and with medication flown in from the UK. I haven't embarked on that sort of trip as a way to see the world since.

5 China

October 1985

In three weeks of travel from Beijing, through Jinan, Quingdao, Shanghai, Nanking, Zungshan, and Canton to Schenzen I saw no derelicts, but I saw three beggars (a woman and two children at the Shanghai Railway Station) and one group of youths who showed signs of recent alcohol consumption. But in the Beijing department store, mannequins were dressed in Western clothes and makeup; in Shanghai, girls were in the Reform School for prostitution; in Canton, male marketers sat catatonically waiting as the opium pipe returned to them, and television advertisements for modern conveniences duplicated the sex-role stereotyping of the West.

The journey from north to south passed through hundreds of miles of farmland, the maize of the north giving way to plot after plot of geometric fields of rice in the south. The fenceless landscape was marked by formed paths along old waterways, which irrigated the fields. Water-buffalo teams lay languidly and half-submerged in ponds until their next task. In uniform white shirts and blue or black pants, peasant men and women crouched, hoeing, in rhythmical, incessant movements, or moved from field to field in temperatures exceeding 30°C, carrying fertilizer, tools, crops, and umbrellas.

On the road we occasionally passed a heavy truck or piece of earthmoving machinery, but other than the omnipresent bicycle, the vehicle we saw was most frequently a converted rotary hoe with a small trailer, a highly adaptable piece of machinery.

Every few miles the landscape was interrupted by another village, with new housing developments and perhaps a brickworks, some factories, and bamboo groves. Bamboo was used everywhere, for staking plants, supporting propagation cloches, supporting work shelters in fields, or used as scaffolding for the largest buildings. There were few wood lots – we saw little afforestation.

In the market in Canton the longest queues were for wood, sold among kittens, dried snakes, flowers, bonsai trees, old crockery, meat, live fish, herbal medicines, grains, skinned ducks, live hens, and tobacco leaves dried and processed on the spot.

Much of our travel involved 'briefings' at selected sights with selected people. We got to visit the Reform School because one of our number had requested a visit to a prison. The doors of the small dormitory rooms for boys and girls in the Reform School in Shanghai were in marked contrast to the general impression I had been given in the talks with the deputy principal. Locks, bolts, and bars signalled an attitude that had not been spoken about.

The school was symptomatic to me of so much about China: on the surface, it was most appropriately described by the now-clichéd adjective in relation to this culture: 'inscrutable.' On another level, it was complex, experimental, conservative, caring, strict, innovative – a combination of qualities and political approaches that a Westerner would not expect to find under one roof.

Children who commit minor crimes (examples given were stealing, gang fighting, and hooliganism) and who are refused help from their family, school, and community might be sent to the Reform School. Six 'chops' (signatures) are required – the headmaster of the original school, the neighbourhood police office, the headmaster of the reformatory school, an officer of the upper level of the district education school, an officer of the upper level of the district education bureau, and the district security bureau. Notice is then served to the student and his/her parents, and according to Reform School regulations passed by the State Council and the Shanghai Municipal Government, the parent's permission is not required.

The deputy principal explained what might be expected by any one of the twenty girls or eighty boys, supervised by fifteen faculty and twenty teachers, in a minimal stay of two years. He said:

> Two-thirds of the time will be spent on study, and one-third of that time working. Four half days of work foster a good habit and cultivate respect for labour and workers.
>
> The first lesson is in judicial education to make them understand that they are hurting themselves, their family, and their future. We invite rehabilitated children to speak of how they realized their crime and to tell of the harm they did to society.
>
> Moral education is offered in two ways. The first is the collective life with the teachers, who stay at the school and teach by example in their quality of work and model values. The students make pen friends with 'model people' and pay visits to them to foster self-confidence. Some children have major qualitative changes.
>
> Usually these children lack education at home, and have bad habits of behaviour making fun, eating, drinking, and playing. They must understand that a personal future is closely linked with the country's future. Besides school education we rely on social efforts. We have heart to heart talks with the children to ask them what they are thinking about.[1]

In spite of the locks on the door, I was told that very few children take liberties with the trust in them. Very few run away. They have summer and winter vacations, state holidays, and visit their home every two weeks. At other schools three good students could enjoy travel privileges during vacation, but at the Reform School all students can travel: last year to Nanjing, this year to Hanchow.

A strict system of punishment and reward operates at the school. There are rewards for labour, academic work, and good behaviour.

---

1 These quotes are from my personal interviews.

Privileges are more holidays – if pupils behave well, they might go home every week: bad behaviour sees the loss of opportunities like seeing a film or travelling. Travel announcements are made two weeks in advance, so that pupils who have not behaved could still improve in time to take the trip. Children who fail to reform are sent to the judicial court.

I was recalling a briefing from Guan, the principal of the Shandong Teachers College, when the deputy principal said, 'We think the reformatory school has characteristics which distinguish it from other schools.' Only days earlier, Guan had been describing how 6,000 students in fourteen departments are trained to take positions in high schools of 2,000 students. In the largest country on earth there is a national shortage of qualified teachers. While the literacy rate in 1982 was 76 per cent, rural women were the majority of the illiterate and semi-illiterate population. It was the rural areas where recruitment of qualified teachers was a problem.

Guan had been at the 'Teachers University' for twenty-eight years and had never had practical teaching experience in a high school. 'Most teachers at the college have not been in high schools, but each department has a group who teach method – in the mathematics department, eight of the ninety teachers teach method and this group are in and out of schools. But students have only five to six weeks practical experience teaching some courses in their fourth year."

Guan spoke perfect English. An internationally renowned mathematician, he had been savagely attacked during the Cultural Revolution, and had locked himself in his room for months on end to write and study. He discussed the course taught in moral education, saying that 'communism is the moral standard' and explaining that politics is a compulsory examination subject. When asked about examinations, he said: 'The open-book examination is now gone. Many people say we must change the system. Students know how to remember but not how to think, or how to create new things. This is not really good for university.'

The students at the Teachers University are not instructed in teaching sex education: 'Not many think this is necessary for high school students,' Guan said.

But this was not the case at the Reform School, where an experimental teaching course had been established. This was possibly a result of the increase of girls sent there for prostitution, which is on the rise for the first time in twenty years. The open-door economic policy bore the brunt of the blame for this: pornographic books and video tapes were arriving in Shanghai. Secondly, the deputy principal claimed, young people mature two years earlier than they used to. At the same time, he claimed that none of the students at the reform school were victims of molestation or incest abuse. Not that he had asked them; he simply claimed it did not happen.

Every district has a Reform School – in Shanghai there were twelve. Students receive no pay for their labour, which on the day I visited was tedious, repetitive assembly work reminiscent of the so-called occupational therapy that I have seen in Western psychiatric institutions.

Our three women interpreters travelled with us for the whole three weeks. Two features of their company are fixed in my memory. One was their collective envy, expressed to us safely as we travelled in our bus, of the income available to the new entrepreneurs in the economic zones. These incomes were many times in excess of the fixed state incomes of our companions. When we reached Schenzen, and visited the large new homes replete with Western appliances and complete with domestic servants from rural China, the envy shifted to contempt.

The other feature was the way in which they became allies as they came to know us and as we heard their life stories. We would ask a question, and the 'big man' would give a reply. Our translator would begin: 'He's saying that ...' in a tone of voice and using body language that relayed immediately that this was not the truth. Of course, they had heard our discussions on the bus after such briefings and were becoming embarrassed at being part of attempted deception which we recognized as such. A little later on the trip, the approach changed. Before the 'big man' had finished, one translator would interrupt and say to him: 'I won't tell them that; they know that it's not true.' At the final dinner in Schenzen, when the 'big man' proudly announced plans for a nuclear power plant, our team was not impressed. All of us were, to some extent, anti-nuclear activists. At a certain point, our translators just became themselves and argued vigorously about claims of safety long after we had stopped talking. I have always wondered if there were any ramifications for them from this exchange. This was the exception. The tone and temperament of the trip can be generally gauged by the records I have of a morning briefing from the All-China Women's Federation.

The social status of Chinese women has improved greatly in the thirty-six years since liberation. Before liberation, a woman had no rights. She was a wife and mother, and was expected to look after her husband, children, and the house. Her marriage was arranged. Her obedience to feudal virtues, from looking after her parents-in-law to being an expert at needlework, was demanded.

At liberation, the majority of Chinese women were preliterate. Only 600,000 women were employed in some independent activity, only 7.5 per cent of the total female workforce. In the land reform campaign, women were allocated land on the same condition as men. They were also employed in construction, and became economically independent.

In Beijing today, there are 4,200,000 women in the city workforce. They make up 36 per cent of the total urban workforce and can be found in practically every field and profession.

Since 1979, women have played a greater role in agriculture, displaying increasing ingenuity. For example, Federation representatives reported a Shanghai woman farmer who, in addition to her crops, was involved in a network of secondary activities. She had 700 chickens, from which she sold eggs, young chickens, and poultry. She used the chicken manure to raise fish, and propagated grapes by the fish pond. While her husband was at the grade-eight level of skilled workers where wages were fixed, she earned far more. Some foreign women think Chinese women have been driven back to their homes and carry out only family duties, but this is not true.

Women are also more politically involved. The Federation has one woman councillor who is president of the Bank of China. One provincial governor and six deputy provincial governors are women. One provincial party secretary was originally a branch president of the All-China Women's Federation. Twenty-one per cent of the National People's Congress are women and one of the vice-chairs is a woman. Although women have made progress, it is not enough, and the Federation wants more women to play a part in the state's political life.

There are plenty of problems. The majority of the preliterate are women. This stems from the feudal ideology that women should not be educated because their only roles are marriage and motherhood. Now, 95 per cent of children aged six to twelve are at school. Overall, female students make up 42 per cent of primary pupils, but only 27 per cent of university students, so there are still problems getting women into higher education. By the year 2000, there will be a nine-year education plan available to all. The Federation runs special classes in the countryside so that women can improve in agricultural production, and factories run classes for the improvement of education in worker's spare time.

But therein lies another problem. The load of family work means women have to make an effort to find time to improve their education and study. Eighty per cent of women of employment age are in the paid workforce. They must also do family chores and care for children. The lack of social services, the time spent on laundry and shopping, and low incomes all cause problems. Many efforts are made, with the provision of kindergartens and childcare centres, but for most of the population the problem still exists. Some factories and service industries ease workers' burdens by preparing take-home processed foods.

The Federation advocates the sharing of household chores between men and women, and tries to improve social services. Recent surveys show women spend an average of three hours a day on family chores, while men spend two hours.

There are also discriminatory recruiting practices. Women workers have to be of a higher standard because they lose work time due to pregnancy and childbirth. The Federation publishes newspaper articles exposing such double standards. Reveal, criticize, and educate is the method, for the whole nation must be made aware of the gap between theory and practice.

The Federation, the largest body of women in China, aims to mobilize women in the country's reconstruction, safeguard women's rights, and promote the realization of equality between men and women. They educate women to develop self-respect, self-esteem, self-confidence, and self-improvement. They believe that although it is required by law, genuine equality will only be achieved by Chinese women fighting for it themselves.

In a broader context, they work to establish contacts with women all over the world, and work for world peace. The Federation believes equality is a goal that women all around the world have not yet achieved.

The Federation is the only national mass organization which has as its purpose the promotion of women's interests. Like other mass organizations in China, it is subordinate to the leadership of the Chinese Communist Party, and has no authority over any government units.

The Federation has a department of 'propaganda,' education and publicity, a department for children, an institute for the training of women cadres, a research centre on the women's movement which undertakes studies on proposed legal changes, and another department which specializes in giving legal advice to women.

One of my travelling companions, Laurie Salas, asked our hosts on our visit to the Federation headquarters, what kind of problems women came to the legal department with for advice. Divorce, property disputes, discrimination in recruitment – any problem, was the answer. The Federation also gives advice to the state legislature. The legal committee of the National People's Congress came to the Federation three times to solicit opinions on recent changes to the law on divorce and matrimonial property. The Federation spokeswoman said:

> The Women's Federation is one of the agencies carrying out the main tasks of the party. We believe that women's liberation and the socialist construction of China are not possible without the participation of women. And although women are an important force in the total revolution, they have special features, so diminishing the gap between men and women in practice is a mark of development. The Federation also enjoys staunch support from the government and gets all its funds from there. Nationally, there are hundreds of special cadres specializing in work on women, and paid for by the government. So the Federation reflects the party, and bears its own features.

The next question was obvious. Is the Federation consulted on the reduction of the number of people in the army, or on the establishment of a new economic zone, since it was obvious from the rhetoric of the Federation that it believed all issues were women's issues? But, of course, 'such things are decided by the National People's Congress, and at the Party Central Committee level the women members of the Politburo can represent the viewpoint of the women.'

(There are 11 women out of 210 members [5.2 per cent] of the Central Committee of the Communist Party, and 13 out of 138 [9.4 per cent] alternate members. There is 1 woman out of 26 members of the Politburo, Deng Yingchao, and one woman alternate, Chen Muhua.)

Another colleague travelling with me, Elisabeth Vaneveld, commented on the mannequins (which were largely European) in department stores. She asked about the long-term effects of Westernization, and explained that such exploitation can reduce women to objects to drape clothes over, and to paint. The Federation spokesperson replied:

> We are already aware of the phenomenon. With the open-door policy some good things have been introduced, but some Western influences are not so healthy. Not all women are conscious of this, some blindly pursue the appearance of Western style. The Federation does not oppose women paying more attention to clothing, maintaining some characteristics of the

Chinese woman, but she should pay more attention to her education and culture. Many advertisements, especially on television, are exploitatively directed towards women. The Federation has made protests to the authorities concerned, but they cannot make an order for women not to touch these things. Television broadcasters do not care about the social effects of advertising.

A number of people of influence have raised the issue – the Women's Federation, newspapers, and the People's Congress. They must educate and convince. Even the Party Central Committee is aware of the unhealthy attitudes sneaking in from the West.

Then there were other answers:

- Legally, there is no discrimination in housing for single women, but in practice there is. Marrying is the only way to avoid living with one's parents or in the workplace dormitory. Marriage is called a 'normal' life. [I heard of only one single woman who had her own apartment. She was a famous novelist, who was child-free].
- Theoretically, work transfers, for example to the new economic zones, are the same for men and women, but that really depends on the authorities; the majority of authorities will obey state laws. [One-third of the population of the new city in Schenzen's economic zone are construction workers – none of them are women.]
- Yes, they have amniocentesis, but there is no evidence of its use for gender determination (and consequent female infanticide) in the one-child family policy. It is used only to determine fetal abnormality, and the doctor is liable to punishment for releasing details of the gender.
- Only 21 per cent of the total population are in one-child families. The policy is far more prevalent in the cities. Pensions are guaranteed in the city, but not in the country, so country families are dependent on their children for support in their old age. Thus, the preference for sons: thus the current practice of female infanticide.

But in the cities, as *nowhere* else in the world, the one-child family means fathering! male parenting! child care! It is in evidence everywhere you turn.

It's remarkable the capacities men have to be so involved when such drastic measures are taken. This will be a most interesting generation of Chinese children.

And they will be a quarter of those their age on the planet.

6 Brazil

October 1987

A meeting of women trade unionists was held in Sao Paolo, Brazil, on a Saturday. The agenda, in Portuguese, was universally recognizable. In this vast country, the largest in South America, 1 per cent of the richest Brazilians receive 50 per cent of the country's income.

Seventy million workers, in a total population of more than 136,000,000, receive minimum wages. While 50 per cent of the economically active are unionized, the proportion of the female labour force in this category is one-third, or 16 million. While the purchasing power of wages decreases, women join the paid labour force in greater numbers, the total tripling in the last ten years. Forty per cent of these women workers have children. An increasing number of them are becoming heads of their families. Thirty per cent are employed as domestic servants. In the meeting, as rural workers, textile workers, clerks, and factory workers articulate impassioned strategies in a language I neither speak nor understand, I am at home, and overwhelmed by my welcome. They ask me how women in New Zealand organize in unions. Are the women in leadership positions? Do labour unions present or represent women's rights and demands? What is the policy, and what is the practice on equal pay, childcare centres, family planning (and, in particular, abortion), hours of work, retirement, night work, maternity leave?

One Brazilian woman approaches to ask if I know of a New Zealand organization called Corso, and explains that Corso funded the first childcare centre in their area, and that this led to their first women's organization.

The meeting with rural women is held in the evening – at the same time that men attending a conference would attend a cocktail party and go to a nightclub. These women have travelled from remote corners of this country to be here. It is these women who continually provide the linkages between such concerns as sex-role stereotyping in textbooks, and the need to have schools. It is these women who remind this conference, calling for more women's television programs, that many still need roads as a basic form of communication. It is these women who represent the poorest of the poor, the largest unpaid economic sector (although 17 per cent of women workers are 'employed' in agriculture), the largest number of the preliterate, the largest number of the malnourished, and those exhausted from incessant childbearing. It is these primary producers who are seldom recognized in any wealth redistribution in land reform policies.

A young woman PhD student, whose thesis is on the unpaid work of rural women, works for hours on translation with us. The strategy is an analysis of the Census of Agriculture and Population. Earlier in the day, some visiting 'overseas experts,' mainly academics and lawyers, were sceptical of its value as feminist policy and practice. But in the space of three hours, the rural Brazilian women have organized how they will work towards the 1990 Census, involving millions of poor, preliterate women in strategies to ensure their numbers and their work are counted.

The meeting with Brazilian women parliamentarians is held in Brasilia, a city of symbolically fascist architecture. These twenty-five parliamentarians (4.9 per cent of the total members), representing six different parties, speak a language that I recognize in the depths of my being.

These women know who their people are. They are united across party lines on the need to have the UN Convention on the Elimination of All Forms of Discrimination Against Women (CEDAW) included in their new constitution. They are united in their opposition to the policies imposed by international bankers regarding their debt crisis. They are united on agrarian reform, land titles, urban drift, and the delegation of power from federal to municipal governments. These are the voices heard reporting on the 36 million homeless and parentless children living in gangs on rubbish heaps, desperate for survival. These are the voices heard describing the disgraceful violation of human rights in penal institutions. These are the voices in the legislature fighting for the environment.

Many of these women were exiled in the years of the junta. Many were imprisoned. Some have risen to leadership from poverty-stricken rural areas, some have spent most of their lives in *favellas* (slums). They are here now for '*diretas Ja*' – free elections. They want to know of the 'nuclear free' movement, for they have certainly heard of that New Zealand campaign. Strength in sharing, strength in precedents, strength in knowing we are not alone, strength in seeing again and again, and over and over, the most powerless organize against seemingly insuperable odds, was part of their process and their praxis.

It was the same in the *favellas*. There, Maria Alice told me: 'When 700 people are killed in South Africa, that is headlines in Brazil. Here, when three times that number are killed, there is no news.'

I was in a sparsely furnished concrete room, in the prostitution district of Rio de Janeiro, near the main prison. Maria Alice's photo was recently in the press, comforting the 'woman' of the latest 'attempted prison escapee' shot dead in the act by the police. In the past six months under a new state government, many criminals have been killed in this way. They have a common characteristic: they were breaking ties with their criminal bosses and beginning to organize their communities politically, but refusing to invite any political party in to assist.

The most recent such killing, of a man with the nickname 'half a kilo,' occurred in the same week as the violent death of the minister of land reform, with whom I had dined and danced only days before. In his post for only three months, he had already concluded a higher percentage of land reform deals than all his predecessors, and had hugely accelerated the pace of change.

I assumed that no one would face any trial or sanction in either killing. Maria Alice explained that it was the same for the seventeen to twenty-five women killed every week in the slum communities. 'There is no police action. If it's a middle-class woman, the investigation doesn't stop until the murder is solved.'

It took some days to set up this meeting. At the preceding evening's gathering at the home of a wealthy white Brazilian feminist, I had met Joselina, Sandra, and Vernia. They were the only black feminists present. In a situation which I have come to recognize as symptomatic, the presence of foreign feminists, asking to meet Brazilian women, had brought these local women together in this grouping for the first time. Two of us asked for these further meetings.

Maria Alice said that after the prison riots, one of the prisoners' demands that was readily met was to allow conjugal visits once a week. Despite a massive television campaign about AIDS (Sao Paulo is said to be the worst-hit city in the world) no condoms were provided to prisoners. 'It's a very effective form of hands-off genocide for the poor,' I am told.

Sandra was twenty-six, a *favela* organizer, and had been a member of a black *favela* women's group for three years. As she moved us on to our next meeting, she explained:

Many *favela* women have been active for years in health, water, and wider issues. 'Women's issues' were always the bottom of the list. I'd go to big assemblies and see women of fifteen or sixteen looking fifty or sixty. I saw women being beaten in their homes. I noticed it as isolated incidents at first, but then we realized this was women's reality, and this attracted women to our movement. We realized the problem was women's consciousness.

We came together with the white Brazilian feminist movement through a big fight. Three years ago, the Latin American Feminist meeting was held in Sao Paulo. We wanted to participate but weren't let in, so we camped outside the gates for three days. We made an alternative conference outside. Guests who went to the conference then came out to talk to us. Things have changed a lot since then, but no group can pretend the class issue doesn't exist.

We have arrived at the bottom of a hill where cardboard, wire, wood, and corrugated iron make up a network of small huts, which perch precariously on mud. There is the stink of sewage, and the pall of hunger, infant and maternal mortality, disease, unemployment, alcoholism, lack of land rights, violence and exploitation. In the North, when we hear news stories of mud slides in Brazilian slums with high death tolls, it is these shanty towns that are the disaster scene.

Anna moved to this *favela* twenty-five years ago, when there was no water or electricity. Since then she has held every elected position in the community, and in the last elections resisted the pressure of her husband and stood successfully for president against three men. Anna joins about forty other women who have been elected as presidents of a *favela*. One of them heads the largest such community in the country, over 200,000 people. It is largely due to their efforts that the 755 slum communities in the state of Rio de Janeiro (there were 455 two years ago) are beginning to work together. Says Anna, 'Women do all the work here.'

Five of us are crowded in a small office cramped in a corner of the second storey of a plain concrete building. It serves as the office of the head teacher and the *favela* president. On the ground floor, beside the queue of people that wait to use the sole public telephone for St Isabel's 20,000 people, is the crèche and childcare centre, and the kitchen, which feeds all the staff and children in the building. On the next two floors are schoolrooms, and we are led proudly to the as-yet-bare third-floor space, sponsored by the Los Angeles Rotary Club. Here, it is hoped with the help of a small private-aid scheme, that schools can be set up to train teenagers in such skills as screen-printing or leatherwork.

Whatever the first impressions of the visitor at the bottom of the hill, here there is humour, generosity, warmth, courage, and resilience. When I ask her priority is as president, Anna says, without hesitation, education.

With education children can have the opportunity to change this place, or to leave it. I was one of six children. I was born in a *favela* but I had a chance at education. That's why I am here. That's where I learned I should change the place. Not in a political party. There are no party politics in this *favela*.

But there are certainly politics, and healthy feminist politics, working among the women of the poorest communities of Brazil. It was for me a day of rare political privilege. I told them I would share it with you as best I could, even though it was not 'news.'

7 The Philippines

December 1988

I went to The Philippines as the guest of a number of women's organizations, and in particular as the guest of Nikki Coseteng, who had been one of the participants in The Women's Summit with Bella Abzug and Gertrude Mongella. She was known there as Manila's answer to Jane Fonda. The daughter of an extremely rich businessman, she was the host of a highly rated, weekly nationwide television program called *Womanwatch*. But Nikki had also run for Congress in the previous election for Kaiba, the first women's political party in the Philippines, and had won the seat of Quezon City, one of the poorest constituencies in metropolitan Manila.

In the fourth district of Quezon City, I am led along a narrow, dark passageway – the only entrance and exit to a typical 'urban poor community.' In this community there are twenty 'houses,' each about the size of a New Zealand bus shelter, with two storeys. They are made, typically, from cardboard, hardboard, corrugated iron, and rubbish. The smell is of constant dampness, urine, feces, dogs, poverty. It is dark. The rats are gone; they are eaten. The women tell me they live in daily fear of a fire. And they would like a real drain. They apologize for the state of the path. There is no electricity. They would like one water pump for the community.

They bear six, seven, or eight children. In the Philippines, abortion is illegal. There are no exceptions: not the life of the mother, not German measles, and not rape. Abortion is a criminal offence for the doctor and the woman. The rights of the fetus are enshrined in the constitution. For Manila, the conservative estimates are that one in four pregnancies ends in abortion. One in five of those abortions end in the death of the woman. These figures are not wild guesses, but are based, according to a leading obstetrician and gynecologist, on hospital admissions for septic abortions.

The women here share what little medication anyone can ever get. Dysentery and tuberculosis are the key diseases from which their children suffer. 'Older' women already stoop with osteoporosis. We stop to talk. How many families live here? (The twenty 'houses' are contained in an area smaller than a 1,000-square-metre section.) Now a man interrupts and replies 'forty-five.' It is at least fifteen minutes later, when a woman tells me that her life is 'just so hard, but not as hard as my sister's,' that the international stereotype is exposed. The sister has two children and was deserted seven years ago. Her domestic unit is not a 'family.'

Now it appears that the 'forty-five' answer I received earlier relates only to units where men are present. But another 100 families live here in woman-headed households. And as I struggle to picture all these women and children in this space, the sisters introduce their mother. Without prompting, she says to me: 'There is no work here, but of course, women work all the time.'

Busloads of Japanese men are conspicuous in Manila. Eighty-five per cent of Japanese tourists here are men on sex tours. The Manila Midtown Hotel passes out sheets printed in Japanese addressed 'To our Japanese guests with ladies.' The sheet lays out the system. The women are to be admitted after 5:00 p.m., through the employees' entrance; they are to leave by 8:00 the next morning; they are not to be taken to any of the public areas of the hotel, and all food and drink orders must be made by room service. Finally, the hotel charges a 'joiner's fee' of $10 for the right to take a woman into the room. The Manila Midtown management has admitted to making 40 per cent of its gross income from the 'joiner' system. Prostitution in the Philippines is technically illegal, yet, by virtue of presidential decree, prostitutes are considered part of the labour force. Women prostitutes report that they have to pay the police every evening that they work.

In the north in the Cordillera I meet one of the two doctors serving one million people. 'What is the major health problem here for women?' my friend asks. In a highly intelligent answer that speaks for the humanity of this small woman, she answers, 'literacy.' And this in a situation where rubber gloves, speculum, syringes, and all basic instruments are only infrequently available to her.

One day she leads me up and down through narrow paths on the typically mountainous terrain, crossing the river, traversing its banks along terraced rice fields to meet her patients. We stop to speak with two women farmers raking peanuts as they dry. The younger of them went to school until the age of twelve; the older one went for only a year. She is bent and toothless. She wants to know if this foreigner has come here to laugh at her. She is reassured. We ask what she would most want to have now in life. She says she would like to learn to read. She explains that the furthest she has ever travelled is to Bontok, the town at the end of the road we had travelled this morning, before we began our long walk. This was a recent trip, for she had gone to Bontok to cast a vote in the last elections. She tells us that one day she would like to go further than Bontok, 'and when I travel,' she says, 'I would like to know where I am going.'

This woman is from one of the tribes that managed to stop the major Chico dam project and are disparagingly referred to as 'head-hunters.' The women did this, first by refusing to feed any of the workforce and then by moving on to remove all survey pegs. The women were determined to take the initiative in this political struggle, for the historical cultural male practice of confrontation would have only meant bloodshed.

To further prevent violence, the women carried out their political work in groups, in daylight, and naked. Naked, their own men would not dare impede their progress; naked, the men who wished to see the dam proceed would not dare attack these political activists. And in this way, over many months, they moved on to destroy camps, dismantle bridges, and impede any construction effort. You will not be surprised to know that they had not been consulted on the dam, that the lands which were to have been flooded had been home to them and their ancestors for centuries, and that no electricity distribution was intended for them, or for any other domestic community.

These pre-literate peasant women of the Cordillera stopped the dam.

Then, back in Manila, in a meeting with members of the Women's Studies Association, we were told, in that cliché now familiar in city-educated privileged liberals, that such peasant women do not understand feminism.

You might recall those televised scenes from Manila, of the tens of thousands of civilians who had thronged at Cardinal Sin's call into the streets outside and between the defence force presence in the capital. The army barracks are on one side of the wide road, and the air force barracks are on the other. There was an expectation that the Marcos loyalists within either force might begin to fight those who had abandoned the corrupt leader. Sin had called for the people to place themselves between the two camps. With the tanks of Marcos loyalists rumbling towards them, they stood firm. I wanted to see the place, the actual space, the walls they surrounded, and so I was taken there. [Marcos was president of the Philippines between 1965 and 1986. His regime was corrupt, despotic, and nepotistic, and control was maintained with ruthless political repression and human rights abuses. He was removed by the People Power Revolution in 1986.]

After some time in the Philippines, I knew that the mass of the protesters against Marcos had been the impoverished, students, workers, farmers, nuns, seminarians, servants, the urban poor. Yet I recalled those television pictures showing large numbers of the middle class and the wealthy on that particular day, outnumbered perhaps only by statues of the Virgin Mary. I remembered folding chairs, coffee, sandwiches, fans – the air of a picnic in the midst of imminent danger. Had I misremembered? I asked myself.

'Oh no,' said my guide finally, 'the elite were here. One maid carried their umbrella, another carried their protest sign. Another ferried the meals to and from the residence in one car. Beyond the demonstration, the chauffeur waited in another car, so that when the elite became tired or hot they could go and rest in the air conditioning.' 'Surely only a few did this?' I asked. 'No again,' said my guide. 'This was how the wealthy participated.' I checked it out with others. She was not making this up.

If the elite liked comfort in their revolution, the Left liked a little fascism. In the feudal hacienda system based on the monocrop multinational production of pineapples, bananas, rice, and sugar, the plantation owners have frequently controlled all the details of the lives of their workers. This was not simply a matter of where and how they lived, and any access they might be given to health care, education, or hospitals. The owners also determined who might marry whom and when, whether they might live together, whether they could have children, whether they could separate. Today the members of the National Democratic Front, the armed insurgency, are fighting, among other things, for freedom from such feudalism and enslavement and have adopted the social decision-making policies of the liberation armies of North Vietnam. Members of the National Democratic Front shall not take a lover, get married, have children, or get a divorce without the NDF committee's approval. The irony escapes the highly placed members with whom I spent time.

In an effort to recuperate from a heavy viral fever, I flew to the island of Boracay. On the island, my companion entered a restaurant, where she interrupted a meeting between the (predominantly white-European and South African) businessmen on the island, and fifty uniformed military personnel.

A German tourist had recently been murdered on the island. The businessmen, who were already all armed, wanted walkie-talkies and an excuse to set up a 'citizens' army.' The military wanted an excuse to get on to the island. Several days later, when I could venture out to the shore, there in pairs, and often in T-shirts, Nike shorts, and sandals, strolled the soldiers – with semi-automatic machine guns over their shoulders. This seemed very strange. Boracay is a very small island. We circumnavigated it in a small boat with an outboard in just over an hour. I noticed that a lot of the other 'guests' on the island were U.S. servicemen, possibly taking time out from Subic Bay.

Subic Bay Naval Base is the largest U.S. naval reservation outside the U.S., and the largest naval supply depot in the world. The Subic Base covers an area of 89,000 hectares of land and 64,000 hectares of water. Stationed at Subic Naval Base are 5,000 military personnel, 560 U.S. civilians, and 5,500 U.S. military and civilian dependents. The U.S. Seventh Fleet, with its 70,000 military personnel, 550 aircraft, and 90 ships regularly visits Subic for repairs, military exercises, food, fuel, ammunition, and rest and recreation. Port stay is usually one to ten days.

Olongapo is a city of approximately 250,000 people. It lies adjacent to the main gate of Subic Bay Naval Base. Olongapo is known as the 'hottest rest and recreation' spot available to the U.S. Navy anywhere in the world. There are an estimated 15,000 to 17,000 prostitutes, with 5,000 registered at the Social Hygiene Clinic. These women work in over 330 bars, massage parlours, and other entertainment establishments, which line the main road and side streets near the main gate of the base.

When hired for the first time in a bar, women must get a mayor's permit (the mayor is a U.S. citizen), which requires a chest X-ray, a VD smear, a blood test, and a stool test. This permit makes them legal, and they are required to carry identification. All legal workers must have a bi-weekly VD smear, a chest X-ray twice a year, an AIDS test twice a year, and a physical checkup to renew the permit each year. The tests are conducted at the Social Hygiene Clinic, a joint project of the city health department and the U.S. Navy. The women pay for the tests themselves. If a smear is positive, the woman's bar (not the woman) is contacted and she must report for treatment and stop working until she is well. If the woman's AIDS test is positive, the servicemen are informed to avoid that woman and that bar. The woman is not informed. The servicemen are not regularly tested for VD or AIDS.

When I was only a little shocked by that – disgusted, but not surprised – I was advised of the series of different bars. I wasn't surprised that there were some bars for officers and some for the rest of the forces. But there are bars for black men and bars for white men. Buddies can, but seldom do, traverse that line. Naval personnel justify it by saying 'some of the prostitutes prefer black men and some prefer white' – as if sexual slaves have choices.

The prostitutes of Olongapo know every movement of the Seventh Fleet.

The hope generated in the Philippines by the election of Corazon Aquino has not resulted in any real political change, particularly for women, in a nation where feudalism and militarism still dominate. For the final stop on the journey, we travelled to the island of Negros. Here, Congresswoman Nikki Coseteng, chair of the Human Rights Committee of the House in the government of Corazon Aquino, was to conduct hearings into abuses on the island.

The first witness arrives. The young woman struggles to hold back tears, to find the words. Her husband has been shot. He had been shot at point-blank range, leading a demonstration in Bacalod, Negros. He was an only child, unusual in a Filipino family, and he is survived by only one child. Compensation for such a death is available, but none has been forthcoming. Japan's Amnesty International chapter has adopted the case and has pressured the president, the Commission on Human Rights, the military for prosecution, the governor and the mayor for explanation. There has been no reply from anyone.

Nomila Sabari appears next, struggling forward on crutches, her right leg amputated at the knee. She recalls the moment on 10 September 1988 when the military opened fire on eleven families in her village. The military had been prepared for a clash with the New People's Army. They opened fire as the families ran before them, stopping only when they finally heard the cries of the survivors: 'We are not rebels.' Five women and one child were dead. Four others were wounded. An officer blamed the shootings on the fact that the victims had hidden and could not be identified.

A military release on 14 September claimed that a company of troops had a battle with a large group of rebels, killing and wounding a number of them. The wounded had been left for dead. But Nomila had been picked up and taken to the hospital in Bacalod, soon enough to save her life – not soon enough to save her leg. Captain Lumbag, who led the military operation, has, as is usual, received no censure.

Coseteng listens, and as the testimony unfolds, her bright Manila mask-smile begins to slip. Her mother's family comes from this island of Negros.

Next to speak are the representatives of the National Union of Sugar Workers. This union is frequently dismissed as a Communist Party front, in red-baiting clichés reminiscent of the McCarthy era in the U.S.

The legislated minimum wage for sugar workers here is 48.5 pesos (U.S.$3.64) a day. Women and children, who are casual workers, do not qualify for this amount. Some planters pay their male workers only 15 pesos a day, and 10 pesos for women and children. The highest number of days a sugar worker can expect to work in a year is between 170 and 180. Such is the power of the union.

Yet the military have been mounting a 'successful' campaign against this union in the haciendas, the plantations of Negros. The military holds meetings of sugar workers, who are all invited to sign a paper and surrender as members of the New People's Army. Those who do not sign are treated as communists. In the three years up to October 1988, under a policy sanctioned by President Aquino, 49 haciendas with 4,311 members have been forced to surrender; 17 haciendas with 2,096 members have been forced to withdraw from the union; 183 union members have been arrested and detained; 24 unionists have been killed and 4 are missing. In the past ten months, five haciendas have been strafed. The military have been assisted in all this by the vigilante armies of the plantation owners.

Although Coseteng is only in her second year of congressional politics, she knows it can be this bad. When I met her, just after arriving in Manila, she had been up most of the night, working for the release of the surviving youth of two who had been shot and left for dead for pasting up anti-nuclear posters.

Lucretia and her two small children are now talking. A fisherwoman, she tells of the night on 8 September when the soldiers came to her home in the village, calling for her husband. 'They forced entry and searched everything, holding their rifles at us.' She raises her arms as if aiming a rifle. 'We do not have anything,' she told them. 'You must have arms or documents,' they replied. The soldiers wanted to take her husband to the precinct: 'No, I cannot allow that. He won't come back,' she said. Finally, he was taken. 'Don't kill him,' she pleaded.

'Come down to our headquarters at 7:00 a.m. and he will be there,' they said. 'We are only going to talk to him.'

But he was not there. They took him to another compound to identify others. Lucretia saw her husband more than a month and a half later. 'He is still behind bars without charges. He has been hit a lot, especially in the stomach.'

Representatives of the Task Force Detainees of the Philippines take up the story. 'We have had a lawyer file a petition for illegal detention,' they tell Coseteng. 'There were seven arrests that night. They were all members of the Federation of Small Fishermen in Negros. Three have been released, four are still in detention, all are family men. All three that have been released had been interrogated and tortured for being subversives.'

The subversion? Forming a federation and agitating against the illegal forms of fishing in and around Negros. Japanese and large Filipino commercial vessels all violate the 10-kilometre local fishing zone. Dynamite fishing is common. The small fishers want a new fishery law to prohibit foreign vessels inside the 200-kilometre offshore zone.

According to the testimony now being given, the military have launched a saturation drive in coastal districts. Anyone found organizing is accused of being part of the Communist Party front. All are pressured to withdraw from the union because it is getting 'too big.' 'Too big' is about 1,000 fisherwomen (out of an estimated 350,000 on Negros) and 3,000 men.

Congresswoman Coseteng begins to respond, with patience and sympathy, explaining her own place in the appeal process, and her own powerlessness. In a litany I am to hear frequently, she is forced in a brief résumé to try to explain how the Government of the Philippines works now, at least in theory.

Coseteng asks: Who is your congressman? (Romeo Guanzan, one of the planters who operates his own vigilante army.) Have you talked or written to him, or your mayor? (Ghay Muntilibano, another landlord who amasses arms and men to form an infamous army to fight the workers.) Or to senators, your governor, your elected public officials?

'We are too scared,' interrupts a woman, sitting quietly at the hearing. 'We are too scared. There have even been two attempts on the life of the bishop of this area.'

Coseteng stops. She needs no other answers.

The congresswoman is an independent. She knows that she is about to be thrown out of the chair of this Human Rights Committee, ostensibly because she refuses to join a political party. More obviously, her position is in jeopardy because, in stark contrast to all but three or four other members of the Philippines Congress, she is sitting in this Catholic church hall, where the priest has twice survived assassination attempts, listening to these submissions. In her colleagues' eyes, her 'error' of independence is compounded because she believes what she is told.

As we leave the hall, we notice a jeep full of soldiers at the gates. They had been seen earlier, but those attending the hearing had thought they were part of Coseteng's security team. Not so, our hosts are told. And those at the meeting spend the night waiting for a knock at the door. This time, so far as we know, no doors are forced open.

The next day, the arrested fishermen are released. At the same time, a group of international experts leave to investigate the deaths of sixty children in the part of Negros where the 61st Infantry Battalion are operating. The government health authorities have classified the deaths as a disease epidemic, but a nurse has smuggled out tissue samples – and her own diagnosis. Although I have no medical expertise, the symptoms sound reminiscent of the defoliant chemical poisonings which killed so many children in Vietnam. But this is Negros, the sugar island of the Philippines and, since the world sugar price collapsed in 1985, this monocrop island has managed to rocket to the top of the global list for starvation, malnutrition, and infant and maternal mortality.

After the fall of Marcos and while the flame of hope still burned in the early Aquino days, multilateral and foreign government aid agencies organized programs to ensure that this wretched record was never matched again. At the forefront of the local response was the organization called the Negros Women for Tomorrow Foundation. They hooked a large quantity of aid money, with the biggest single contributor being CIDA, the Canadian government's aid agency which poured in some U.S.$150 million.

The foundation did not want to give testimony to Congresswoman Coseteng. In fact, this group refused to meet her. Surprisingly, they agreed to host a lunch for me and to spend an afternoon showing me their projects.

The surprise lasted until I realized that they believed I was still a member of the New Zealand Parliament, and until I understood that the recently appointed New Zealand Ambassador to the Philippines,

Alison Stokes, had been their speaker at a Chamber of Commerce function, and that New Zealand had contributed in a modest way to one of the Unicef gardening/nutrition schemes promoted by these Women for Tomorrow.

They were, with one exception, very pleasant and straightforward with me. With one exception, I even liked them, and in many ways I felt enormously sorry for them. And while every fibre of my intellect, heart, and spirit screamed its internal resistance, I even maintained my equanimity with them. You see, the Negros Women for Tomorrow Foundation is an organization of planters' wives.

At lunch, I am seated near a very white woman. She is an Australian, and, in that perversity of too many cultures, is envied as a prize; it is a matter of some status for a Filipino planter to marry a white woman.

The Australian is married to Ghay Muntilibano, president of the Planters Association and mayor of Bacalod. In my background reading on the Marcos regime, I had encountered his name as one of those who had borrowed substantial sums of overseas funds and squandered them, adding to the national debt.

Mrs Muntilibano tells me there are no right-wing vigilantes or private armies, that 'volunteers' guard the haciendas (Amnesty International disagrees), that only 12 per cent of the Negros haciendas are large and that families continue to run haciendas in cooperatives because their division into individual entitlements would mean plots as small as six hectares.

When she declares that no one pays workers only 15 pesos a day, she is corrected by other planters' wives who suggest that there are a few who still do.

Then part of the Foundation's work in Bacalod is explained. There are immunization programs for polio, tuberculosis, and diphtheria. More than 5,000 children are fed in the city once a day with particular attention to their intake of vitamin A and carbohydrates.

Also under way is a 'values education program,' the main thrust of which is to encourage self-sufficiency and independence. Some of its aims, in nutrition, infant care, subsistence crop growing, and environmental preservation, are undeniably admirable. But as I listen, a cynicism grows, that women who have nannies, cleaners, cooks, domestics, laundresses, gardeners, and chauffeurs should be responsible for defining 'values.'

After lunch, they take me to a pavilion selling products made by poor women in a business run by the Women for Tomorrow. Later, we tour the outskirts of Bacalod and a chosen hacienda. As we travel the roads, the planters' wives point out the rapidly expanding operations of a freshwater-prawn farm. These are a major part of a diversification program the governor of the province has promoted since the collapse of sugar prices in 1985.

The farms are also specifically exempted from any land reform program for ten years, because they are so capital intensive and their monthly harvest is all exported. The farms generate work and income – and delay the reform that would give land to the workers. Contaminated water from the farm ponds also pollutes the meagre freshwater supply of the villages nearby, forcing the poor women to walk ever further to meet their families' needs.

Another part of the 'values education' program involves reforestation. Only 6.3 per cent of the forest cover is left on Negros, the educators explain. It takes 40 per cent forest cover to provide the ideal biosphere to support sugar cane growth, so the island must be replanted.

According to my guides, peasant farmers are to blame for the devastation of the Negros forest. Yet later that afternoon I learn that the large sugar refining company that we visit is fuelled by logs obtained from another major company engaged in illegal felling operations in the hill country.

Well, yes, the women concede, but look at those trees along the road – look at the way they have been cut. I had been looking at them. They attract attention because they all appear to have been cut at a height of between 1.2 and 1.8 (about 3 feet) metres from the ground.

This seems very odd, but as Typhoon Ruby (which hit our area while travelling) breaks up the next day, I understand. The typhoon snaps these trees like matchsticks, at just that height. The poor people clear the broken limbs immediately (they are valuable) and the rest of the tree is left to regenerate.

We enter a road leading to a sugar mill and haciendas, passing a roadblock mounted by a group of 'scout rangers.' Using unprovocative language, knowing that these are vigilantes, I ask: 'Is this a private security firm?'

'Oh, no,' is the response, 'these are men recommended by the army.'

One of the major thrusts of the Negros Women for Tomorrow Foundation is to encourage self-sufficient cooperatives, or so they say. But no training is given or information imparted on how to apply to any form of aid agency for funding. When a cooperative becomes 'independent,' its application for assistance still passes through the Foundation. And the Foundation still charges 12 per cent in brokerage fees for service.

Another aim is to 'free the sugar workers from their womb to tomb dependency.' But the planters and landowners have 'worked so hard' that they want to see their province remain productive. The workers do not know how to farm. If workers gained title to their own land in the much-vaunted reform program, who would pay for the irrigation systems, health care, hospitals, schools? The government has no alternative support system, cannot afford to provide even the surveyors, and the schools and hospitals are still 'given' by wealthy landowners.

Now we have arrived at the hacienda where the UNICEF garden project is in operation. Three hundred square metres are allocated for individual plots and the focus of effort is on crops other than rice or grain. This is the showcase project. There is no cooperative farming here as there is on the haciendas where the unions are strong.

Dr Cecilia del Castillo, the executive director of the Negros Women for Tomorrow Foundation, is particularly proud of this project. A Filipina who was trained as a psychologist and who spent seven years working in Washington, DC, she returned to Negros after the fall of Marcos and spent 'a year travelling about, thinking what I might do, where the need was.'

A single woman, del Castillo was elected recently to the Provincial Council. She explains to me that her next project is the establishment of a Poor People's Bank. The bank's initial working capital is to be U.S.$5 million and she expects it will be provided from the Canadian Government's aid scheme. The bank will be based on 'the Bangladesh model.'

Dr del Castillo does not talk as frequently as the planters' wives and she occasionally voices some disquiet at things we pass. At the sugar mill, she comments on the phenomenal waste of using logs to fuel the boilers, at the heat and energy passing unharnessed up the smoke stacks, at the failure to dry the wood of the cane to use as fuel.

In almost a month in the Philippines, as guests of the women's movement there, we were engaged in hearings, visits, and dialogues in a number of areas, from Bagio to Davao. In many instances, our visit was the first occasion since the fall of Marcos that different local organizations had cooperated to talk and work together. That was true everywhere, however, except on Negros.

There, no amount of persuasion could induce groups as diverse as those who testified to Congresswoman Coseteng and the Women of Tomorrow to speak to each other.

On Negros, there is a boundary that very few ever cross. Some do. There is the son of one landowning family who now works for Amnesty

International in New York but who dares not go home. There is one woman landowner who has joined the land reform program and the umbrella women's organization Gabriela, which works vigorously for the reform and against the abuse of human rights under the Aquino administration. She has been ostracized.

Negros, I was told, is the social volcano of the Philippines. I believe it, as I also believe that, until the feudal life of Negros is changed, there is no sense in which the fall of Marcos can be seen as a revolution. To my personal distress, I see no way in which the hope generated by the election of a woman president has been realized in genuine political change.

A Vigorous Vigilance

In 1984, the Labour Government was elected with a key policy platform of legislating for a nuclear free New Zealand. The Anzus meeting to establish a security alliance between the U.S., Australia, and New Zealand was to follow within weeks of the election. The pressure would come immediately from the so-called allies against the nuclear free policy. There would be no waiting for draft legislation.

After the introduction of the nuclear free legislation, the propaganda and scare tactics reached a frenzied peak. Some years before the Bavandra-led government in Fiji had had a nuclear free policy, but this was never enacted before the first Fiji coup in 1987. Nuclear free activists in Japan had mobilized, as had those in the Philippines. Washington officials despaired at the possible spread of the 'New Zealand disease.' These two essays were written during this period.

1 Big Brothers, We're Watching You

28 July 1984

The big brothers were scheduled to assemble last week in Wellington for the latest Anzus round. This agreement, signed in 1951 and designed to 'strengthen the fabric of peace in the Pacific area,' brings to the table one partner with missile weaponry sufficient to destroy the planet Earth many times over, one partner with expanding investment and interest in uranium mining and enough bases to represent a permanent accession to U.S. global nuclear defences – and then there is New Zealand.

And what sort of a treaty partner is New Zealand? What can we say when three of the four main parties contesting the New Zealand elections – representing between them the majority of voters – no longer want to join the Anzus ritual of providing a base for U.S. nuclear warriors with their rest and recreation? This must worry the brethren who like their relationships so cut and dried that they even draft their final communiqués before these assemblies start. This time, let us ask them a few more basic questions.

Who is our enemy? Since we are of no current strategic importance in the global scheme of things, the answer must be 'no one' or 'anyone.' I have always been briefed that our security is an economic one, dependent on our ability to trade with all political blocs. When I put this point to the deputy director of the United States Disarmament and Arms Control

Agency, his response was: 'I've never heard that line before.' The under-the-table kick launched in his direction by a U.S. diplomat at the dinner would have served as a model for any self-defence class.

Where would our enemy come from? According to a recently leaked major defence document adopted by the Australian government, any potential enemies are seen to be coming from north of Australia.

How will they arrive? If the Falklands War is any indicator, by ship. And, since we are reasonably large islands, lots of ships. So some eye-in-the-sky would see them coming.

Then does Anzus spring into action? Article Three of the Treaty, the only effective operative article in the small document, says the 'parties will consult together whenever in the opinion of any of them the territorial integrity, political independence, or security of any of the parties is threatened in the Pacific.' At the signing ceremony in 1951, the New Zealand representative said: 'Finally the treaty has no effect unless and until one of its parties is attacked.'

But wait. Why is it that the same recently leaked Australian defence document also sees that those enemies from the north are to be coped with ... without expectation of or desire for support from Anzus partners? Australia must be prepared to stand alone.

Now let us presume that 'anyone' or 'no one' is advancing on New Zealand shores. Admiral Crowe, commander-in-chief of Pacific and American forces, admiral in command and responsible for carrying out Anzus obligations, is contacted. This admiral has been much quoted in the debate over visits by nuclear-powered and nuclear-weapons-capable ships.

'As a military commander,' he is reported as saying, 'it seems difficult for me to see how I could fulfil any military obligation that we may have under Anzus where I would have to deploy forces to this part of the world if they did not have access to the ports of our allies ... when I say it is difficult, I do not understand how I can do it.'

(Of course he can't. From the moment you enter the military, you are taught to take orders. Imagine if all the brothers trained to press the button were encouraged to consider the consequences of what they were doing!)

Why is it difficult for Admiral Crowe to see how he can help us if we decide we do not want visits by the nuclear navy? These ships come here for rest and recreation, nothing else. The grand, wonderful total of this cornerstone of access in thirty-three years is: 1960 – one submarine; 1964 – three ships; 1976 – two cruisers; 1978 – one submarine; 1979 – one submarine; 1980 – one cruiser; 1982 – one cruiser; and 1983 – one cruiser.

If calling a halt to these rest-and-recreation visits would pose difficulties for the admiral, what problems lie waiting for him in our official policies towards nuclear weaponry? Has he ever been advised that New Zealand refuses to manufacture, possess, or permit to be stored any form of nuclear weapon in this country? Has he been told we are totally opposed to their use anywhere in the world? Has it been pointed out to him that New Zealand could not possibly be defended by the use of nuclear weapons and that New Zealanders do not wish to see themselves defended by their use?

(If anyone advances on these shores, I'm not sure that these American nuclear warriors will be all that useful anyway. British soldiers landed in the Falklands at night to disguise themselves as farmhands before engaging the enemy. We'll be after the British again, to slip on to our industrial sites as riggers and boilermakers, and Aussie lads will fly in unobtrusively as horse-racing gansters (or punters) and surfers. The mind boggles. I must return to Admiral Crowe's navy ...)

My understanding is that the New Zealand government receives a list of vessels that might call and the proposed dates. It then indicates whether or not it will receive such a visit. Publications are freely available that show whether or not a particular vessel is likely to be carrying nuclear weapons. So, if the New Zealand government wanted to ensure that this country was nuclear free at all times, it has the opportunity to do so. We don't even need legislation (though I would vehemently support it), only the political will.

But, we have been told, Anzus is threatened if such visits do not continue. Since this is patently untrue, I can't work out whether I am being bullied or treated like an idiot. If we are being bullied then two can play at that game. Maybe we could tell our Anzus allies to just push off – and get their intelligence on the south-west Pacific (for which New Zealand has a reputation par excellence) from somewhere else. But if it's an idiot I'm seen to be, would the brethren please desist. I was told at an early age the story of the emperor who had no clothes, and I can't escape the feeling that I am hearing the same story whenever I ask these simple questions.

2 I Think I'm Getting the Message

26 July 1986

Admiral James Lyons, commander-in-chief of the United States Pacific Fleet, said recently that utopianism was threatening the 'fabric of deterrence' in the South Pacific. Reading New Zealand Prime Minister Lange's speeches, he concludes that 'he is leading his country on a path of essential neutralism.'

Meanwhile, a State Department official in Washington supports moves to end the *Rainbow Warrior* dispute between New Zealand and France. 'We welcome the news that this dispute between two key Western democracies may soon be resolved.' [French security agents blew up the Greenpeace ship the *Rainbow Warrior* at Auckland's Wharf.]

Richard Perle, the U.S. Assistant Secretary of Defense, has said – (in the context of the European allies, but very interesting nonetheless) – 'Democracies will not sacrifice to protect their security in the absence of a sense of danger. And every time we create the impression that we and the Soviets are co-operating and moderating the competition, we diminish that sense of apprehension.'

(That would be dreadful for the arms trade, and the U.S. economy, too.)

I'm just lining up relevant quotations and pondering on the meeting of Prime Minister Lange and the U.S. Secretary of State Schultz. The United States administration has problems with clause 9 of the New Zealand Nuclear Free Zone, Disarmament and Arms Control Bill. This is because of the policy of neither confirming nor denying the presence of nuclear weapons on board U.S. ships and aircraft.

For many years, this policy has enabled the United States to fly in the face of the expressed wishes of allies to be nuclear-weapons free at all times (for example New Zealand, Sweden, Norway) and to breach international treaties (such as with Japan).

This policy no longer has logistical credibility. Two senior U.S. officials have publicly confirmed that Soviet satellites could detect the presence of nuclear weapons on U.S. vessels well before they reach the South Pacific. The two officials were James Kelly, the deputy secretary of the U.S. Navy, and Fred Brown, senior staffer at the Senate Foreign Relations Committee.

An alert opposition spokesperson on foreign affairs would question the prime minister as to why, then, the New Zealand government continues to leave that U.S. policy unchallenged.

Because it would not be supported in its challenge by any other country? Because of fears of reprisals, or even, as the jargon has it, 'destabilization'?

Perhaps there's nothing in it, but Dr Ray Klein has recently visited New Zealand. Klein, who has no specialist Pacific background, was named as the head of a special Anzus project at the Centre for Strategic and International Studies at Georgetown University in Washington,

DC. He is best remembered as a major figure in planning the over-throw of the Allende Chilean government when he was director of the Bureau of Intelligence and Research in the U.S. Department of State.

I'm not suggesting that there is nothing wrong with clause 9 of the bill. There is a problem: there is no criminal sanction on a prime minister who does not perform in accordance with the provisions of the bill, or who lies. It would seem to me that the only suitable charge would be treason, and this is a nightmare scenario.

The nuclear free policy displays such 'uncommon' sense; perhaps that is why it's so difficult to understand. In light of the bombing of Libya, failed Titan, Cruise and Challenger launchings, and the melt-down at Chernobyl, it seems strange that the New Zealand model is perceived as a destabilizing model for the planet.

Accidents, debris, iodide tablets, pregnant women and children con-fined indoors; radioactive air; banned food; dumped milk, vegetables, and meat; poisoned water; alerts, fallout, and fear all seem to be trying to tell us something.

The final text of section 9 of the New Zealand Nuclear Free Zone, Disarmament and Arms Control Act 1987 reads as follows:

9. Entry into internal waters of New Zealand – (1) When the Prime Minister is considering whether to grant approval to the entry of foreign warships into the internal waters of New Zealand, the Prime Minister shall have regard to all relevant information and advice that may be available to the Prime Minister including information and advice concerning the strategic and security interests of New Zealand.

(2) The Prime Minister may only grant approval for the entry into the internal waters of New Zealand by foreign warships if the Prime Minister is satisfied that the warships will not be carrying any nuclear explosive device upon their entry into the internal waters of New Zealand.

3 Suffrage Sufferance

11 April 1987

The next series of essays follows my own process and biases as I move to support a change in New Zealand's voting system to proportional representation.

The first is written as we approached the election of 1987, an election which brought me as close as I have ever been to not bothering to cast a vote. The country had been rocked by the first three years of the period that came to be termed 'Rogernomics' – named after the finance minister, Roger Douglas. My sentiments were pretty much disgust and repulsion at the deception foisted on the people of New Zealand, and the bald-faced lies. Cabinet minister Richard Prebble had led the charge to sell off the 'strategic' assets (railways, electricity generators) of the country after maintaining in 1986: 'The Government opposes the suggestion ... that they will sell off taxpayer's assets. The Government does not regard itself as the owner ... of the State Corporations affected. The Government is the guardian on behalf of the people. No Government has the right to sell off State trading enterprises to its cronies.' Roger Douglas was subsequently hired by Ralph Klein to continue the same policies in Alberta.

I am not facing the impending prospect of exercising my freedom to vote with any joy. It seems to me that asking me to endorse the policies or practices of any current New Zealand political party is asking a bit much. And since I don't live in one of those seats where candidates hold their breath until the 'special' votes are counted, my endorsement of anyone will not make much difference.

As a feminist, political scientist, and activist, I am much discomforted by this feeling. I will, of course, vote. Men and women died for the suffrage, more than a billion still don't have this right to exercise it freely, and while it's far from the be-all and end-all of human freedom, it's a practical symbol. And we do exercise this process in this country, and in numbers proportionally exceeding most countries.

That is one of the reasons that we baffle the U.S. administration – not because they can't see 'democracy' in front of their eyes beyond their shores, but because they don't have it to recognize within their shores.

One cannot say, after an election in the U.S., that 'the American people have spoken.' The 1986 election showed that about 37 per cent of those eligible to vote did. The result does not represent the views of the 112 million non-voters. The non-voter is alienated from the American political process. The system operates so that only the people who have influential and wealthy friends can be in the Senate.

A recently retired senator, Missouri Democrat Thomas Eagleton, explained of the Capitol building where representatives have their offices: 'There's the stench of money around this building ... You're not getting that money out of the Red Cross or the Little Sisters of the Poor. They [those who give it] expect something for that money. And when you receive that money, you know those folks have an expectation. You're not blind.'

And while Australia has a healthy percentage of turnouts during elections (assisted by 'compulsory voting' legislation), I've always felt sorry for voters there, even more so these days, when the choice is between the Right, the Further Right, and the Far Right, and whatever else they choose to call themselves.

But none of this helps me decide how to vote. So far from the National Party I've heard a call for law-and-order policy based on blame and fear. I heard the spokesperson say the threat of harsher penalties was a deterrent to criminal activity, because the fear of being caught was of major importance. Well, there's an enormous body of social science literature which concludes that is not the case. The fear of being caught and the possible penalties are not always operative when men, like those who are elected to Parliament, commit adultery, and I might have thought there was an analogy that could be made there.

The Labour government's policy can be observed in action. There is still no law declaring New Zealand a nuclear-weapons free zone, and I am anticipating more mud in the waters on this issue before the election. And in a week recently passed, 2,000 coalminers in Huntly were informed they no longer had work. I felt Huntly's blow keenly, for I was initially elected to Parliament while living there. Two things struck me immediately. First, isn't there supposed to be an energy resources levy paid for coal extraction, and has the state ever paid that to Huntly? Second, did you notice the global politics operative in microcosm in the immediate offer of re-siting the proposed Mangere irradiation plant from Auckland to Huntly?

Around the globe we see multinationals exporting pesticide, pharmaceutical, and major dangerous pollutant manufacturing to the economically depressed parts of the world where there is a readily available, exploitable labour force. I don't doubt Huntly people want work, or that a site couldn't be found a safe distance from worker's homes. But on any site near Huntly the earth might move, because there are centuries-old peat swamps creating an instability within old coalmine shafts and holes.

Huntly used to vote five-to-one for Labour. In the 1950s, National Party meetings there turned into riots, and shopkeepers' windows were smashed. In my first campaign there, we had separate signs from the rest of the electorate, replacing the party logo with a reference to my being a 'local.' I wonder what the voting patterns will be

in Huntly this year, or in Ohau, or in the salt-of-the-earth parts of
New Zealand where the quality as opposed to the quantity of life still
means something.

I still don't know who the candidates are in this electorate, and I do
remember rashly vowing, whilst still inside the parliamentary institution, that since the party affiliations of the brotherhood were relatively
indistinct from each other in terms of the issues of freedom which concerned me, I would always vote for the candidate, not the policies or
party. But the nuclear-weapons free policy and the homosexual law
reform, for example, have demonstrated some distinction.

Besides, that was in those days when, with a broad grin on my face, I
would vote for myself. The consequences of that may not have brought
me much joy, but I was saved from this current dilemma.

*In the election, Labour was returned with 48 per cent of the vote and fifty-
eight parliamentary seats. National had 44 per cent of the vote and thirty-nine
seats. There was little consolation for the disillusioned in the result, but I did
try to find some. I was misguided in believing that the rise in the number of
women in the House and on the Labour benches might ease the right-wing
juggernaut unleashed in the previous term.*

4 A New Convert

12 September 1987

I'm glad the election is over. It was interesting how many people in the
weeks before asked me, 'How will we get on on August 15?' I was
never sure just who they meant by 'we.'

But 'we' are now 14 out of 97 parliamentarians and 11 out of 56 in
the government caucus. After the 1978 election we had only four
women in Parliament, and I was alone in the government caucus. This
is a good rate of progress if we can maintain it. From where I sit now, it
is a decidedly more interesting situation in terms of possibilities. We
will wait and see.

That Judy Keall, Ann Fraser, and Annette King would get a swing in
their favour was one of my predictions. I forecast Labour would get
fifty-five seats, National forty-one, and the Social Democrats one. Jenny

Kirk's victory in Birkenhead was a good reason to celebrate losing the election sweepstakes.

While it seems invidious to pick out one but not all, I want to honour the election to the New Zealand Parliament of Sonja Davies. It is inevitable that a woman who has shown so much leadership in so many facets of society should enter that institution carrying our hope for a change in the direction of many people – women in particular. I trust she will not find that hope a burden and will realize that my concern comes to her with a wry smile and good humour. For Sonja Davies, Parliament is not the pinnacle; it's just another place we have to be, and I'm awfully pleased she's there.

In my experience, parties seldom call for a keen analysis of an election campaign, but here are some points anyway.

First, we were very bored. Our leaders were not stars in a continual soap for three or four weeks. They were tediously repetitive and their scripts lacked substance and humour. I found the ads extraordinarily patronizing. I'm not interested in being told how to think, which is why I liked Mana Motuhake's Maori-based party's invitation to 'imagine.'

Second, National Party stalwarts dreaded getting back into office with Muldoon still in their ranks. They said it like a broken record. They believed they would not be able to win with him in the team. But the problem runs deeper. There is, out here in the real world, disquiet about the 'team.' National Party leader Bolger may well have extracted himself from public perception as a yes-man for former prime minister Muldoon, but none of the other former National cabinet ministers who remain have. So they are seen as men who could change political horses and ride off in a different direction very quickly. In George Gair, solitary and getting older, they see the remaining face of what used to be a considerable liberal element in the National Party.

Third, in the National caucus the doctrinaire and ill-conceived policies on education and social welfare were the cause of much unease. The authors of these programs still seem persuaded by the late nineteenth-century scientific approach that there is a clinical analysis of social issues. The public are intelligent enough to know that life doesn't pigeonhole like that. Promoting social division in the guise of freedom and responsibility are old tricks and not the answers they are looking for. So, it interested me that Labour took lots of votes without a policy.

The fourth point of analysis: when 'liberals' looked at National's slate and potential caucus line-up, they saw an opportunistic call for a referendum for capital punishment (a big political mistake), they saw only three members who thought that gay people should have the same

rights as them to a job or to housing, and they saw all the other discriminations still current on the grounds of gender preference. They saw one
future caucus member who, as an electoral official, had stabbed his MP
in the back to become the candidate; they saw a winner who led legiti-
mized assaults on New Zealand citizens in the Police Red Squad and
other winners whose political self-control is analogous to an unguided
missile. There was the failure of many National Party constituencies to
select candidates who might have contributed effectively at not only the
local but also the national level. This flows from a lack of liberal input at
the grass roots. There really wasn't any 'caring' in National's campaign.
New Zealanders are fairly resistant to 'fear campaigning' at the moment.

This doesn't mean to say there aren't chaps in the government caucus who send chills up and down my spine. Nor does it ignore for the
large part the role that the nuclear free New Zealand issue played in
the campaign. That issue epitomizes something proud and growing
and intensely political. It is a flavour the National Party hasn't tasted
for some time. While it may not be the flavour of the month in this new
government, it is still visible.

In case some people are getting upset about my election analysis, let
me assure them that this is exactly how I used to talk to the National
Party, at meetings and inside its caucus. They did not take any notice of
me then, either. The Labour Party never takes any notice of me because
I used to be on the other side. Besides, I'm a farmer and a feminist. A
double whammy on Rogernomics.

This election did cause me to make a new political commitment. I
am now a convert to more seats in Parliament and to proportional representation. If New Zealand runs true to stubborn form, a raft of really
interesting independents might turn up. It would do wonders for the
television ratings during the election campaign.

5 Party Animals

6 February 1988

*The Royal Commission on the Electoral System reported in December 1986. A
year later, New Zealanders a government circular with information on the findings and recommendations of the Commission as a prelude to the referenda we*

*would be involved in. These would be held to determine if New Zealanders
wanted a change in their voting system and, if so, what system they preferred.
The dice were already loaded to push the Mixed Member Proportional system
favoured by the Commission.*

Did you read your copy of *The New Zealand Voter* in the mailbox just
before Christmas? Did you discard it as junk mail or put it aside to read
in the holiday period and never got around to it? I wouldn't be surprised, for neither the circular nor the *Report of the Royal Commission on
the Electoral System*[1] are an easy read. But the issue is vitally important.

In 1981, the Labour Party took more votes than National but didn't
win the majority of seats in the House. In the same election, 20.7 per
cent of New Zealand voters supported Social Credit candidates, but
that party won only two (2.2 per cent) of the seats. In 1975 the Values
Party and in 1984 the New Zealand Party took a percentage of votes
without gaining any representation. It is to such results that the Royal
Commission has, substantially, addressed itself. This current system of
ours is termed 'plurality.' The Commission comments in the report:
'Plurality systems everywhere have a poor record in terms of the election of women, ethnic and other minorities, and those from certain
occupational and socio-economic groups.'[2]

Several alternative voting systems fall under the generic term of
'proportional representation,' designed, says the Commission, 'to provide that the seats a *party* receives in Parliament are in reasonable proportion to the number of votes that that *party* receives in the election.'[3]

The Royal Commission recommended one option in particular – the
mixed member proportional (MMP) system. This was done in the
belief that 'the process of choice should to the fullest extent possible
give each member of the community an equal part in the choice of
government.' The effect of the recommendations does not give each
member of the community an equal opportunity to participate in government, for the possibility of an independent standing for other than
a constituency seat under the new system is not considered, and ren-
dered impossible.

1 New Zealand, Report of the *Royal Commission on the Electoral System: Towards a Better
   Democracy* (Wellington: Government Printer, 1986).
2 Ibid., 28.
3 Ibid., 34. My italics.

The Commission proposes an increase in parliamentary seats to 120. There would be boundary changes so that there would be 60 constituency seats elected on the same basis as the last election, and 60 seats elected on a nationwide party list system. The political parties would draw up lists of names in a preferential order as their nominations to take seats up to the number equivalent to the percentage of votes they each received.

We, the voters, get to vote for the constituency candidate, then for a party – and an automatic acceptance of their selection of people. The ballot paper wouldn't even list the names. The commission says that 'it would be impractical to allow independent candidates to appear on the list section of the ballot.'[4]

So this landmark reform suggests that half of our parliamentary seats be cut off from independents. As if parties are the be-all and end-all of our political process; as if by any stretch of the imagination the economic policy alternatives, which are available to this country, are currently represented by the parties in office; as if the 'loyalty' (a euphemism for tyranny) of party candidates contributes constructively to policy. This presumption about (male, white, conservative, hierarchical) political parties being political cornerstones is no more than that – a presumption, ritually assumed in the language of political philosophies.

Yes, we need a form of proportional representation here, but not one which excludes me from going to the ballot box and indicating that in those sixty seats I want to see Gwenny Davies or Brenda Cuttress or Vicki Duncan or Annie Ballin or Eva Rickard, and that I don't expect them to run the gauntlet of a party system in order to stand. I want it possible for MPs who establish themselves, as Mike Minogue did in a constituency seat, to stand as independents in one of the proportional-representation seats. I want it to be possible for Sonya Davies to stand as an independent and feel free to give public voice to her feelings about Rogernomics, rather than sit silently on Labour's backbenches. The last election was no recommendation for any party, and the New Zealand voting public deserve an alternative. But if they want it, then they'll have to work for it, for both political parties (somewhat misguidedly, given the heavy-handed party endorsement of the Commission and the entrenchment offered with MMP) voted at their annual conferences this year to oppose change. So stand back to receive loads of 'fear-and-loathing' propaganda.

---

4 Ibid., 27.

In defence of their preference for MMP, the commissioners have a childlike quality in their defence of the *party* – none of them has had the experience of openly working within a political party or standing as a candidate, which was basic to their selection for this role.

The Commission dismisses the 'single transferable vote' system as less preferable than MMP, but for no good reason. In the STV system (used to elect the Australian Senate, for example), each one of us would vote in a multimember constituency and would vote for five members from a slate of candidates. We would number them in order of preference. In this system, voters choose their members of Parliament, not parties. The possibility exists to a much larger extent of real representation of the diversity of views, people, issues, and opinions in this country.

No one can doubt that our Parliament needs such a change. I don't doubt that there are enough other political battles for us all in 1988, particularly on the evidence of this government's frightening Christmas 1987 financial package. The other battles, in some ways, require less work and are far more readily condensed to clichés of the mindless kind. But we need to be at work, and hard, on electoral reform. So shake off the vacation torpor, and find out what you think about this now. If we, the people, want this change, we've got a lot of work ahead.

6 The Stink of Success

22 October 1988

Whatever my own sentiments about which electoral system was preferable, concern and despair rose with the increased poverty and powerlessness of our people. (Inflation rates had risen to over 15 per cent.) Just surviving left little time to catch one's breath to be active against the government's policies. As Finance Minister Roger Douglas disclosed in his book Unfinished Business,[5] *this was entirely the intention. He wrote: 'Do not try to advance a step at a time. Define your objectives clearly and move towards them in quantum leaps.*

5 (Auckland: Random House, 1993).

*Otherwise the interest groups will have time to mobilise and drag you down
... Once the programme begins to be implemented, don't stop until you have
completed it. The fire of opponents is much less accurate if they have to shoot
at a rapidly moving target.'*

I have told myself, for the past few years, that since I was no longer on
the circuit and in receipt of vast volumes of mail that I was unlikely to
have a good sense of the political mood. It was as if one could 'smell'
particular odours in the nation's political consciousness. And while my
comparatively reclusive lifestyle these days does bring me into contact
with very diverse and somewhat eclectic sections of the community, I
choose to be with these people. There was little choice involved in the
old days, so that I could be sure that it was a truly representative cho-
rus of voices I was hearing.

So, it was with considerable interest that I began the obligatory book
tour for my recently published *Counting for Nothing*[6] throughout
Aotearoa. It was also with considerable trepidation. It has been some
years since I have been 'on the road' in my own country, and the prospect
awakened in me old resistances and resentments. This was in spite of
what I also knew lay ahead: wonderful reunions with old friends, new
meetings, support, love, and warmth. But one cannot write a book about
'value' without beginning from home, so I wrapped myself in the safety of
my childhood mountain, Taupiri, and went out to meet that world again.

To discover that I did know, could still smell, the political consciousness is troubling to me. I should prefer to have lost the scent from the
distance of the farm. But poverty smells, and once you have had that
stench in your nostrils, you never forget it. It is not a smell apparent in
Molesworth Street or the Terrace in Wellington. Here concrete, clay,
salaries, long (paid) working days, patriarchy, textbook ideology, and
air conditioners combine to refine and filter air from contamination by
unemployed people, the homeless, the devastated provinces and
impoverishment in the rural sector. When encountered by the MPs and
ministry officials of the Beehive and the Treasury, these smells are
called 'welfare' and 'crime,' not government policy.

---

6   *Counting for Nothing* (Wellington: Allen and Unwin and Port Nicholson Press, 1988)
    is about the international accounting framework which ignores the environmental
    import and omits all unpaid work from a country's GDP, while valuing war and all
    forms of illegal market activity.

Never in my lifetime has there been so large a group of the people of this country so classically alienated. The sense of powerlessness is the most rapidly increasing movement discernible. The formerly politically active working (as distinct from the poor) and middle classes are stuck for a political response. This is chronic among Pakeha male leaders in these groups, from farming to unions. Maori and women are so used to political activity from points of powerlessness; they spend less time gasping fish-like when they have been pummelled yet again.

The confusion in the New Zealand population is not that they can't accept or can't adapt to or don't understand Rogernomics. For them it is all too clear: they live with and beside its effects every day. They notice and observe, they are part of it, they smell it. For an increasing number, it is suffocating. The confusion is that in such a readily socially observable country, the government's accounting doctrine and practise is so blind and unresponsive to what is really happening out here! The outrage at, for example, tax cuts for those on higher incomes, even from those in that income bracket, is real, and injected with a stubborn Kiwi streak for fairness. [New Zealanders are known as Kiwis; a kiwi is a flightless native bird.]

Rather, why not government-subsidized jobs like PEP (Project Employment Programme), or making sure that a health department is able to prosecute for food contamination, or that rural hospitals remain open, or even national superannuation. Why instead, tax cuts? It was a point of pride not to have very wealthy Kiwis, and not to have destitute ones either. It was a point of pride that services were provided as a first priority, and then, if necessary, incomes were supplemented. Abandoning the services, and then heaving money at those who miss out, is not the Kiwi way.

The perception generally that nothing would change under a National government is probably why there is a desperation out there for a strong third party. I see the problem, but not that as a response. Parties are a major part of the problem, and their collective wit seldom equals that of the people – witness the nuclear free New Zealand campaign. And the poor membership and poor financial position of the parties gives cause for alarm in two important areas.

The first is the likelihood that Parliament will attempt in the next two years to pass legislation to make taxpayers partially fund election campaigns. (Not that we don't already fund the government's ongoing campaigns and party political broadcasts.) The second is that any move Parliament makes towards proportional representation will entrench parties, not provide for strong independent parliamentarians.

It is simply not true that parties offer the most stability. They offer coercion, intimidation, lack of principle, a void of courage, and a dearth of consciousness about people and their lives. A good flood of personally unambitious, publicly well-supported independents is what this Parliament needs until political parties can offer members and candidates the space to be representatives, instead of cliché-ridden automatons. It is also perfectly obvious which seats will fall in the next election – which means constituency takeovers are in order if we are to avoid having boring party hacks win these seats.

Creative subversions or integrated anarchy are called for from the ranks of the seemingly powerless. The opportunities for such activity are endless, provided one maintains a sense of humour. Without such activity, the only sense to be enhanced in the months ahead will be that of smell. As the seasons go, we do know that an acrid smell left unattended in winter can foment to stench proportions by summer.

7 Voting Reform: The Conspiracy Theory

31 August 1992

By 1992, and despite the opposition to change from the two major political parties, New Zealand moved towards a historic referendum on electoral reform. While the public education campaign was to put the issues before the electors 'fairly and without bias,' the fact that the Royal Commission had recommended the mixed member proportional (MMP) system meant that it had the most publicity.

It may have been the Women's Electoral Lobby's misguided endorsement of the mixed member proportional (MMP) option in the forthcoming electoral referendum that sparked a plethora of letters and telephone calls to me asking what option to support. It appears that many join me in not being a part of the generic 'most people' frequently invoked by the Royal Commission.

It is appropriate to put the Royal Commission in historical context. Appointed in February 1985, four Pakeha men – a high court judge, a former government statistician, a professor of law, and a professor of politics – were joined by a Maori woman research officer and reported in December 1986, four prime ministers ago, before we had thought of pausing for a breather and a cup of tea. It is not idle to suggest that were a Royal Commission to hold hearings today, significant proportions of submissions made in 1985 and 1986 would differ markedly in tone and emphasis. The performance of the two major parties, and parliamentarians, has altered the focus of discontent.

Historically, I also recall that the Electoral Reform Coalition was, from the outset, a proponent of the MMP system, a system which gives even more power to major political parties than does the first past the post (FFP) system. The Coalition emerged with its leadership firmly based in members of the Labour Party executive, then drawn from the Western Hutt constituency of Mr John Terris, Labour's deputy speaker.

As we approach the referendum on Saturday, 19 September – (the bitter irony of holding this exercise on Suffrage Day is not lost on me) – Parliament has agreed on a major debate on standing orders and parliamentary procedure, as if the problems lie in that arena. This is a distraction: parliamentarians can fiddle with those rules all they like, but not much will change.

Overwhelmingly, the suffocation of a responsive representative Parliament can be attributed directly to the calibre of people the parties dish up to us as candidates. For any electoral reform my priority is the option which best addresses this problem. That immediately eliminates the supplementary member system, the preferential voting system, FFP, and, most emphatically, MMP.

The *Report of the Royal Commission on the Electoral System* bypasses human nature in its discussion of voting behaviour, political stability, and the behaviour of political parties and individual MPs. 'Most people vote for political parties,' the Report claims. Based on what evidence? What alternatives have we ever had? While my own experience in Raglan and Waipa is but one instance, significant numbers of National Party supporters – and even members of the National Party – voted for Social Credit and against me. Meanwhile the Labour Party vote collapsed as constituents, particularly women who were lifelong Labour Party supporters, and even Labour Party members voted for me.

When I go to vote, it is the calibre of the individual candidates on offer, not a political party, that is uppermost in my mind. Will this be just another hack, compromising principles beyond existence, taking refuge in the caucus majority (always a middle-aged white male majority regardless of the party in office)? Will political ambition prevail over the interests of constituents, or even minority or special-interest groups?

Oddly, at a time when membership of the National and Labour Parties is constantly falling, the Royal Commission concludes that MMP 'is fairer to supporters of significant political parties and likely to provide more effective representation of Maori and other minority and special-interest groups.'[7] While the latter claim is patently absurd and demonstrates a major incomprehension of how candidate selection procedures really work, I cannot see where women, the majority of New Zealand voters, and hardly 'minority or special-interest groups' are included in this hypothesis.

The single transferable vote system (STV) would mean that we vote by putting candidates in order of preference. Voters can choose across party lines and within parties. Voters will not have party lists, ordered by parties, foisted on them. STV is the only system that gives an independent a good chance to win. (Under MMP, independents cannot even stand for 50 per cent of the seats, and this is supposed to be a 'democratic option'!) More voters participate in electing members under STV than any other system. Constituents are far more likely to be represented by at least one parliamentarian they have voted for. There would be no safe seats. If MPs did not perform, they would be out next time. In 1986, for example, in Tasmania, which uses the STV system, 17 of the 35 members of the House lost their seats while the party distribution in the House (19 Liberal, 14 Labour, and 2 others) remained unchanged. And before the textbook boys race to describe this as unstable or providing problems in selecting a cabinet, what is the difference between that and the results in the 1975 and 1990 elections in New Zealand?[8]

The Royal Commission claimed that STV did not deliver proportionality as well as MMP. But as journalist David McLoughlin has demonstrated using the Royal Commission's own figures, STV averages out just as proportionally as MMP.

While the Royal Commission recommended that the Maori roll might disappear in the STV option, there is no reason a number of the

---

7 New Zealand, *Report of the Royal Commission on the Electoral System*, 120.
8 In the FPP election of 1975, there were eighty-seven MPs in the House and thirty were new. In the FPP election of 1990, there were ninety-seven MPs in the House and thirty-nine were new.

electorates could not be the Maori roll. This would no more disenfranchise a number of *iwi* (tribe members) than the present system, and as well I would expect the Maori and Pacific communities to have representatives elected in general electorates.

The abuses of power the public complain of most are the result of the personalities in power. Few elected to political office – whether in minor parties, major parties, or as independents – ever leave on a matter of principle. They like power, the trappings, the acknowledgment – and lots more. I have no patience with suggestions that STV is a more 'unstable' system requiring coalitions. Human nature makes constitutional crises no more likely than in any other electoral system.

MMP is a disastrous option, entrenching dominance of political parties and separating half the representatives from any real form of accountability. And as for the suggestion that STV will promote regional as opposed to national issues, where does the Royal Commission think we are? Just over three million people at the bottom of the planet, our total electorate is just a borough in a large foreign city. The west coast of the South Island is entitled to have a representative in Parliament, just as Aucklanders deserve a system where they can dismiss Richard Prebble when they've had enough of him.

The propagandists have pushed MMP to such an extent that I suspect a conspiracy. If it is chosen as the major option in September, by the election in November next year when we are invited to engage in yet another referendum on the issue, its real character will be exposed as a horrendous movement towards more power to political parties. In the run-off next year, many who in theory support proportional representation will find themselves supporting the first-past-the-post system to prevent it. That scenario will leave us with what we have – after all this exercise – which is what the two major political parties supported originally in submissions to the Royal Commission. Surprise, surprise.

So I will be voting STV and not in self-interest. There is no system under which I would be persuaded to stand again for office. But a wealth of high-class candidates would then be persuaded to stand, free from party nonsense. It is the only system that would force political parties to really clean up their performances, so that we go to the polls to vote for candidates and policies rather than against the worst on offer.

MMP won a resounding victory in the first referendum, taking 70.5 per cent of the votes with STV taking second with 17.4 per cent. The second referendum was between the old first past the post (FPP) system and MMP, with a margin of 53.9 per cent for MMP and 46.1 per cent for FPP.

The number of seats in Parliament was increased to 120. In the 1996 election, record increases were made in the numbers of women and Maori and Pacific Island representatives, and it saw the election of the first ever Asian representative. Women won 35 of 120 seats, the majority of these (24) on party lists. Seven of the 15 Maori elected won constituency seats. Two of the three Pacific Island representatives were on lists, as was the first Asian representative.

In 1999 the number of seats won by women increased by two to 37, but the distribution of constituency (16) and list (21) seats changed: The percentages of the total number of seats held by Maori (13.3 per cent) and Pacific Island (2.5 per cent) representatives remained the same. No 'party hoppers' were re-elected.

8 Being Prime Ministerial

26 August 1996

The last in this series is a letter to the then prime minister Jim Bolger as he sought to establish himself on the world stage. With many other nations, New Zealand had performed dismally in respect to its relations with Indonesia. The lust for trading opportunities with the world's fourth largest nation outweighed principled actions at the government level. When New Zealand student Kamal Bamadhaj was gunned down in the Santa Cruz Cemetery in the massacre of 271 unarmed people in Dili, East Timor, by the Indonesian military, the New Zealand reaction was disgraceful. Bolger was about to meet President Suharto; I thought he might like a little advice. [Suharto was the corrupt president of Indonesia from 1967 to 1998. He and his family embezzled massive amounts of funds from Indonesia's government coffers, and Suharto's genocidal regime occupied East Timor for twenty-four years.]

Dear Jim,

After a few years in office, there seems to be a prime ministerial pattern characterized by a polite boredom for domestic affairs, and a search for an international role and the designation 'statesman.' (Of course, former prime minister David Lange did it backwards and never got beyond boredom in domestic matters until we hit catastrophe.) I suppose the Commonwealth Heads of Government Meeting gave you a taste for it, and your conversion to the nuclear free movement, and your late apology for the 'mistake' of being a vicarious apartheid supporter, suggest a desire to do a Malcolm Fraser. [A reference to the former Australian prime minister who changed his policy stance on leaving office.]

Now there are one or two issues in our backyard demanding attention, and this time you could be up to speed – not from the beginning – because Suharto has been getting away with murder since 1965. As the quest for democracy in Indonesia heats up, Suharto and his family make Marcos of the Philippines look as if he never left kindergarten. The corruption is in your face at every turn, profits from the much-vaunted growth directed into the pockets of a few, the repression is outrageous and relentless.

I worked in Indonesia during the last elections in 1992. Every candidate for any party had to be screened to identify and disqualify any 'communist' (i.e., supporter of democracy or human rights or political decency). A presidential decree prohibited political parties from criticising the (desperately inadequate) state ideology consisting of the five principles of Pancasila and the constitution, or from 'insulting' the government and its officials. Do you remember that the Dutch Embassy staff and all Dutch working on a variety of projects were tossed out of the country during the campaign because they supported non-government groups who wanted to debate democracy and human rights?

At the level of farce, each of the three permitted parties was allocated the same number of days to rally in the long streets of Jakarta, and these alternated. 'Supporters' blocked most major roads in overloaded buses and jeeps, T-shirts were supplied, and supporters were paid. In the spirit of personal survival, the security guards in my housing complex in Jakarta changed their T-shirts appropriately each day.

There was a movement by a number of Indonesians to effectively invalidate their voting papers to indicate their support for free and fair elections. A young woman I knew did this. The police arrived at the door and took her away for questioning before the 'secret' balloting had finished on election day.

Have you seen or heard about the labour conditions? The factories on the island of Java look like Mt Eden jail, the only thing different is men with machine guns at the entrance. Even with a United Nations passport, and working for the International Labour Organisation, you cannot get inside the factory gates. The toxic fumes and noise levels outside are unhealthy. Inside, women workers speak of the access to toilets being locked throughout their shifts; in some cases, workers have been chained to machines. When deadlines approach for orders to be met, no one gets to leave. Attempts to organize workers usually end with bullet-ridden bodies floating in rivers.

I never imagined I would find Indonesia the most rampantly racist country I had ever visited (no, I didn't need to go to South Africa to 'see' for myself, as the line went in 1981). Javanese, describing themselves as the most white, believe themselves superior to the Balinese, who think they are paler than those from Lombok – and so it goes. Staff at the Ministry of Agriculture where I worked (in the building burned to the ground a fortnight ago) described the Melanesian people of Irian Jaya as black primitive ignorants.

Have you heard of the genocide in Irian Jaya, Jim? I was told about it in the presence of the counsellor of the Canadian Embassy, a Canadian documentary film crew, and a representative of one of the Canadian timber giants raping the rain forests. The government isn't too concerned for the boys with guns in Irian Jaya. It's the significant number of different tribes, dialects, proud peoples that's of concern. So, to decimate a tribe, is to decimate the equivalent of the tohunga, the kaimatua, the kuia – those who are the repositories of the dialects, stories, dances, history are those who 'disappear.' Then the area is logged, then thousands of Javanese are 'resettled' in schemes that, at the end of two years, see women and children abandoned with no support in virtual wastelands as the men go back to Java.

Do you know that the combined estimated wealth of three Suharto children is now $4 billion? And that the tyrant is now in his late seventies? And that one of the sons is the owner of a substantial block of land in the South Island? Now, for a statesmanlike start, Jim, I want to be assured that neither he nor any of his retinue could last a day here when the tyrant falls and the family is called to account. Such an action is after the event though, and we're looking for leadership.

At your church, have they mentioned the wonderful Pax Christi peace campaigners recently before the Liverpool Crown Court? Last year the four women caused $3 million of damage to a hawk fighter at British Aerospace by attacking the weapons control system and the wings and fuselage with hammers. The jet was due for export to Indonesia. The women argued that they had 'lawful excuse to disarm Hawk ZH955 because they were using reasonable force to prevent a crime.' They cited international and British law against genocide and particularly argued that the jet's export would flout repeated United Nations condemnations of repression of Timur Timor, where more than a third of the population have died since the Indonesian military invasion of 1975.

The women freely admitted their attack, defended themselves, and the jury and judge cleared them of the charges. Now, if effectively powerless Catholic women can make the point on the other side of the planet, imagine what a statesman close at hand might be able to do. Don't give me the 'afraid of trade' or 'keep communicating' type answers. Don't be forced to make another mistaken apology.

Shall I send you a little hammer? You'll be surprised how fragile tyranny is.

In anticipation,

Marilyn

Having a Real Life

1 Joining the Bucket Brigade

February 1987

Throughout the years of my representing the Raglan and Waipa rural constituencies (1975–84), I would dream about the possibility of living in a rural area, with the seasons and with the fresh air and the physical work, and far away from the phone and demands of complete strangers. I longed to live with the colours and topography of this beautiful country, and I wanted to sense some freedom. I had been thrust on to a national and international stage in my early twenties. Much of what I did was predetermined hour by hour for months at a time. I was weary. I had been in a demanding role for a long time, and I wondered who might be there inside if I had the space and time for recovery. In the last years of Parliament I read a great deal about alternative possibilities for farming – trees, flowers, cattle, and goats. I finally saved enough money to buy a small farm and to fulfil this promise to myself. And yes, those years did provide that respite, and for many of them I begrudged having to leave to engage with the world of people again. From time to time I would write the Listener *columns about this life, and this is where this collection comes from.*

The forecast is again for temperatures in the mid to high 20s accompanied by incessant wind. The news says that nowhere in the country has there been heavy rain since mid-October and that this pattern occurs only once every hundred years or so. In a description, which always seems especially pedantic, the Weather Office has invited me for some days to expect 'passing' showers, which is certainly what they do if they exist – go passing right by.

So water has become an obsession for me, along with the thousands whose domestic tank supplies are dry, the hundreds who were turned away from camping grounds because of a lack of fresh water, the farming community who feed hay and silage now and build in a winter feed problem, the thousands of household gardeners who watch their summer crops and flowers wilt from lack of water and restrictions on hoses, and the millions in Europe who still spend U.S.$5 a week on fresh water since Chernobyl, and the probable billion who have little or no fresh water at all.

But I have options and good health and parents who give me 9,000 litres of water at Christmas and neighbours who connect the water pipe at the cattle trough to a tap for water for the garden. This sees an end to the thrice-daily chore of straddling the barbed-wire fence and emptying the trough contents into buckets and thence onto the plants. A continuous trickle through the hose, moved every ten minutes during daylight hours, allows a circumnavigation of living things in the house garden every forty-eight hours.

I make concessions. The dishes are done by hand (not that a machine lies idle as an option) once a day. This gives me the opportunity to observe that the flies are not as thick on the ground or as familiar as Australian ones – that is, they don't land on me all the time – and are more evident when the neighbours' stock are close by or when silage is being fed out. The lavatory is flushed when necessary so that 'doing what nice people do' becomes a matter to remember when I visit city friends. I don't want them to think I've lost my manners along with a variety of 'things' some of them appear to have concluded I have 'lost' in this move to the country. There is one large bath per night and guests arrive at various levels of cleanliness, according to when they get to wash in the relay order.

Much of our dirt is thus returned to the soil from whence it came in the bucket brigade the next morning. Dirty washing is stored for days and finally sorted into two piles – 'grubby' and 'filthy.'

Maximizing the laundry water is an exercise in speed, strength, and logistics. One cycle per load of course, and as well as a plug for the tub one needs a minimum of four buckets, which I fill immediately once the spin cycle starts, so that the tub, which collects the rest of the water, does not overflow.

Then, one buckets this water up – after running about emptying the first four loads – so that the tub and buckets are empty and ready to collect the rinse water of the 'grubby' washing. This is poured back into the machine to become the washing water for the 'filthy' washing. Then both the washing and rinsing water from this load are ferried hurriedly about the herbs and vegetables. This is food for my pectorals as well as for plants, I tell myself.

I consider myself lucky. I do not take this water for granted. I reflect constantly on the lives that women who must live and die with a fraction of what I have in a day. The World Health Organization (WHO) estimates that water-related diseases claim as many as 25 million lives a year and cause untold illness. The United Nations Children's Fund (UNICEF) calculates that 15 million children die every year before reaching their fifth birthday. Half could be saved if they had access to safe drinking water. According to WHO, approximately 80 per cent of all disease can be attributed to inadequate water or sanitation. Typical of these diseases are diarrhoea, trachoma, parasitic worms, and malaria.

Only 8 per cent of the world's water supply is fresh or potable. Projections under the International Drinking Water Supply and Sanitation Decade 1981–90 program estimate that approximately U.S.$600 billion is required to provide clean water and adequate sanitation during the ten-year period. The money seems a modest sum compared with military budgets.

A woman peaceworker in Paraguay reported what she saw in the following way: 'In one particular colony area the only water supply for at least ten to 15 kilometres was a large puddle of clear water. Other than just swamp water, there were no wells of any sort. In this one puddle of water there were women washing clothes, women washing babies, numerous pigs wallowing, several boys washing their horses, girls drawing water, and the local malaria control team washing out their DDT spray can.' Where water is available on this planet, we contaminate it with chemical and nuclear wastes, domestic and industrial sewage, and, in the case of the Rhine River recently, with 'accidental spillage' from a factory of the third-largest pharmaceutical multinational in the world.

So, my buckets of water are not carried in the yuppie yearly camping adventure manner, but in earnest. And the weather is not just something I talk about to be polite.

2 Orderly Chaos?

June 1987

There is the semblance here of chaos, I think to myself. And then add quickly, reassuringly: 'A violent disorder is an order' – and vice versa.

I thought the good weather had packed up and gone, trailing leaves, and I had moved inside, to gibbing, plastering, sanding, stripping old paint and varnish, hanging curtains, painting – alternating with unpacking cartons of papers, books, and maps collected in the past few years, just waiting for rainy days. Goats, china, the Solomon Islands, growing edible bamboo, many feminist abstracts, music, vegetables, agriculture (miscellaneous), Irangate, Pearly Gate, the CIA-Libya connection, nuclear free New Zealand, other newsletters; the large piles become subgroups. In another room is the litter of good intentions: letters to answer, accounts to pay, tax receipts to action, and the index cards to check the footnotes and a bibliography for the book.

All of this proceeded at points during the day since, unlike mothering, most of the characteristics of the work require that I can only do one thing at a time, but, like mothering, no task is ever wholly completed.

Then the sun came out again bringing bright, clear, frosted, green autumn mornings day after day, and three more yet are forecast. So the life of the interior was abandoned at its particular point of disorder. I leave it in the mornings, visit it en route to bed in the evenings, and it's a bit grim. And I'm expecting visitors.

But now there are echoes of the interior outside. Autumn growth is rampant so that, as I hoe and fork my way through forests of weeds everywhere, there is much separating of growing things to be done, and in the immediate vicinity this is a losing battle. But I do have the latest seedlings – borage, catnap, chervil, and chives – planted at last, along with the proteas, hibiscus, and tree lucerne now out of their pots and bedded in 'the nursery.' The garden might have a chance, except that there are acres beyond that need attention.

Beyond the garden fence there are still many felled pine boughs to saw, collect, and stack for the winter's fires, though this is now a second consideration to the major chainsaw exercise. Three macrocarpa trees have been felled, and for hours a day I prune off the vegetation for fires that maintain a stubborn resistance to flame except when boosted by diesel or petrol. The weather is not the only imperative in this chore. The trees act as an abortifacient for cows and goats, and it's that time of year.

And, yes, the kids need attention. It's time for their booster injection, which is a performance, as they cry and kick and jump and carry on.

Then, all the hooves will need trimming again. The fencing isn't finished. I haven't completely cleaned the silage out of the wintering barn. There are a pump shed, goat shelters, and a hen-run to build. I want to trim and spray around the paddock trees and shelter belts.

But I'm harvesting mushrooms, tomatoes, carrots, cabbages, zucchini, basil, tarragon, coriander, corn, and sunflower seeds (in anticipation of hens) and pot pourri ingredients, and I'm drying lemon grass, camomile, and bergamot for my organic tea, and gathering flowers, and watching trees planted less than a year ago stretching out. The earth rewards the hours spent working with her, down to producing sea-sand-covered mushrooms from the lower silage layers of the summer-laid asparagus bed.

I postpone thinking about the list of tasks that should be done on a visit to my local town. It is as formidable as the list of phone calls to be made.

I cannot quite characterize what it is about this life that is most difficult to cope with. It has to do with learning that there's no point in going in every direction and the logistical impossibility of working in a linear fashion, so there's a certain panic about life that has no place. But where is it isolated? Is it in the recognition of the impossibility of control? Is it that I can no longer do multiple chores at once? That the pace of life is different does not mean that it is not as productive; quite the contrary. And it has a deliberate rhythm. It is more subsistent and less materially endowed than anything I have known for a decade, but my life is much richer.

And, before I tell you I've just been hooked by some guru, let me reassure you, it's just fresh air and space and a change of lifestyle that I'm celebrating. It's just that if anyone from the old life saw this it might look very out of control, and perhaps it is. But the old life gave the contrast to the new. A violent order is a disorder?

3 Minor Miracles and Heroic Days

November 1987

The young man answered one of the continual phone calls received at the small farm. 'No, she's not here,' he said. 'She's in Brazil for four weeks.' He returned to the table where the young woman, the two small children, and the cat and the dog were variously seated. 'That was the *Listener*,' he said. 'She's late with her column. They wanted to know where she was.' The young woman said, 'We should write it, about all the changes going on here.' And so they should have.

It's a pretty long way from Sao Paulo, Brazil, to Auckland, via a five-hour stopover in Los Angeles, but I was determined to get home in daylight and walk around a large, quiet space in sweet air before I collapsed.

I hadn't foreseen my fascination with a clear, blue sky – unseen in a month. It's almost a week since my return and, besides recognizing which trees have survived their first year, after assaults by cattle or perilous encounters with a rampant rotary hoe, I'm still noticing the real care and attention invested here in my absence.

For a start, you now reach the back door by a small brick path, rather than dancing through puddles. There's a large wood-box now at the other door, full of pine cones gathered along the driveway, and sawn kanuka from fallen boughs fetched from the bush. Inside, there are signs of heroic days. Of these the most amazing to me are the bathroom and kitchen, now stripped by hot-air gun of the lead-based, thickly coated paint which covered the rimu woodwork. I loathed this job and had, with others, made a slow start on it. I think it now looks extraordinary – as do the passage and sitting room, recently gibbed and now displaying a white undercoat. Paintings, photos, mats, rugs, have been rescued from the 'not-yet-unpacked' area. This is far more comfortable than I had left it.

Daily, as I open cupboards, I find them restored to an ordered regularity. Many more things are accessible. Included among these is the piano – which, though not inside a cupboard, had been lost under the piles of 'not yet unpacked.'

Outside, thistles have been grubbed and the shed is thoroughly clean. There is abundant, spring birdlife, and within twenty-four hours of my arrival home the first kids of the season dropped, a set of triplets. The orchard, with the exception of some avocado trees, has survived a morning invasion by a herd of goats. There are puppies in the garage, ducklings on the dam, and living things here seem to be thriving.

Especially in the garden, where there are minor miracles. Bricks, old railway sleepers, and old, bent fenceposts had been abandoned by me in the middle of framing a large garden on one side of the house. They are all now in place, exactly as I had envisaged them. The very large, old, framed glass door, which I had left leaning on the front of the house to use as the cover of a small, disorganized glasshouse to raise seedlings, now performs precisely that function, and beneath it, trays sprout tomatoes, thyme, violets, Canterbury bells, sage, and calla lilies.

The trays were here. The gardens had largely been fallowed for the winter. The seeds were here. Even a trailer-load of manure from the wintering barn was here. The four weeks of my absence had been full of rain, gales, winds, storms, and power failures. Yet imagine the scene. Topsoil has been added to the herb garden, where the perennials are shooting nicely and the eau-de-cologne mint, feverfew, and camomile have been split. The artichokes, too, have been split and transplanted.

Borage, chervil, campanula, basil, and pyrethrum have also been planted. Close by are asparagus fern and a ring of forget-me-nots. There are lobelia seeds, and courgette and cucumber seedlings in planters. Further down this garden there are rows of gladioli, statice, and calendulas.

The vegetable garden, newly and neatly framed, is the most extraordinary feature, and I can see that I shall have an interesting battle with the rabbits and the roving turkeys in months to come. Already clearly recognizable, there are rows of peas, carrots, lettuce, spring onions, broccoli, dwarf beans, onions, corn, garlic, parsnips, and beetroot. The asparagus planted in its bed, has sprouted. So have the pumpkins in their hillock. And against the house there are sunflowers, morning glory, and lupins. And much more.

It was a very moving welcome home. On my desk was a small handwritten diary of the sojourn here. One of the typical entries addressed to me read:

> Lay in bath and decided farming is possibly one of the best holiday/professions one could undertake. There's always a chore to be done, and one can usually pick and choose the mood/weather. Like the other day – driving along the road in torrential rain – saw an old guy parked under trees on his tractor – seeking shelter – and admired his ability to have time to stop for the weather. So many don't stop for nothing – pardon the grammar – you know what I mean.

Yes, I know what that means. But there didn't seem to have been too much stopping going on here in my absence.

And I forgot to mention: on my bed were four homespun shanks of mohair fleece.

Yes, they should have written and told you what was going on here when the *Listener* called for a column.

4 Soulless Cities

March 1988

I begin to get grumpy a good twenty-four hours before I have to leave the farm for the city – any city. It is a little easier if I use public transport

144 Way 2 C the World

and avoid the stress of driving. I used to think I loved driving and that the tens of thousands of kilometres I'd run up in a rural constituency were pleasurable. Now I recognize it was not the driving at all, but my moments of solitude that were guaranteed in the car. As well, while the surfaces of the roads in the Raglan and Otorohanga counties left room for improvement, the countryside itself refreshed me, moved me, filled me with awe.

Glass, concrete, asphalt, exhaust fumes, incessant noise do not have the same effect. Because my nose is now sensitized to sweet fresh air, I can smell the stench of Auckland in the south from the Bombay Hills until I clear the East Coast Bays sewage ponds in the north. My subconscious conspires against my going anywhere. A kilometre down the road I realize I have left office keys at home. I turn back. Five kilometres down the road on the second attempt I realize I have forgotten my toiletries. I turn back.

In the last year I have systematically left without lecture notes, clothes (hanging behind the door), wallet, sunglasses. My briefcase is about the only thing I can guarantee not to forget, a habit of my institutionalized years. If I take only sandals with me (my feet now resist anything that might not be casually worn across a paddock), the temperature will drop ten degrees and I'll come home with a cold. If I take no raincoat, it will pour. If I take warm sensible clothes, there'll be a heatwave. If I make a real effort and rehabilitate the 'dressed for success' clothes of the last life, the iron will fail at my city abode and I'll have that perpetually 'crushed' look. When I do go into cities and emerge from the confusion of new one-way streets, when I have given up on parking legally and need to leave the farm utility truck on a loading zone, I venture forth. I observe these city beings with a wide-eyed rural curiosity which slows me to a pace that upsets the flow. If I do not hurry, head bent, face intent and unobservant, I am continually bunted and shoved about. When I choose to spend time in pens with goats, I expect this. I do not expect this in the city from human sheep, but then goats are more intelligent and certainly more polite.

Sometimes I try to persuade myself that this city trip will be an adventure. As the list of things to do and things to get builds up (after putting off the inevitable as long as possible), it certainly has interesting prospects. There's carpet to collect and photos to get developed. Paintings will be ready at the framers, I need another filing cabinet and there are sales at plant nurseries. An approaching autumn signals the next round of sand papering, stripping, painting, so stops will be made for these supplies. Then there's the list of goods that are not stocked in the local store which supplies my rural delivery: Trade Aid decaffeinated coffee, a good olive oil, a treat of bagels, and possibly a mango. Such rewards I promise myself for the effort of getting there at all.

'Indeed,' one part of me says, as the other stamps its foot and starts to throw a tantrum about going to town, 'if you get all these things done you may go to a movie, or take in a play as a reward.' So I check the newspaper and discover, without surprise, that there is not a feature film in town that would not offend with gratuitous sex and violence. But a friend is performing in a new theatre production, so I try for a seat, and that night the show is entirely booked by a school party. This does not assist the pre-city disposition.

From the moment I leave home I feel I am going in the wrong direction, and as the day wears on, and I begin to run late, and my shoulders begin the journey upwards to the bottom of my ear lobes, I am overwhelmed with a new kind of panic that bubbles in my stomach and journeys to my throat. I recklessly decide to leave the necessities until 'next time'. I collapse a multitude of tasks into one. Like Virginia Woolf's *Orlando,* I am likely to find myself in the right part of a department store by chance, not intent, and quite unable to stay long enough to purchase everything on the list. But unlike Orlando, who would forget the requirements of her dogs in her panic to leave, my dear goats are assured that the only shopping I do will be for them.

Teeth grinding and my adrenaline shot up with the speed of the city, I find myself running to my driver's seat, desperate to turn home again. It takes some kilometres to face the number of chores that will repeat themselves on the list next time. It takes a ten more kilometres before I pass the city environs and stop driving like its inhabitants. And then as vistas widen to reveal real living things, and as the life around becomes visible and luscious and languid, my soul comes out of hiding. We're going home she whispers, easing into the seat with me at last. She sighs with relief and joy. There were years of hiding for her when expediency dictated that this little body liked life in the fast lane.

Given room to breathe, she has spread her wings. And now, with compassion, we both wish for a world without cities, without these empty shells for soulless automatons that this century and its values has built.

5 Tupping Time

April 1988

She has been away for sixteen days in cities and is due home this evening. She's called several times to ask how we were and to say she
missed us and all that. Says she's been so busy keeping a cash flow
going to keep us in the manner to which we've become accustomed –
which I hope doesn't mean the manner in which she left us, in the
middle of that cyclone. She says perfect strangers come up to her and
say, 'Hello, Marilyn, how are the goats?'

Well, we're fine as we could be, which is not always how she would
have us. It's tupping time, you see, and it's not just us goats who are at
it; there are mating dances and much honking from the shores of the
dam. It means from time to time there's quite some excitement down
here. The worst bit is (and this will make her cranky), this smelly G4,
who isn't wethered properly, jumped the fence into what is called
around here 'the fluffy paddock' (that's the one with all the kids and
some of the mothers because the kids haven't been weaned yet) and
he's making a great noisy nuisance of himself. Still, if she arrives in the
daylight, she'll probably see him and leap out and separate him off or
something. She's like that.

I wouldn't like to be him. I mean, it seems to me that some of these
wethers – not M3 who's a pet and has a beautiful fleece – are here only
as long as they don't create too much trouble. I notice that they don't
get visited or talked to as much as us, or get as many sheep nuts, even
though they're all bigger. Ariel, who's my full brother and so in a different paddock from me, and Atom, who's in my paddock, are bucks,
and they get more attention than the wethers. Currently they're in little
pink harnesses and look ridiculous. Every three weeks or so they
bother us with their spraying and snorting and mounting and leave us
as marked does: it's all over in a moment, but what a performance
from them. Ariel is running with more does than Atom and he looks
hangdog all the time.

That group hasn't been too bad. Well, Tahi's got in there and must
have abandoned her wether kid Wiremu back in the fluffy paddock,
but he was older than most of the kids so that's okay. I didn't see her
get there – that's two fences – but she's a pretty good jumper. And then

one of the other does that Ariel had already marked is in the fluffy paddock, too. I didn't see her shift either, probably because my group has been quite distracted and had a wonderful time.

And I have to say we deserved it after those endless wretched days of wind and rain. I keep thinking how miserable I was, but then I remember all those poor goats around Gisborne and Wairoa and the East Coast. We hate the wind and that driving rain, and we hate getting our feet wet. We weren't too bad in the wintering barn and she brought us hay.

When she left for the city, she left the back door of the barn open, so we've had a marvellous time. We found lots of blackberry bushes and thistles and barberry hedge to eat. We wandered throughout three paddocks and, even though it's not goat proof, we never went through the boundary fence. In the evening we all lay around in the big ashen pit, where she sometimes lights fires, and we looked at the stars. Yes, well, we're sort of grey goats right now, but we were shorn recently so we'll clean up in time. When she comes back, she'll put us all in a properly fenced paddock, which can be dull.

She'll also have to do something about the roof from the piggeries she converted into a goat shed. The roof has been a great joy to all of us at some time. It's iron and very warm to sit on, but the best part is running down the hill, leaping onto the roof, thundering across and hurtling into space and down to the ground again. It's great goat fun. But one day the inevitable happened – we started to make holes it. So during the cyclone, water came in and created lakes on the floor, and she had to make interim plank bridges inside the shed.

Then there are piles of unopened mail, feet high – we know, she tells us. She comes down here to escape the telephone and worldly responsibility. And we know that she's missing her deadlines for writing her letters to her sisters because of all that stuff. So she'll have plenty to do when she gets here, which is just as well.

Because we're due for drenching, which I really *hate.* Some of the older does just take it in their stride. But *everyone* hates the foot bath, and we're due for that, too. She drives us into this bath in the race – 'Move, move, move,' she shouts, waving her arms. We stand there for ten minutes like a crowd in an elevator at rush hour. 'Good goats,' she says, and then gives us nuts. What does she think we are, Pavlov's dogs?

Anyway, I do go on a bit, because life is pretty good for us here. We've been looked after splendidly while she's been away. But it will be good to see her again. I mean, I know it sounds silly, but you can get very attached to these humans.

So long for now,

Sybil Goat

6 From the Farm

October 1988

There has been so much activity here on the farm and I don't just mean all the human construction-type work. It's been a very busy and difficult time for we goats, what with kidding and nursing. She decided that we had to kid early because of her book tour, and that landed all but the last seven or eight does with rotten rain and wet paddocks and the cold. Now evening is a cacophonous nightmare, with every one bleating and trying to sort out mothers and kids.

She thinks she has her hands full just with Tofu, who was one of a premature set of twins and never stood up and drank. M2 had them in the middle of a rainstorm, and she and her mother were just driving out the gate and she came to check 'cos M2 seemed upset. My, then what a sight, because she took off the football jersey she was wearing under her overalls and wrapped up this miniature kid whose mouth had already clenched shut, and thrust it through the car window at her mother to take home to dry. Then, half-naked, she ran across the farm to pin down a very pregnant Saanen that she keeps for such occasions and stripped some milk off her and then ran up the hill with it so it could be the first thing the little goat had to drink – but she was too late. Her mother had poured whisky down the kid's throat! I didn't see all the next bit but apparently, using an eyedropper, she slipped drops of milk and honey and whisky into the kid, and laid him in a plastic basin on top of a hot-water bottle wrapped in a towel (just like a water bed) and covered with a little rug. Anyway Tofu lived, and (shades of Konrad Lorenz and imprinting) for days he thought his mother was a pair of black gumboots. He trots down here at her heel on her rounds and I think he's probably a very mixed-up little goat. She thinks he ties her down, but she ought to have two or three like most of the does here, then she would really have problems.

Not everything has been OK. Two little kids died from exposure in a storm, and I had a terribly long and hard labour and my kid was born dead, which was very devastating. When she came down with the spade and dug a hole, I cried and cried and she cried, too. But she told me she was just happy I was OK and that I wouldn't be sold just because I'd lost my first kid.

This weather has been hell on our feet, so she's been making us stand in those zinc baths again, which I just hate. And in a week or two we're going to be shorn again which is a relief, I suppose, but it's such a performance. Mind you, nothing is like the performance of the big day with the kids in the shed when they all get an ear-tag and an injection and their first drench and some of the buck kids have the ring put on them so that their balls drop off and they become wethers. What a racket that is. They're all screaming, even when they haven't even been touched yet, and their mothers are all screaming; anyone would think she was a callous, rough brute, which she isn't at all, but I guess we all hate those injections. (Actually, several times someone has shifted violently at the last moment and she's injected herself, so I don't suppose she'll have any risk of worms, liver fluke, pulpy kidney, or any of those other things.)

Tofu is going to live somewhere else for six weeks or so, until he's weaned. Another kid who was also human imprinted has gone to live somewhere else, too. He arrived one night in the pouring rain at dusk when, truly, it rained kids. About ten kids arrived at once and some to very flighty does and they were all mixed up and all were finally sorted out except two and she grabbed one and wrapped it in the afterbirth of M10, who's one of her favourites and had just had a single doe kid, and M10 took it on but the other little buck got treated to the old whisky trick before he was given away.

Even though Tofu is going away and is very small, he has already distinguished himself. I noticed that on the one fine day we had recently, when she was gardening, every time she knelt down he jumped on her shoulders, which was great fun for him, but not terribly helpful for her, and though he tried to make up for it by sticking his tongue in her ear, which is apparently a turn-on for some humans, it didn't work. But his best trick was when he wrestled with the screen at the back door while she was in town getting some work typed, and when she came home he was on the kitchen table eating the freesias, having relieved himself all over the draft of her manuscript. That shows you what he thought of it. Frankly, I would probably have eaten it myself.

On that front we've done rather well. We've managed to eat some beautiful flowering native trees like pohutukawa and kowhai, and we like flax when we can get at it. We've decimated the agapanthus and irises on the fence line and 'pruned' the climbing roses. M4, who can jump in a way that none of the rest of us can, and who is lucky that she's a fine-looking goat with a great fleece and so gets to stay, has done a pretty good job on the avocado trees. And the other day we all had a great breakout into the neighbours' but got caught before we could get into their orchard.

In case you're wondering about me, I have my photo on the back cover of her book *Counting for Nothing*, although I've grown since then. But it does give me ideas, and I think I could fancy myself as a writer one day, if anyone would give me a contract. I might get another chance to write to you before then, though, and let you know the news from the doe's mouth.

Cheers,

Sybil Goat

7 The Precious Planet

A while ago a wonderful television documentary covered the effort by Don Merton to conserve the black robin, a species reduced to five birds. A recent count has shown that seven years of effort and dedication have boosted the robin population to more than 100. Lucky little robin. Be grateful your rescue started before the power brokers went market-mad. In terms of their propaganda, you can't be bought or sold, you don't add to a tourism market, you can't even be considered a qualitative indicator in the biosphere. I don't know what it cost to save you, but as far as the prevailing power ideology is concerned, it was all a bad investment.

Do you often think that the market-mad are like blinkered racehorses – no lateral vision at all? Do they think they're immune from the effects of deforestation, ozone-layer depletion, toxic waste, nuclear fallout, air and water pollution? Do you suppose they're the least bit aware that their slack business and private standards will come back to haunt them?

They remind me of the business giants of Cubaton, near Sao Paulo in Brazil. The yellow, orange, brown soup mix there that is euphemistically referred to as air is expelled from a vast web of petroleum, chemical, smelting, and processing companies. The town is lodged in a valley and the colourful hue of smoke hangs permanently over it. Depending on the wind direction, you can smell Cubaton more than 100 kilometres away.

The 'bosses,' who knew of illness, leukemic death, diarrhoea, and birth defects, chose to live up out of the valley and, as it were, around the corner. They were stupid enough to think they were safe. When all the trees started dying around their homes and their own early cancers were diagnosed, they rushed in consultants to report that whole industries should be shifted 'because of the lack of sufficiently supportive infrastructure.' Yet I would wager that the true agenda was 'get the hell out of here' before the illnesses of whole generations could be loaded at the door of the blinkered boys and their contaminants.

They were caught in their own crap. Others would escape too easily. It is unlikely that the legal and illegal lumber company bosses of those who have raped the forests of the Himalayas, or the Philippines, are those who drown, starve, are left homeless or afflicted with cholera after the floods, after the rains.

Those in developed countries who unthinkingly dumped toxic waste in their own backyards for years, and now seek to ship it off to dump it in the backyard of a developing country – with the assistance of corrupt leadership there – or simply tip it over the side of the boat in the southern hemisphere, may get some of their poisons back through their water supply. But so, unfortunately, will the community about them.

Those who seek to scar our landscape for short-term market gain won't be around to have to explain the scars they leave when ozone-layer depletion changes weather patterns and the trees – vital to the essence of life in cleansing air, stabilizing ground, and giving us oxygen – are gone.

The market has nothing useful to say about the sustenance of life in the biosphere (and, given Star Wars, beyond). It is a pathological ideology. I don't need to read what it says it does or would do about the environment – its activities speak explicitly for themselves. Noise is one of its favourite products, so is filth. Some of the filth is dirt, some of it is poisonous, much of it is deadly. None of it is good. Waste is another key feature of market growth, as is exploitation. The marketeers believe that since none of them 'owns' the water, the rivers, the oceans, or Antarctica – or anywhere we're not looking at any particular time – they are free dumping grounds. In the way of all such ideologies, its practitioners have no need for a sense of responsibility for life: the only language they understand is coercion.

So how convenient it is for all of them that the usual framework of such coercion is the antithesis of their precious market madness. Regulation, or the levying of pollution taxes or statutory standards is the usual unimaginative responses that brothers in government come up with for brothers in the market.

The brothers must stop crunching the numbers, except those that are qualitative indicators of their death wish for the planet, and exercise (if they can locate any in their mechanistic superficial intellects) some judgment and some courage. Cleaning up the planet and preventing further destruction is more important than any chairman of the board or the retention of any seat in any elected office. It requires that all too infrequent characteristic called leadership. It requires action, no more words. The planet is exhausted by the fumes of rhetoric as well as those of so-called growth. No one can 'value' something and simultaneously be indifferent to its degradation, whether it is 'mother' nature or a female person or even a black robin. The planet could do with many more Don Mertons and his team who saved the black robin. The kakapo – our beautiful flightless parrot that loves the night – is a very lucky species if that is where he is next to direct his love and his care. I would nominate him for prime minister, and his desire not to contemplate the job would emphasize his suitability.

But it's not something to leave to others. It's the responsibility of us all now. When did you last buy an aerosol can, throw plastic in the sea, forget to return bottles or cans, needlessly light an incinerator fire, take a car when you could have bussed, avoided signing the petition, or writing the letter, neglect to pay your tramping hut fees [small accommodation huts in national parks]? Every episode matters, every failure counts for the planet. It's only a matter of degree. The black robin may have been saved for the planet, but can the planet be saved for the black robin?

Don Merton worked for the New Zealand Wildlife Service and spent fifty years dedicated to saving endangered birds. In 1980 there were only five black robins left. In 2008, the number was over 250.

Canada O Canada

1 Open Letter to the G7 Leaders

In June 1995, the G7 Summit was held in Halifax, Nova Scotia. The National Film Board of Canada had decided to premiere the documentary Who's Counting? *at the People's Summit held in conjunction with the leader's meeting. As a consequence, I was asked to write the Open Letter from the 'people' to the 'leaders.'*

17 May 1995

Gentlemen,

Last Sunday I was in Waitomo in New Zealand. I was dressed in a winter-weight wetsuit and handed an old inflated tire tube. With me, similarly garbed, were two adults and four children, one of whom was an eight-year-old boy, Sam. We descended a small path through native bush to a tomo (underground cave), wound our way down to a tunnel entrance, and launched ourselves afloat on a small river.

On the ceiling, lit by a myriad of glow-worms, their fishing lines suspended, the fossilized remains of shells were clearly visible in the limestone left there by the ocean millions of years ago. They lit the glistening stalactites and stalagmites, their staggering shapes and textures alive with the slow constant water dripping its 'growth,' that would progress a cubic inch every three hundred years.

The farmland above had preserved bushstands. The farmland above had not been poisoned with fertilizers and chemicals, but it had sustained indigenous people in traditional and modern farming practices for 800 years. It produced food. The caves lived on below.

We followed the path of the river for a kilometre underground to emerge through more bushland, teaming with nesting birdlife, and returned with our hosts to a traditional family marae (a meeting place where Maori protocol is used), where we showered and were fed soup and toast. All tribal protocol was observed, simply, without pretension.

On this Sunday, 14 May, New Zealand had won the America's Cup in yachting. In this country it was churlish not to follow the news. I turned on the radio.

More cases of Ebola fever were counted in Zaire. The disease had spread because of the lack of absolutely basic medical supplies in a hospital. I remembered that two-thirds of Zaire's GDP is controlled by Unilever and other multinationals. I flashed to recall being in the field on UN mission work in Bangladesh and coming upon the WHO vaccination team in a village. I watched the same needle and syringe being used repeatedly. I grimaced. 'Its OK,' the team leader assured me, 'on children this age, you can use the needle up to ten times before it gets blunt.'

The news continued. China had conducted another nuclear test, and France was rumoured to be commencing underground testing at Mururoa in the South Pacific. Japan had increased its storage of nuclear 'waste' material. The International War Crimes Tribunal had announced a list of Serbian leaders whom it wished to prosecute in a war in which it was long ago agreed that no weapons would be supplied. In Iraq there continued to be a shortage of basic medicines, as a result of the Gulf War.

I remembered that our countries rallied to defend 'democracy' in the Gulf War, in Saudi Arabia where there is no universal suffrage, and in Kuwait, where half of us are not entitled to vote. I compared this with G7 resolutions in respect to South Africa. I remember Ben, in the nuclear silo in the film *Who's Counting?* practising his drill to fire a nuclear weapon. He says: 'We're trained so highly in our recurrent training that we take in simulators like this that if we had to do it, it would be an almost automatic thing. There wouldn't be time for any reflection until after we turned the key.'

Finally, on the radio, there's an interview with the New Zealander who designed the mast of the yacht that won the world's oldest sporting event. What was his proudest moment? he was asked. 'People said nice things about the mast,' he said. 'It didn't give any trouble. It never fell down.' When asked how he had competed with the likes of designers from NASA from his basement garage, he quipped: 'If you don't have money, you've got to have ideas.'

Gathered together at the 1995 G7 Summit, you will count your growth statistics, your GDP figures, your currency values, your unemployed, your interest rates, your investments, your surpluses or deficits, your export receipts. You will count your money.

Outside, we wait for the ideas – those that spring from the real world, where too many of us are refugees, too many of us are pre-literate, too many of us are anaemic or malnourished. Where too many trees are felled, too many of us are poisoned by the by-products of what qualifies as production, too many of us are dependent, too many of us are the subjects of corrupt political regimes which you welcome for their business and capacity for exploitation. Too many of us have no fresh air anymore.

Most of us are women and children. Most of our lives and our work don't count in your statistics.

We notice that you are all men. Do you remember from your childhood the sense of wonder in the experience of Sam last Sunday in the cave – the awe, the amazement, the capacity for utter humility in the face of millions of years of unalloyed drama in the kind of world from which your office now excludes you? Do you remember this boy in you, and what he valued?

Outside your room, there is a different sense of values operating for most of the people on the planet. Six weeks ago Sam was with me in the ancient kauri forests of northern New Zealand. In the early autumn here, the cones of the tall conifers had exploded, showering seeds on the ground. Sam picked them up, more than 400 of them, and is planting the offspring of 800-year-old magnificence (that we viewed for free) to sustain life and to defy the political and economic pathology that governs your agenda and your lives.

Gentlemen, I do not address you cynically or lightly. I retired after three terms in the New Zealand Parliament. I have some small experience in that profession. Close friends say I am a consummate apologist for politicians.

So I ask you, from a place that politicians know: Do you have the political will and the personal commitment to plant trees that may live 800 years, or to preserve living growing fossilized caves for millenniums?

Or is all imagination spent?

Yours sincerely,

Marilyn Waring

2 Civil Society, Community Participation, and Empowerment in the Era of Globalization

On two occasions I was lucky enough to be invited to be the visiting scholar at the Toronto office of the Association for Women's Rights in Development (AWID). It was fabulous to work in an office with younger feminists who were passionate and committed, in an organization that I have found exceptional in its cutting-edge outcome work, an organization so different in its approach from so many I have known. While AWID always had some issues which they wanted me to work on, I also had the space for some cathartic writing about issues that gnawed at me. One of these was the emergence of the phrase 'civil society' in the development discourse, and this essay was published as an occasional paper for AWID.

The Early Days

In the early days of the second wave of the women's movement, we had our own stories of community participatory development. In 1978 we knew of Lois Gibbs and the women of the Love Canal region of Upper New York State whose houses were built on twenty thousand tons of toxic waste; the entire neighbourhood was sick. Gibbs identified that men, women, and children in the area suffered from many conditions – cancer, miscarriages, stillbirths, birth defects, and urinary-tract diseases. She collected the evidence. Through petitions, public meetings and use of the media, the Love Canal community took on the school board, the state and federal governments, and, finally, the president. They were rehoused and compensated, and left a legacy to the U.S. in the form of the Environmental Protection Agency.[1]

Similarly, the work of Maria Mies and her students in the early 1980s in Cologne, Germany, introduced us to 'action research.' Their research involved contacting women across the city as they collected evidence of domestic violence that was sufficient enough to convince the police and city councillors of the urgent need for the first shelters for battered women.

As those who followed in this wave were to find while working for the first women's health clinics, for the examination of victims of sexual assault by women police officers and doctors, for rape crisis centres, for breastfeeding in public places, and for workplaces free from sexual harassment and stereotyping in employment, the community participation of women was necessary because there were no statistics kept. There was no reputable research available, no empirical, statistically valid 'evidence' to backup policymakers when they wanted to address these needs with public funds.

In myriad ways, the women of my generation collected our own evidence from our sisters, demonstrating that the experts on these subjects were not those with degrees, bureaucratic appointments, or clinical coats. The 'experts' were those who had lived through the experiences.

---

1 Lois Marie Gibbs, *Love Canal: The Story Continues* (Gabriola Island, BC: New Society, 1998).

We collected narratives and photographs, held focus groups and demonstrations, engaged in street theatre and conducted key information interviews with powerful people. We thought locally and acted globally, as we knew that these issues were challenges engaged by a worldwide women's movement. We were most certainly 'civil society' activists, but we were seldom invited to engage in dialogue with power brokers. We frequently needed to be 'uncivil' to be heard.

Because I have 'grown up' through this wave of the feminist movement and learned the stories of those who went before, I believe it is simply impossible to claim that 'the rise of transnational civil society – NGOs linked across borders in issues-based advocacy networks – [is] an important development in the international context.'[2] Such networks might well work with more speed in the twenty-first century, but I have stood in the library archives of Ishikawa Fusae (feminist, journalist, union activist, and independent senator) in Tokyo, Japan, and examined letters and magazines she was receiving from suffrage leaders in New Zealand about the first women elected as mayors and councillors in local government elections there, and also her correspondence with Jeanette Rankin, the first woman elected to the United States Congress in 1917. I saw archived correspondence from women throughout the Pacific congratulating Ishikawa Fusae on establishing the first union for women in Japan. They wrote by hand or antique typewriter, and travelled to international feminist gatherings by ship, yet their language and their issues have resonance in our era of notebook computers and business-class air travel.

Thus, for many women there is nothing new in 'transnational civil society.' For generations now, we women would have described our methods as transparent, community-based, empowering, and political. We are doing what women have always had to do.

The Emergence of 'Participation' in the Development Sector

Academic social scientists were first influenced by the work of Paulo Freire in the 1960s.[3] He outlined a philosophy of actively involving the

---

2 Report of Comments by Thomas Carothers, Vice-President for Studies, Carnegie Endowment Symposium, retrieved 14 December 2000 from www.ceip.org/files/events.
3 Paulo Freire, *Pedagogy of the Oppressed,* trans. Myra Bergman Ramos (New York: Herder and Herder, 1972).

poor in critically analysing their social situation, creating from this the potential to challenge and transform their environments. From this strand of thought participatory action research evolved. This was described as the process when 'self conscious people, those who are currently poor and oppressed, will progressively transform their environment by their own praxis. In this process others may play a catalytic role but will not dominate.'[4] Not a great deal of feminist analysis informed this work, though feminist writers could easily adopt Freire's approach, since the herstory of women has been redolent with such examples.

Throughout the same period, Rapid Rural Appraisal (RRA) was emerging as an environmental scoping tool in development practice. The polite explanation for its emergence was that the assessment methods being used were too lengthy; the reality was that they were laughable. Mostly designed in Western donor capitals, the assessments operated as if (a) there was data available across a wide sectoral field, and (b) that it was remotely reliable. In my experience nothing much – including GDP figures, census of population data, literacy rates, numbers of women involved in agriculture, numbers of men or women working in the informal sector, and numbers of children enrolled in or attending schools – could be believed. In the absence of data, officials just made it up.

In addition, national counterparts I worked with 'elevated plagiarism to an art form' (as a good Filipina friend described it). Ironically, they stole from Western academic books about their own country. In many countries the idea that a national counterpart, even on an agricultural project, might actually have to travel to areas beyond a comfortable day trip from the office, was anathema to them. And the prospect that pre-literate rural people might actually know more than the Western experts about water volumes, pelagic species in the river for a dam or irrigation project, or about the flora and fauna of forested areas was completely out of the question.

Somehow more reliable insights and information had to be brought to the growing litany of development disasters. When Participatory Rural Appraisal (PRA) emerged in the late 1970s as a research tool in development programs, Robert Chambers's work was often cited.[5] Initially, PRA

---

4 Orland Fals-Borda and Muhammad Anisur Rahman, eds., *Action and Knowledge: Breaking the Monopoly with Participatory Action Research* (New York: Apex Press, 1991).
5 Robert Chambers, *Whose Reality Counts? Putting the Last First* (London: Intermediate Technology Publications, 1997).

used the local people (the experts) as repositories of information, but did not engage them in project feasibility, implementation, or monitoring and evaluation. In fact, those using PRA had usually predetermined the parameters of the project and did not bother to ask what the priorities for development might actually be. But during this period there was an evolution of the research methods themselves: social mapping, transect walks, scoring and ranking with seeds, stones or sticks, and institutional diagramming emerged. The 'lab-rat' approach, backed by technology, was failing. Communities were different from each other, had different histories/herstories, different power dynamics, different ways of working with, and uses for, their natural environments. And they were the experts on all of this information. Field methods evolved to reflect this reality, and to change the dynamic of the research.

By 1997 Chambers's work was evolving into a more detailed and sophisticated power analysis. PRA was not just about gathering more textured information. It meant giving up control and power, and this was very threatening to the Western 'experts' in the field. National bureaucrats also thought it completely out of the question.

What They Don't Tell You about Development

I have learnt from my experiences over the years that there are many vital reasons to be engaged in participatory development, most of which are usually not mentioned in the textbooks. Not all countries fall into each of the following categories, and some fall into one or two and not others, but I can certainly identify some that exemplify each category.

When the government regularly says yes to any project offered: This usually means that communities are not consulted about what their priorities are at any stage. The project priority is often to create a dependency on donor country producers, for materials, machinery, infrastructure development, vehicles, or computer hardware and software, for example. In this way, a great percentage of the donor package is actually spent on the donor's own experts and production. This approach presents major ongoing capability challenges from the project's inception because dependency, not capacity-building, is the silent agenda. In the Asian region for example, I have frequently named certain projects of the Japanese government's development agency, JICA, as demonstrative of this approach.

The spin-off for the recipient minister, or the project leader's national counterpart, is another driver and vehicle at the family's disposal.

When the recipient government refuses to have cross-sectoral focal points: This might happen when you are engaged in an ecotourism development on offshore islands, for example. You sign the project agreement only with the minister of tourism, and it is the ministry of tourism that gets the four-wheel drives, mobile phones, and computer packages, that appoints the national counterparts to be paid in U.S. dollars, and that hosts all of the training. You know you will need plenty of cooperation from either the Ministry of the Environment or Conservation, but there is nothing in it for them and you will not get the information you need from them at all. The same will happen inside the Ministry of Transport, which is in charge of policy in respect of air or sea transport to the islands; you can just whistle in the wind for any assistance you may require.

When the bureaucrats in the public service were at university or in the civil service during a period of major repression in the country: I have seen helicopter gunships hovering over a university killing students. I have seen a university surrounded by tanks with students manning the gates in balaclavas, and have read of the deaths in the days before and after. I have had a woman say to me: 'Missus, I too 'fraid to speak. No one speak here – not mother to son, not sister to brother.' In cases like these, speaking, thinking, or acting independently was *literally* more than your life was worth. When a university education consists of the discipline of regurgitation of the party line, and when a government agency's job is to protect the government and nothing else, it takes two generations for the people who become government servants to move on from the agencies where they rise to be senior managers and hence for institutional change to happen.

Those fighting the repression seldom become influential bureaucrats; they take the political or NGO route when there is change. Even ten or twenty years after a move to something resembling democracy, you will not find a transparently honest senior bureaucrat to work with as a counterpart. If counterparts are recruited from the private sector, the game of withholding information will be played out until you recognize their power and importance. Such persons will be losing power and realizing that they do not have a role in the new country. They will be holding on every inch of the way. These counterparts are usually obeyed but despised by communities. They cannot be trusted at any point to participate in community participation exercises because they will not give up power. But neither can they be trusted to have a single innovative, challenging idea.

When the bureaucrat is also a 'civil society' leader: Many of us will have worked in countries where all NGOs have to be registered with the government; where all donors' funds are strictly monitored and approved by the government; where NGOs are a lucrative, foreign-exchange earning small business sector, rife with nepotism and corruption. In Bangladesh and the Philippines, for example, I have heard conversations between women of the capitals' elites asking each other: 'How are your NGOs? Six now? I've just had another idea for one, too.' In some countries the office holders of NGOs also hold bureaucratic positions, but wages are so low (if they are paid regularly at all) that everyone who can find something has another job. And if you speak English, and if your relatives are office holders in the right places, to also be an NGO professional is a desirable option.

When the donor knows best 'what is good for them': I have also had the opportunity to observe genuine politically active grass-roots organizations being invited to take on the philanthropic donor's agenda in order to receive funding. An application – which is about empowered capacity-building and has been arrived at through rigorous, lengthy, engaged community meetings – becomes a vehicle for an attempted hijack, with a conference, international speakers, and a publication in the donor counterbid. Outcomes for which the community has no need, no resources, and no energy are proffered as conditions. I have never heard of the Global Fund for Women doing this. I have, however, been present to hear it in the offices of the Ford Foundation. I have also led a Food and Agricultural Organization (FAO) project where the pressure from Rome and the recipient capital were for activities that bore no relationship to the project document.

When no one knows how to move from information to policy to implementation: Actually, this is not a problem confined to national bureaucrats in recipient countries. It is particularly evident among the project leaders from Ivy League universities on some of the multilateral schemes with the biggest budgets. The truth is they have not made or implemented a policy at a national level in their lives. In my experience, great Western agronomists, engineers, or economists appointed as multi- or bilateral project leaders do not regularly brief themselves on national constitutions and rights-based legislation, the last several years of Amnesty International or Human Rights Watch country reports, the nature and functioning of the domestic political system, or any international legal obligations entered into by the recipient country. They certainly do not ask for the latest Status of Women documents. Consultation with civil society is not part of their service contract nor are they tasked with it in their terms of reference. The best analysts available are the communities to be affected by the project, but as far as these foreigners are concerned, the analysis should be done by 'social science' experts; engaging with the local people is not something from which they could possibly learn.

When your national counterparts will accept some locations for civil society engagement through pilot projects but not others: If you are working on a national project in Indonesia, your counterparts will argue very hard for training or pilot programs to be held in Bali. If in Nepal, they would prefer to be on the terai, within a day's trip of Kathmandu. This means that the same communities are the basis of all the student theses, the NGO projects, and the ministry's data collection. The available micro-data, therefore, is severely flawed because (a) the micro-economy grows from being everyone's pilot study; (b) respondent fatigue, or the 'professional respondent'; and (c) wily village leaders are on the take. In the absence of anything else available, 'data' collected from these communities are then generalized to entire regions or the whole of the country as 'indicative.'

On rare occasions, you strike the bureaucratic exception in both the international contractor and the national counterpart, revealing the many issues about having so-called international experts involved at all. But while this remains an exception, there is a place for consultants who can pressure projects into consultation with the real people affected by programs and projects and to pressure for projects to respond to the analyses of the local people. The international consultant as feminist action researcher can force a project to 'discover the poor.' Through a combination of human rights conventions ratified by the recipient country, boosted by the rhetoric of their constitution, and a pedantic reading of the donor's policies on development assistance, you can usually bring a project or a program to a complete halt and force it to adhere to the language of those documents before it continues. It does not require specific skill, just a little strategic forethought as to when to play that card and then some stubborn resilience. This usually means that the poor have to be 'consulted.'

The World Bank Discovers the Poor

In the late 1990s, the World Bank sponsored consultations with more than 60,000 poor men and women from over fifty countries and discovered *that poor people were the real experts on the multidimensional and complex issues of poverty!* The research was published in a three-volume series.[6] The researchers did ask the gender question, but not many of the narratives are rights-based or make explicit links with human rights covered by United Nations covenants.

Despite this massive study, there is little evidence that the voices of the poor have markedly influenced World Bank policy or practice. Senior World Bank officials do not have the skills to convert triangulated qualitative research into targeted policy programs for outcomes negotiated with the *actual experts* on poverty, that is, the poor. The growing emphasis on participatory evaluation should be a major concern, given that no genuine grass-roots participation has occurred in the identification of the goals and the objectives, the parameters of the project, or the outcomes desired of the project by those directly affected. Agencies expect communities to respond to an evaluation of someone else's agenda. It has not been at all clear that the World Bank's exercise has gone beyond the opening of spaces for those whose voices are rarely heard.

The Problem with Civil Society[7]

While many of the 'voices of the poor' in the World Bank study used rights-based language, development initiatives have been phrased in the international community's language of cop-out: civil society (and just what is uncivil society?), governance, or strengthening institutions. Projects and programs have titles such as 'Civil Society Empowerment for Poverty Reduction,' 'The Case for Constructive Engagement,' 'Human Resources Development and Utilization,' 'Capacity Building,' 'Modernization of the Legislative Assembly,' and 'Institutional Strengthening Initiatives.' Occasionally, a human right will be mentioned – for example, you might find the words 'literacy' or 'poverty' in a project document,

---

6 Deepa Narayan et al., *Voices of the Poor*, vol. 1, *Can Anyone Hear Us?* (Washington, DC: World Bank, 2000); Deepa Narayan et al., *Voices of the Poor*, vol. 2, *Crying Out for Change* (Washington, DC: World Bank, 2001); and Deepa Narayan and Patti Petesch, eds., *Voices of the Poor: From Many Lands* (Washington, DC: World Bank, 2002).

7 I am not going to bother here with the academic dispute about whether 'civil society' is about NGO's or civil society movements or organizations. For coverage of this, see the London School of Economics (LSE), *Global Society Year Book*, vol. 2 (2002), 5; retrieved 28 August 2003 from www.lse.ac.uk/Depts/global/Yearbook/yearbook.htm.

and 'supporting democratic electoral processes' gets dangerously
close. But usually, it is just more 'citizen security and justice,' or 'transparency and accountability in government practices,' and now lots of
'judicial training.'

This has birthed a whole new industry of different NGOs, civil society
organizations, academics and experts, who are chasing the development
dollar and creating another monstrous layer between implementers and
grass-roots experts. There is something very unsettling about reading a
sentence that claims 'the emergence and growth of civil society over the
past two decades has been one of the most significant trends in international development,'[8] when social history reveals that political movements of communities of people organized in pursuit of their rights is
nothing new. The fact that 'international development' power brokers
now claim that 'partnerships, among governments, private sector and
civil society [are] the most effective way to achieve sustainable *economic*
and *social* benefits for the poorest people'[9] conveys two messages to me.
The first is that 'civil and political' benefits are excluded. The second is
that engaging with 'transnational civil society' should not be confused
with, or considered a valid replacement for, consulting with the poor, the
overwhelming majority of whom are women.

In the current circumstances, we are often invited to be grateful for
the consultation that does occur. Most certainly, as Yasmine Shamsie
describes, the engagement between civil society and governments is

> tentative and fraught with a mix of apprehension and grudging necessity.
> The growing sense of necessity stems from a belated appreciation for the
> fact that a strong and active citizenry is the indispensable foundation of
> democratic governance. The apprehension [is about] ... representivity [*sic*]
> accountability and [the] legitimacy of civil society organisations.[10]

There is obviously a distinction in terms of these characteristics between,
say, Oxfam, some groups of academics organizing themselves as a public

---

8 Carnegie Endowment Symposium, see note 2.
9 The World Bank, 'The Growth of Civil Society,' retrieved 28 August 2003 from http:/
   /web.worldbank.org/WBSITE/EXTERNAL/NEWS/0,,contentMDK:20040873~
   menuPK:34480~pagePK:36694~piPK:116742~theSitePK:4607,00.html.
10 Yasmine Shamsie, *Mutual Misgivings: Civil Society Inclusion in the Americas* (Ottawa:
    North-South Institute, 2003). Available online from www.nsi-ins.ca/english/pdf/
    mutual_misgivings.pdf.

policy institute, and a textile workers' union. Yet each of these is organized, has some access, and has a form of prescribed legitimacy and
accountability. Such organizations like to have 'consultative mecha-
nisms' in place. But does that mean that the voices of the poor are heard,
as moderated through these middle men and women? Isn't that all a bit
too cozy?

Where Has the Rights Agenda Gone?

Personally, I cannot avoid a perspective that suspects that the focus on
civil society and governance is *not* an exercise in the subtle use of
euphemisms by donors to insert civil and political rights into their programs. It is about *avoiding* a rights-based approach and is an exercise in
control of NGO or civil society groups. A program by a donor will usually include at least two steps: (1) 'developing NGOs and their capacity' and (2) 'sustaining partnerships' with them. Money will flow from
donors to groups that have agendas that suit. NGOs do like to sustain
themselves and know where their next job is coming from. At times,
this can lead NGO governing bodies to make policy decisions to
refrain from any activities that could be considered advocacy. The
mantra is then: At the nation-state level, by all means train and participate, but do not take political action. At the international level, multilaterals will take care of those 'transnational civil society groups' that
have a solid base of citizenry support and are not donor dependent by
engaging them at the top table in civil society dialogues, as long as
they 'behave.' They will even staff whole units for this 'engagement,'
as the World Bank has done since 2002.

Now, let me hastily add some caveats here. I do not want Greenpeace,
Amnesty International, or Save the Children to change their mandates
or stop their work. I also realize that there are some very important
exceptions to the organization of civil society NGOs, where the active
political participation of the poor is the rule as opposed to the exception.
Here, I would cite the case of India. I have also met stunningly courageous feminists on the leading edge of civil society groups in Eastern
Europe, for example, who do not back down on an agenda in order to
placate the donor. Furthermore, I am not absurdly romantic about the
capacity of all the poor to participate and respond constructively all the
time. Some will always have been too recently terrorized, too impoverished, or have been without fundamental rights for so long that they do
not have the capacity for constructive participation in that project at that

time. The presence, then, of an NGO of integrity with the ability to represent these groups for a sustained period without 'taking charge' is a critical factor to help prevent further abuse.

We also 'have to be there,' as was demonstrated by the Civil Society Declaration at the World Summit on the Information Society (WSIS) in Geneva, 10–12 December 2003. In an effort to overcome the narrow understanding of information and communication technologies as only telecommunications and the Internet, and because the preparatory process for a summit was more than two years old, the WSIS Civil Society Plenary adopted the document *Shaping Information Societies for Human Needs*.[11] There were two key issues on which governments seemed hopelessly divided: how to deal with imbalances in and among nations to overcome the 'digital divide' and agreeing on a commitment to international human rights (in particular 'freedom of information') as the foundation for the WSIS *Declaration of Principles* and *Plan of Action*. The civil society group has produced a list of essential benchmarks against which it will further assess developments and outcomes in the WSIS process.

There are good examples of significant successes by international civil society. Take the case studies used by the Centre for Global Governance at the London School of Economics (LSE) in their *Global Society Year Book 2002*. These were the cases of movements around corporate social responsibility, HIV/AIDS, and the International Criminal Court. The case study on the International Criminal Court details the 'institutional' and 'formal' history of getting to the Rome Conference (June–July 1998) to adopt the definitive treaty. It points out that half of the 236 NGOs represented legal, professional, or human rights groups. Others, either at the domestic level or within the preparatory conferences, included women's organizations, peace and conflict resolution groups, church and religious groups, and UN organizations.[12]

When I think about what mobilized my own support for the International Criminal Court, I remember the Mothers of the Disappeared, banging pots or dancing alone. I remember the comfort women of southeast Asia during the Second World War. I remember the testimonies of the raped Bosnian women in the conflict in the former-Yugoslavia. Now maybe a handful of those women made it to Rome, but their grass-roots

---

11 Available online from www.itu.int/wsis/documents/doc_single-en-1179.asp.
12 LSE, *Global Society Year Book*, see note 7.

civil and political action and their testimonies, along with other evidence, made it possible for others to translate this *expertise born of experience* into the language of advocacy required on the floor of a UN conference. What is amazing is that with the exception of the human carpet demonstration led by Amnesty International during the Rome conference, the lives and experiences of these women have disappeared from the civil society case study of the LSE's prestigious centre. [In the AI demonstration, demonstrators lay down on the ground and used their bodies to represent the victims of genocide, war crimes, and crimes against humanity.]

Contrast this with the front-line engagement of activists in the mobilizations for the rights of People Living with AIDS (PWA).[13] Civil society mobilization in the late 1980s began in the United States in an environment of judgment and stigma, as the disease was so linked with the gay male community. The resort to direct action by groups such as Act Up saw those with AIDS finally invited to the conferences that discussed them. In the South, a major issue has been the access to drugs for those living with AIDS, when so many of those who have the disease are so poor. But the activism of PWA, and their friends and families, persuaded the governments of India, Brazil, and Thailand to allow generic production of otherwise expensive drugs, against WTO regulations. At the same time, northern civil society has sustained pressure on its governments and multinationals to support the PWA voices from the South. However, as Hakan Seckinelgin concludes: 'After a long advocacy and service-based involvement of civil society in the developing world, the picture is not too optimistic. Therefore it has become imperative for people to voice – indeed shout – their needs, formulated as rights.'[14]

Seckinelgin's comment reminds me of further questions that arise from unease. What is the difference between NGOs that stay with the language of rights and social justice, and others that are happy to compliantly abandon it for 'recognition'? How is it that so many who capture the donor dollar have abandoned the rights language and now appear as civil society 'partners'?

---

13 Ibid., chap. 5, 'Time to Stop and Think: HIV/AIDS, Global Civil Society, and People's Politics,' available online from www.lse.ac.uk/Depts/global/Yearbook/PDF/PDF2002/GCS2002%20pages%20[05]%20.pdf.

14 Ibid.

Standing in Their Sunshine

And there's a further issue that demands attention: the question of the timing. When should an NGO, which has used its institutional operating skills to command some inner-circle space, step aside and leave that area to be occupied by the expert voices of those from the grassroots? This reminds me again of a path we have travelled as academic researchers in this wave of the feminist movement. In the 1970s, as feminist work was trashed as being subjective, lacking clinical detachment, being qualitative or too participatory, our methods threw the practice and process of much mainstream research into relief. There was a pattern in terms of the distance of the white coated professor from the actual collection of data. The professor might design the research, but would keep himself several steps removed from any of the repetitive and boring recording, note taking, or observational steps. These might instead be done by a series of assistants. Then he would lead the analysis of the data, having been engaged in none of that frontline activity.[15] And the analysis would be regarded as rigorous and reputable, although it comprehensively was neither.

Now in the embrace of the projects and programs for 'civil society engagement,' 'community participation,' and 'governance,' too many academics, multilaterals, donors, and NGOs are operating on the basis that *the* significant partnerships, engagements, and communications can occur one or more steps removed from the primary experts. At that level, the politics is lost. The expert and primary statement is translated into something less challenging to the new, comfortable order. The 'voices of the poor' are often being betrayed by those who purport to represent them!

There is a great line in a song by the Australian feminist Judy Small which is 'you don't speak for me.' I suspect that for much of the cacophony of sound from civil society's inner circle, this line is an adequate repost. I know there are no simple solutions to these issues. The 'simple' approach has been the homogenizing of civil society. The beat up about civil society and its processes, as if it is a relatively recent phenomena discovered in Eastern Europe in the last twenty years, is

---

15 See, for example, R. Arditti, *Science and Liberation* (Boston: South End, 1980), and Mary Margaret Fonow, ed., *Beyond Methodology: Feminist Scholarship as Lived Research* (Bloomington: Indiana University Press, 1991).

laughable to any feminist with a remote sense of the planet's social history. But there are pitfalls on this route, and co-option attractions aplenty. Sure we have to 'be there' – and in as many guises (and disguises) as possible. But let's not for one moment relax our vigilance, or our sense of risk, or our sense of humour. We'll need them all for this round.

3 A Reflection on Propaganda

In November 2003, I was invited to give the keynote speech at the New Zealand Peace Foundation's Media Peace Awards. It was just months after the 2003 invasion of Iraq, and the world was coming to terms with the lies and propaganda used to justify the war.

Earlier in the year I had flown to Havana from Toronto, taking an opportunity to be hosted by a friend working in Cuba for a Canadian multinational company. Canada has always had a very different relationship with Cuba compared with that of the U.S., and these clear differences extend back to the nineteenth century. The 'propoganda' that emanates from the U.S. in regards to Cuba never mentions the reality of the strong ties that have been established between Canada and Cuba. But my visit gave me the opportunity to be reflective about the effects that propaganda about Cuba had had on me in my lifetime.

In 2003, we citizens of the planet coped with Western world leaders misleading populations over supposed attempts by Iraq to buy uranium from Africa, and claims of a forty-five-minute launch time for Iraq's weapons, quite apart from possession of weapons of mass destruction. In Australia, voters in the federal election were asked to believe, complete with naval photographs, that refugee boat people threw their children into the sea in a desperate bid for asylum, and that refugee groups didn't communicate that they were seeking asylum until they had been forced outside Australian territorial waters.

I didn't fall for any of those, but the extent of these lies, and their use to breach fundamental human rights law, did invite questions as to why so many people do believe them. Certainly we are advised that there are more sources of news than before – if you have enough time in the day to chase the credible ones. I was lucky to be in the UK through late May and early June 2003 to hear the full length of *that* Andrew Gilligan interview. Gilligan's BBC report that the PM's department had 'sexed up' and exaggerated intelligence in the Iraq dossier was leaked to him by Dr David Kelly, who in turn committed suicide when his name was leaked to the press. I was always disappointed that there was no effort to run the full text of that radio report. I was riveted by it.

I was in London to see the BBC features running night after night: documentaries such as *Here's One We Invaded Earlier* – Peter Osborne in Afghanistan; *The War We Never Saw* – Sam Riley with the Kurds and peshmerga retaking Kirkuk; *Virgin Soldiers*, the documentary about India Company, Third Battalion, Seventh Marine Regiment, which was truly frightening; *Battle Stations Iraq*, which was about the use of bombing as an introductory battle measure, and the correspondent piece, – *Al Jazeera Exclusive*, in which BBC cameras followed Al Jazeera journalists reporting from Iraq. I doubt that many of these were ever available for a New Zealand public, and while the BBC is terrific, I always have to remind myself that the tabloid press is the highest seller and the greatest source of news for the citizenry of the UK.

But these experiences of 2003 mean we always have to be vigilant about our information sources. Personally, it means a need for me to set a very high threshold about 'evidence' for the post-graduate students that I teach, supervise, and mentor. But it has also been an invitation to ask myself how and where I have been propagandized. One such opportunity came for me in September.

At about 5:30 a.m. on 9 September I arrived back in New Zealand after some weeks overseas. On other occasions, I've arrived home having been in some countries during harrowing times: Ethiopia in the famine in 1984, various countries in stages of civil war, or countries known as the base for major drug-trafficking routes. But I have never been asked 'And what were you doing there?' at customs.

This time, though, I had spent a week on holiday in Cuba. 'And what were you doing in Cuba?' the young man asked, and I felt as if I was in some sort of time warp. What could I be doing in Cuba that he could possibly be concerned about? Was it the policy of Customs and Immigration to ask that of everyone who has been to Cuba, or was there some propagandized itch in this young fellow's head?

It was of interest to me because I had had cause to wonder where some of my own information about and attitudes towards Cuba might have come from. I consider myself reasonably agnostic when propaganda is about. I'm curious about the world, but extremely fussy about my sources for information. This makes most media highly suspect in my mind.

But of course, I didn't always know that, so I was forced to think about the influences in my lifetime.

In October 1962, at the age of eleven, I would have read the story in the New Zealand Herald of President John F. Kennedy informing the world that the Soviet Union was building secret missile bases in Cuba, 144 kilometres off the shores of Florida. In addition to demanding that Russian Premier Nikita S. Khrushchev remove all the missile bases and their deadly contents, Kennedy ordered a naval blockade of Cuba in order to prevent Russian ships from bringing additional missiles and construction materials to the island. In response to the American naval blockade, Premier Khrushchev authorized his Soviet field commanders in Cuba to launch their tactical nuclear weapons if invaded by U.S. forces. I listened to the adults around me. My father certainly thought we were on the brink of nuclear war. These days we know that the deadlock was broken when Khrushchev received a secret assurance from Kennedy that Cuba would not be invaded, and so he turned the ships around and ordered the missiles dismantled.

The depth of this crisis for me as a child was not associated with Cuba, but with nuclear weapons. That stayed with me, but I was too young to take on board the Cuban Revolution, or the work of Castro and Che Guevara in the Congo, Mozambique, and Bolivia. The missile crisis appeared again in my life as a second-year student of international politics at Victoria University, and I wrote one of my assignments on it, totally influenced by the writings of Adlai Stevenson and Robert McNamara, so there was nothing about Cuba in my analysis.

By 1975 I was just a little more worldly, since the first obligatory OE (overseas experience) had taken me to Thailand and Turkey where the military were shooting students, and to study music in London and do the European tour. So the month I was elected to Parliament for the first time, I did know that it was Cuban soldiers who had gone to Angola to inflict the first military defeat on the apartheid South African military, who wanted to install a client regime before independence and access the diamond mines.

References to Cuba in New Zealand politics have been rare, but largely because of the Angolan involvement, Castro became leader of the Non-Aligned Movement for three years from 1979, and there was increased coverage. Throughout this period from time to time, and I've never understood why, New Zealand's Prime Minister Muldoon would report to the National Party government caucus, in conspiratorial tones, the names of New Zealanders who had recently returned from Cuba or Libya. I guess this information was given to him at Security Intelligence Service (SIS) briefings, and it was wasted on me for effect, but I can certainly remember colleagues who thought this was a threat to our national security.

The semester I spent as a 'Fellow' at the Kennedy School of Government at Harvard in 1981 was my next frame of reference. There I was blitzed by the rabid U.S. anti-Castro media on the one hand, while working daily in a community where there were scholars (a mere handful) and activists who worked seriously at presenting an alternative picture on the other. The politics of Nicaragua, Guatemala, and Cuba became the subject of my attention for that brief period.

Of course, from time to time, Amnesty International or Human Rights Watch would adopt a particular prisoner of conscience in Cuba, and that was also an avenue of information for me. By the mid-1980s I knew one Cuban woman who worked at the United Nations who published poetry and one or two essays about women in Cuba, but under a pseudonym. She was gay, and spoke of persecution of gay men and women under the Castro leadership. It did occur to me after seeing the film *Strawberry and Chocolate* in 1993 that things must have changed somewhat. This film, set and filmed in Cuba, followed an unlikely friendship between David, an uptight conservative, and Diego, his flamboyantly gay neighbour. At first David balked at Diego's anti-Castro leanings (which had grown especially strong in light of the government's suppression of homosexuality). However, David soon found Diego's access to American contraband (magazines, alcohol, etc.), irresistible. The film provided a light but realistic look at the Cuban Revolution and government persecution of marginalized groups. But the actors, writers, and crew were all still there, and the film had been very popular in Cuba.

Like many others, I developed a new-found interest after seeing Wim Wenders's documentary, *The Buena Vista Social Club*, about the legendary Cuban musicians who, two years earlier, had released a Grammy-winning album of the same name with help from American musician Ry Cooder. Ibrahim Ferrar, Ruben Gonzalez, Compay Segundo, and Omara Portuondo became household names in New Zealand, and the album topped the best-seller charts for weeks. I started going to the documentaries about Cuba at the film festival. In 2003, that included the Spanish documentary made by Carlos Bosch and Josep Maria Domenech called *Balseros*, which followed seven Cuban emigrants who left Cuba by raft in 1994 after Castro announced he would not stop anyone leaving by sea.

All these years later, I wondered what the politically aware and interested teenager might know about Cuba, so with the help of staff at my university library we set out to find what a New Zealander might have learned in 2003. Not much was the answer. Bob Edlin had the first mention in the *Independent*. This was a long piece about GATS requests, and noted that among the EU, requests for repeals of local laws was the 49 per cent limit on foreign investment in joint enterprises in Cuba.[16] For those who have dealt with China in the past twenty years, this couldn't come as a shock. But the careful reader would notice that, while the U.S. had a trade embargo against Cuba, what the EU was interested in was raising the limit for investment.

In May, Bill Ralston wrote a piece for the *Independent* on the ten worst places to be a journalist[17] and wrote about Cuba, but failed to make it clear if it was one of the ten. Zimbabwe wasn't, so Cuba would be hard pressed to be up there, although in March 2003, twenty-eight journalists were sent to prison for terms ranging from fourteen to twenty-seven years. But to me, the interesting part of the article was the lazy insinuation – the reader might believe Cuba was one of the ten from past propaganda.

Radio New Zealand ran stories on 14 October 2003 from BBC reporter Steven Gibbs in Havana when President Bush announced the U.S. travel ban to Cuba was to be more strictly enforced, and that the U.S. was to extend information campaigns inside the country. For the rest of us, that is particularly nice. It's remarkable how much less sound there is in a tourist resort without citizens of the United States around. Officially, Americans can visit Cuba only with special permits from the U.S. Treasury Department under sanctions dating from 1962. The travel ban does not bar visits, but prohibits U.S. citizens from spending dollars in Cuba. Under pressure from the U.S. travel industry, the U.S. Congress has voted four years in a row to end the travel restrictions, and the Senate supports their removal, but Bush has vowed to veto this, because he doesn't want U.S. dollars 'propping up a repressive regime in Cuba.'

Whatever the rules are, they don't work. In my hotel in Havana, guests included four U.S. high school football teams, which were playing each other in a tournament. Foreigners can only pay for goods and

16 Bob Edlin, *Independent*, 19 March 2003, 21.
17 Bill Ralston, *Independent*, 7 May 2003, 25.

services in U.S. dollars, whether that was the cartons of bottled water they needed each day or the Che Guevara T-shirts the boys wore after their visits to the markets. Significant numbers of U.S. citizens now travel to Cuba for medical treatment. It is not unusual to find U.S. pre-clearance customs agents in Canadian airports, trying to catch American citizens travelling to Cuba in defiance of U.S. law.

The final New Zealand story was the fact that Rongo Wetere had some Cuban advisers at the *wananga* (education institution) in Te Awamutu to help set up a model to reduce 'illiteracy' among Maori. This gave Cuba 'expert' Rodney Hide (leader of the right wing party in NZ's Parliament) the opportunity to say he 'was staggered to think Cuba could teach New Zealand anything.' He called Cuba a 'basket case.' 'Their programme is not to teach people to read to free them,' he said. 'The only thing they get to read is what a great man Castro is. People are climbing on boats to get out of it. That's not the model we want for New Zealand in any way shape or form.'[18]

To their credit, *Herald* reporters Ainsley Thompson and Helen Tunnah did run comparative literacy figures to demonstrate that NZ did not lead Cuba in generic literacy scores, and material available certainly pointed to Cuba's figures being better than Maori figures. They followed up with a report from the Cuban Ambassador the next day, which was about as accurate as Hide's.[19] But since the Cubans were paying the consultants, the story came to an end. What a pity, because there is so much more to tell.

So a New Zealander wouldn't have much to enlighten her if Cuba was of interest. But that was the context in which I went to Cuba for a holiday, and at every point it gave me cause to reflect on what I had expected to find, and why I had that expectation.

When I am going somewhere new, it finally gives me the time to check out those questions that have been bugging me for a while, and in this case it was Guantanamo Bay. In the last years of the 1800s, the Second War of Independence in Cuba failed, but the Spanish were considering home rule for Cuba under the Spanish flag. I make no apology for my reliance at this point, on the history as outlined in my copy of

---

18 Helen Tunnah, 'Cuban Educators Teaching Reading Skills to Maori,' *New Zealand Herald*, 21 October 2003, A5.
19 Ainsley Thompson and Helen Tunnah, 'Cuba Foots Bill to Teach Kiwis Literacy,' *New Zealand Herald*, 23 October 2003.

the *Lonely Planet* guidebook. (I did have it checked by a historian as well.) The author wrote:

> The U.S. government had been biding its time … and largely to increase their circulation the U.S. tabloid press stoked war pressure through 1897, printing sensational and often inaccurate articles about Spanish atrocities. When William Randolph Hearst's illustrator Frederick Remington asked permission to return from Havana as all was quiet (the reply was) 'Please remain. You furnish the pictures and I'll furnish the war.' Hearst's ally in this campaign was assistant secretary of the navy, Theodore Roosevelt.

In 1898, the U.S. sent the battleship *Maine* to Havana to protect U.S. citizens. The U.S. offered to buy Cuba for U.S. $300 million, and the Spanish turned it down. Events escalated until a peace treaty was signed between Spain and France in Paris. The Cubans were not invited. Fortunately, the Teller Resolution, 'passed in the U.S. Senate at the declaration of war on Spain, committed the U.S. to respect Cuban self determination … Cuba was placed under U.S. military occupation instead.'

In 1900, the first U.S. governor of Cuba convened a conference of elected Cuban delegates that drew up a constitution, but before this was adopted, another U.S. Senator, Platt, attached a rider to the U.S. Army Appropriations Bill of 1901, giving the U.S. the right to intervene militarily in Cuba's internal affairs whenever the U.S. decided it was warranted. The Cubans were given the choice of accepting the Platt amendment or remaining under U.S. military occupation. They accepted the Platt amendment, and the U.S. used this immediately to obtain a naval base at Guantanamo Bay.

In 1933, Franklin D. Roosevelt arranged to abrogate the Platt amendment as part of his 'good neighbour' policy toward Latin America. In this deal, the lease on the Guantanamo base was extended for ninety-nine years, though a clause stipulates that both sides have to agree before the lease can ever be terminated.

Then there's the Cuban Adjustment Act of 1966, which encourages people to leave Cuba for the United States by providing virtually automatic asylum to any Cuban who lands on Florida's shores, regardless of crimes they may have committed to get there, and offering them expedited permanent residency status. About 1,000 Cubans receive visas and a green card each year. The number of Cuban Americans in the U.S., according to the Census, is 1.2 million. There are over 11 million Cubans in their own country, which is the same size as New Zealand, but we have only 4 million people here. We have a million of us overseas as well, but the U.S. hasn't offered all Kiwis asylum!

The next fun arrived in 1996. From this time, U.S. law not only forbade American companies from doing business in or trading with Cuba, it also sought to penalize foreign companies who traded with Cuba. The law put forward by Senators Helms and Burton (later to become known as the Cuban Democracy Act) sought to impose sanctions on any country that traded with Cuba. I had to go to Cuba to appreciate how mad the U.S. policy is. It means that, for example, the members of the Board of Sherritt International Corporation, the Canadian company that mines nickel in Cuba, are banned from entry into the United States.

Whatever crusade the U.S. has followed in respect of diplomatic withdrawals or trade embargoes with Cuba, they have been pretty much alone. Mexico and Canada have never severed ties. The 'Embassy Rows' in Havana are spectacular. It makes sense for most of the so-called developing world to be there. But almost everyone you can think of is there. And when even the Principality of Monaco has a consulate, you get a handle on how popular Cuba is. Maybe world leaders love cigars, maybe they know here they really can have a safe holiday – lots of them want a photo opportunity with Fidel while he is still alive and well and in control: whatever the reason, the rest of the world is there in droves.

The Immigration and Customs folk at the airport in Havana did not stamp my passport. They don't stamp anyones.' This is very useful for the Cubans who visit family and live in the States, and useful for the U.S. citizens who are not supposed to visit but do, and I am sure that it has its uses for folks engaged in nefarious activities. The next flights were due in from London, Paris and Cancun. There were no soldiers or guns at the airport. I had expected them to be there. I mean, they are just two a penny right through airports across the planet, and with all the hype about Cuba …? In fact, there are more armed police on the streets of Sydney and Melbourne on any given day than I saw in a week in Havana. Where had that idea come from? Was it just because, in most of the early pictures of Castro I ever saw, he was wearing army fatigues? (But then, he wore them to play golf, though I didn't know that at the time.)

On the first drive into the city from the airport, I noticed women standing at intersections looking into approaching cars. We two women were ignored, but my mind had already determined what this meant, influenced by stories from the book *Cuba Diaries*.[20] And it was only mid-morning! I was shocked.

Later in the day, in the centre of Havana, I learned how wrong I was. All cars in Cuba have a coloured number plate which identifies whether they belong to a tourist, a foreign national working in Cuba, if they are taxi, or belong to the interior ministry or military, or another government department. If you are driving a departmental car, you must fill it up with people travelling in your direction and let them off at a public transport or other convenient stop along your route. How eminently sensible. I thought about the selfish aversion to carpooling Kiwis have, and how this Cuban policy, far from presenting a threat from strangers in your car, actually operates as a form of security, of people looking out for one another. It was part of the response to an energy crisis, and many of the billboards along the roads urge energy conservation. You get used to the fact that every billboard is a government one. 'The spirit of Salvador Allende is with us' calls out one; '200 million street children in the world and not one of them is Cuban' another claims quite truthfully. With a family planning program of long duration, free medical care, free education, and yes, a literacy rate as high as New Zealand's, every child is a wanted child. (It's not just in literacy program that New Zealand might learn from the Cubans.)

Some things are typical of anywhere else. There was a call at some stage to recognize and remember the sacrifices made by women in the revolution – the male heroes were on bank notes. So Lucia Sachez is on the 20 peso note, but you have to hold the note up to the light to see her: she's the water mark.

In the Patayas Cigar Factory there are more than 700 workers. They are paid by the piece, plus two cigars for an eight-hour day. They attend a 'school' for nine months to train, and 80 per cent of them drop out. The best can roll a cigar in about three minutes, but those I watched had their own little production line operating. The 'testers' smoke about seven cigars a day! The factory is clean and well-lit, but stiflingly hot. The work is monotonous and boring, our guide told us. Which is why, every day, actors, authors, radio personalities and others are in the factory. All major national and international news is read to the cigar makers every morning, and every afternoon there are readings from the Spanish classics. (Take that, Rodney!)

---

20 Isadora Tattlin, *Cuba Diaries: An American Housewife in Havana* (Chapel Hill, NC: Algonquin Books, 2002).

I'm not pretending to be an apologist for a country with no opposition parties, no free press, no autonomous trade unions, and where every lawyer is employed by the government. Currently, Amnesty International estimates that there are about fifty people on death row. There have been no executions carried out since 1999. This is pale in comparison with the same figures for the U.S.. And unlike regimes currently supported by the U.S., there are no 'death squads,' no lethal 'disappearances' off the street, and police violence and official corruption are probably on par with our erstwhile Pacific neighbours. And while the island houses a centre where flagrant breaches of the Geneva Conventions and civil and political rights are carried out daily, the violator is not Cuba.

Politically, there's a bizarre circularity of an opinion, which goes like this: Fidel stays popular in Cuba because the activities of the CIA and the Cuban emigrants in Miami serve to consolidate patriotism in Cuba. If he ever went to an election, he would win easily. But the destabilization of the country by these and other outsiders in that situation would be far too high a price to pay. Cubans told me this, Western academics there on sabbatical told me this, private business people told me this, Western diplomats told me this.

It is very hard to take seriously the fact that nearly everywhere you go and everyone you meet is part of the government. Taxes on the few licensed private entrepreneurs are ruinously high. Licensing regulations protect inefficient state enterprises. And people can't survive on the average monthly wage. So the Cubans 'resolve' this in the usual way. Any construction will take twice as long with twice as much material, which resolves the inadequate labour wages. I had a number of 'resolving' experiences. My camera and films were 'resolved' in Cuban customs, and never made it back to Toronto. I wasn't bothered by the camera, but they could have left me with the used films.

For some reason, the art of cuisine has pretty much passed Cuba by, and this remains one of life's mysteries. Absolutely delicious food can be had at a *palidero*, a restaurant set up in a private home, but you have to know where to find them because they cannot advertise, even on their street entrance. On my second night we went to one that served outstanding food, and some of the most stunning salads I have ever seen or tasted anywhere. This was of note, because for the remainder of my visit it was tough to find fruit or vegetables other than cucumber. Chicken, rice, beans, and plaintain was the score at the best government restaurant. But there is a point to this story. In Varadero, we had been having *mojitos* in the Dupont house when we spotted 'the most famous Cuban father in America' across the room. It was Juan Migual Gonzalez, father of Elian Gonzalez, who, my host advised, was said to work in an Italian restaurant nearby, although she had never seen him there. We decided the following day to go to that restaurant, as I was getting pretty desperate for almost any vegetable, and it was supposed to do a good bruschetta with olive oil and tomatoes. So we went to the restaurant, and although the most famous Cuban father in the U.S. was at work, the restaurant had no tomatoes! They hadn't arrived this week. Undoubtedly, they had been 'resolved' to a *palidero* close by or in Havana.

One of the more memorable resolving stories I heard was about the resistance of the undertakers to accept the delivery of their new Mercedes Benz hearses. These were diesel fuelled, whereas the old hearses filled up with gasoline, and gas was a better 'resolver' than diesel.

My other resolving experience was significant. I used my credit card three times. Once at the duty-free shop on departure, and once at the desk of each of the hotels for Western tourists where I stayed. Several days after my return to New Zealand, a significant five figure amount was withdrawn in six or seven transactions, one after another – in Moscow!

But for someone who loves the arts and creative work as much as she loves peace, I was bowled over by Cuban culture. Ever since the revolution (and there is very good authority that Che and Fidel agreed on the arts and culture policy during a game of golf), there has been unrelenting support of Cuban culture and the arts. Music, dance, (the son, salsa, rumba, mambo and cha-cha all originated in Cuba), theatre, film, literature – all have a remarkable level of international attainment.

Others love it, too. Hemingway spent years there, and now a beautiful villa is maintained by the government for Gabriel García Márquez, who spends significant time in Havana regularly. The architecture is spectacular. Old Havana was declared a UNESCO World Heritage site in 1982, and the *palacio* (palace) and forts are incomparable. The El Malecón is staggeringly beautiful, and there's a particular beauty throughout the country we have all forgotten: the beauty of having no flashing neon advertising lights, of having no globally recognized labels or junk food outlets, the ravages of another kind of propaganda. It's impossible not to think of how hard it will be for the Cuban people to preserve this, when the world is waiting to pounce at the moment of any change in laws on property, and when it is so difficult for Cubans to travel anywhere and see the nightmares some regard as progress. Some of the UNESCO architects have been desperate that Havana should not turn into yet another bland island resort littered with shopping malls. But as Jonathan

Glancey wrote in the *Guardian Weekly*, 'The word in Havana is that when Fidel Castro dies, and the U.S. finally lifts its embargo, Havana will be transformed, and not necessarily for the better.'[21]

I learned that many years ago in Taupiri and Huntly – probably right across New Zealand – we all sang a poem written by Cuba's national hero José Martí. He was a spectacular essayist, and during his life he warned constantly of the threat to Cuba from U.S. imperialism, particularly in his work in New York City, where he was a correspondent for major newspapers in Argentina and Mexico. He was a relentless advocate of Cuban independence, and was killed by the Spanish in 1895 at Dos Rios, after having landed in eastern Cuba to launch the Second War of Independence.

The lines we sang were from Martí's 'Versos Sencillos,' written in 1891:

Yo soy un hombre sincero de donde crece la palma
Y antes de morirme quiero echar mis versos del alma.
Con los pobres de la tierra quiero yo mi suerte echar
Y el arroyo de la sierra me complace mas que el mar.

You might recognize these as words from *Guajira Guantanamera.*

Finally, let me tell you about something I saw, not through the media, but in a powerful medium of communication. The Castillo de la Real Fuerza is the oldest colonial fortress still standing in the Americas. It was built between 1558 and 1577. It cost U.S. $1 to get in, both for a great view of the harbour entrance and to see the Museo de la Cerámica Artistica Cubana. It had one of the most beautiful collections of twentieth-century pottery I have ever seen, particularly the work from the potters of the Cubanacan studio.

Among these was a piece by Angel Rogelio Oliva made in 1952. I walked up to it as soon as I entered that room. From afar, it looked like a round loaf on a table setting. As I got closer, the 'bread' became a military helmet, and then even closer I could see the southern hemisphere etched into the surface. The place mat was diagonal, with a knife and fork on either side.

I had already stopped and now stood very still, coping with the impact a special work of art or piece of music can have on me. Then I looked at the place mat more closely. It was made of more than 170 pieces as small as my thumbnail, all placed in lines that were quietly

---

21 Jonathan Glancey, *Guardian Weekly*, 25 September–1 October 2003.

offset one from the other. They were skulls. The piece was called *Our Daily Bread*.

It was one of the most breathtaking pieces of art that honoured peace that I have ever seen. I went to Cuba to find it.

4 Do Unpaid Workers Have Rights?

I wrote the proposal for Counting for Nothing/ If Women Counted *in Australia in 1984. I had not written a thesis, or anything of a significant length before. I was an avid researcher, but I had absolutely no idea what lay ahead in asking what seemed to be an obvious question, about the confusion between 'well-being' and 'growth' and the manifestly shocking outcomes of the policy process as a result of this.*

I had had an extraordinary decade of a prime seat in the interstices of all this: I heard tens of thousands of stories from the front line; I chaired the Parliamentary Select Committee on Public Expenditure, the Committee of Public Accounts and Financial Expenditure Review; I was unapologetic about adopting a feminist analysis – and I was not suffocated by the straitjackets of academia. I didn't understand how big the question was, or just how out of line it was. Those of you who are young have never met the pre-Google social science index – physical encyclopedic listings of papers in academic journals. Fortunately, the questions I was asking had never been taken seriously, so it wasn't a huge job to track the few relevant comments down in the realm of journals at that time.

I've never had the space for that extent of textured thinking again. I have had to add academia to my work in women and politics, multilateral development projects, and feminist political work, especially in the human rights field. I am certainly not in daily contact with scores of men and women whose lives were the intellectual and emotional fuel for Counting for Nothing/ If Women Counted. *So I now rely, to a great extent, on the front-line research others are able to do. Some of this work is active and participatory, aimed at policy change. I try to keep abreast of these publications, and use invitations to speak as the agent provocateur to bring myself up to date. One of these invitations came from the University of Western Ontario's Centre for Research on Violence Against Women and from the Women's Community House to give a speech entitled 'Women and Power and a Rights-Based Approach to Unpaid Work' in June 2004. Much of the essay which follows was assembled for that address, during my time as a visiting scholar with Association for Women's Rights in Development (AWID) in Toronto. In the past, I have usually written and spoken about unpaid work in the global context, but this essay is focused on so-called Western and developed nations.*

We all know that workers have rights. Well – we know that paid workers have rights. They have rights to healthy and safe working conditions, rights to paid holidays, and to some sick leave on an annual basis. They have the right to belong to an organized labour group such as a union, and much, much more, set out in national laws and in international covenants and conventions. The International Labour Organization (ILO) has been on the case since the Treaty of Versailles in 1919. The ILO was the sole survivor of the League of Nations and became the first specialized agency of the United Nations in 1946.

The ILO is special internationally, in terms of the membership of its delegations. There are usually four representatives for each country – two from government and one each from the employers and the workers – and the national representatives can vote quite independently of each other. Of course, many don't, because that would literally be more than your life is worth, but in theory, they are independent. As you can imagine, this organization was totally male dominated from the beginning, so it's not surprising that the ILO never paid any attention to the single largest group of workers on the planet – women in unpaid work. So women have never been able to look to the ILO with respect to their rights as unpaid workers.

What do I mean by rights? The usual discourse has been about our rights to do/access something, and the Aristotelian approach was that we were all born with an equal opportunity to access these rights, and only when that access was inhibited was there a breach. Fortunately (and largely thanks to the Canadian Supreme Court), we have moved on from such a fundamentally unsound approach. We can speak of 'substantive equality,'[22] or we can look at the 'capability' approach, which is my focus here.

The capability approach is based on the writings of the 1998 Nobel Laureate Amartya Sen. What is important in the capability model is not what people are or what they do, but what they can or cannot be, and what they can or cannot do, given the opportunities or the freedoms. Capabilities are a means to an end. They reflect access and the

---

22 I have written about this at length in my book *Three Masquerades: Essays on Equality, Work and Human Rights* (Toronto: University of Toronto Press, 1997).

time to participate, the access and the time to make informed choices, or in other words, the freedoms to function effectively.

It is the absence of rights that is of most concern to me when I think about unpaid workers. The availability and accessibility of many rights are in question for *full-time unpaid* workers, dependent on the nature of their work, and their own circumstances. The key impediment to recognition of rights has been the restriction of the words 'work' and 'worker' in international human rights texts to those who are in paid work. The definition of the 'economically active population' is 'all persons of either sex who furnish the supply of labour for the production of economic goods and services.'[23]

What do *we* think it encompasses? Well, it's patently obvious to us that unpaid work is the foundation of the supply of labour for the production of economic goods and services. But those doing the defining mean that there is only economic activity if there is a market transaction, that is, if cash is exchanged. So illegal or morally reprehensible work can count in this system, but most of the productive, reproductive, and service activity that women furnish for the world in an unpaid capacity is 'unproductive.'

Economic Activity

There are four categories of work that are excluded or marginal to the definition of 'economic activity.' Subsistence production is very large in many regions of the world, with many communities dependent on this for survival, but in Canada or New Zealand, our home-grown fruit and vegetables are in this category. The household economy includes unpaid productive, reproductive, and service work, then there's the voluntary and community work category, and finally there's the informal sector, which includes, for example, a lot of the regular 'babysitting' arrangements made in our communities, where cash is exchanged that is not reported anywhere. But how has the continued exclusion of household work, caring work, and voluntary and community work been achieved?

The 1993 rules of the United Nations System of National Accounts (UNSNA) expanded the boundary of production so that the accounts included the subsistence and informal work sectors. It recommended

---

23 International Labour Organization, *International Recommendations on Labour Statistics* (Geneva: ILO, 1976), 32.

that all production of *goods* in households for their own consumption be included, but it still excluded own-account production of *services*. This means that (subsistence) agriculture and non-market production of goods for household consumption now fall inside the production boundary, but that household work (including meal preparation, child and elderly care, and other family-related services) is still excluded.[24] This leads to the remarkable feats accomplished with one bucket of water: wash the dishes, wash the child, cook the rice=non-productive. Use the same water to wash the spray pack, water the corn, wash the pig=productive.

There are, of course, some major technical, logistical, and measurement problems with respect to this, and so in the countries where this change was most relevant, the boundary shifted in theory but not in practice. And you might think that since the subsistence and informal work categories are not key concerns in the 'Northern' or richer' economies, there aren't any problems with the revision, however appalling the politics of the situation are. But the demarcations are increasingly blurred.[25] In 2006, the Greek government surprised its EU colleagues when it announced a 25 per cent upward revision in its GDP, because the Greek statisticians finally rebased their accounts according to this boundary.[26] The increase owed much to counting prostitution and money laundering as part of the service sector. The revision made a significant difference to both the budget deficit and to public debt as a proportion of GDP. This has not yet led to any OECD imitation in revision of SNA boundaries.

Add Research and Stir

Since I finished the first edition of *Counting for Nothing* in 1988, there have been some extraordinary changes in the economic environment in which we live. Changes in technology, in women's paid labour-force participation, in government provision of social services, and in structural adjustment policies and globalization agreements are all of

---

24 United Nations, *System of National Accounts* (New York: UN, 1993).
25 For example, most Human Rights Commissions accept sexual harassment complaints from people working for free in the voluntary and community sectors, treating them as 'workers.'
26 *Ecoanalysts Newsletter*, 29 September 2006.

enormous significance. So just how resistant and entrenched have the patriarchal rules around unpaid work been?

There's been some interesting research adding some texture to the gendered economics of paid work. In 1994, women in waged work in the UK did forty-six hours a week of household work compared to twenty-five hours done by men. When either men or women had an increase in economic power, they were likely to do less household work. Increasing levels of economic power of the man, compared with their female partner, was significantly associated with decreases in the level of sharing work within the household.[27] The number of hours of paid work for men made no difference to how much they shared in the household work; but sharing significantly increased with greater female hours in paid work. Generally, the lower the social class of the man, the greater the time his partner spent on household work.[28]

In 1998, researchers reported that in the UK

... there (were) outstanding patterns with respect to child-rearing. Perhaps the strongest relate(d) to males: men who ha(d) a youngest dependent child between the ages of 0 and 4, (were) far more likely than men who ha(d) no children, or men who ha(d) older children, to undertake paid overtime.[29]

A generous interpretation of this might be that they felt the responsibility to add to their family income. A woman's response might be that they wanted to avoid the most trying hours of the day in dealing with very young children.

The UK Census of 2001 was the first to include a question on health, disability, and the provision of care. It showed that more than a million people were working more than fifty unpaid hours a week to care for family members, friends, neighbours, or others because of long-term physical or mental ill health or disability, or problems related to old age. More than 175,000 children under eighteen were acting as caregivers, including 13,000 children under eighteen who provided more than fifty hours of care a week.

27 Sue Bond and Jill Sales, 'Household Work in the UK: An Analysis of the British Household Panel Survey 1994,' *Work, Employment and Society* 15, no. 2 (1994), 243.
28 Ibid., 242.
29 David N.F. Bell and Robert A. Hart, 'Unpaid Work,' *Economica* 66 (1999), 286.

Just for a moment, reflect on the question of rights and imagine the compromised rights of these children – to 'safe and healthy working conditions,' to leisure, to education, to their own health, or to full enjoyment of life. This is how the capability approach works. We don't presume that these children were born 'equal' and so have the same chance, as every other child, to enjoy these rights. We understand that something has intervened so that circumstances make it impossible for them to have access to those rights which are theirs by birth. We don't have an accurate reading on the gender of these children, but there is no doubt about the gender of those who contribute the most unpaid work hours, even in countries that are lauded as having very gender-sensitive public policies.

In 1999, one of the leading time use researchers, Michael Bittman, wrote that 'Finland represent(ed) an instance of a country that combine(d) a high level of expenditure on the public provision of social services and a remarkably high proportion of the female population in full-time employment.'[30] Yet women spent 25.78 hours and men spent 15.17 hours a week in unpaid work. In a situation where the majority of women (were) in full-time, as opposed to part-time paid employment, men in Finland seldom (took) parental leave. There were major divisions of labour by gender in the paid workforce, more so than anywhere else in Europe. Women were paid, on average, 80 per cent of the male wage for full-time work. Men still occupied most managerial positions in the public and private sectors, and only 2 per cent of the top managers in big enterprises were women.[31]

Bittman reported that, almost regardless of their position at any time in their life, Finnish men's weekly hours of unpaid work tended to be a fixed quantity, while the amount of time women spent in unpaid work varied:

A reduction in men's paid work hours generally results in greater leisure time, so that men literally can choose between (paid) work and leisure. The best predictors of the hours men make available for leisure are the hours they must commit to paid work. For women, however, it is statistically more likely to be a choice between paid and unpaid work.[32]

30 Michael Bittman, 'Parenthood without Penalty: Time Use and Public Policy in Australia and Finland,' *Feminist Economics* 5, no. 3 (1999), 37.
31 CEDAW, *Finland Fourth Country Report*, available online at http://daccessdds.un.org.doc/UNDOC/GEN/N00/292/69/IMG/N0029269/pdf.
32 Ibid., 28.

By 1999, in Bittman's own country of Australia, the gap between men's and women's average time spent in unpaid work at home had decreased. This came about because of a sharp reduction in women's hours of work in the kitchen and in washing and ironing, not because of any large change in the time men spent doing housework. The major reason for the change in women's participation was attributed to 'increased reliance on market substitutes for women's domestic labour.'[33] Women had also increased their activity in home maintenance and car care.

> While men ha(d) increased the hours they devote(d) to child care, their share of this responsibility ha(d) not grown because women's time spent in child care ha(d) increased at the same rate. Parents ha(d) been devoting an ever increasing amount of time to primary face-to-face child care despite falling family size.[34]

In Canada

Since 1988, Canada has sustained a high level of advocacy, lobbying, research, statistical innovation, and alternative indicator development. Some of this has been coordinated into strategic combinations, some of it has been isolated and dispersed, but Canadians have provided leadership across the spectrum of questions rising from the treatment of unpaid work by economists and policymakers. There are still significant gaps in analysis and policy response, but the work that provides the evidence for this has been ongoing.

The 2001 Canada Year Book reported that in 1998, women spent 15.2 hours on unpaid housework (not counting childcare) per week, compared to 8.3 hours for men. Mothers aged twenty-five to forty-four who were working full time spent nearly thirty-five hours a week at unpaid work.

Academic studies of tracking data in Canada revealed that between married couples, few husbands took over their wives' unpaid work responsibilities when the wives' paid work hours increased.[35] At the

---

33 Bittman, 'Parenthood without Penalty,' 27.
34 Ibid., 30.
35 Shelley Phipps, Peter Burton, and Lars Osberg, 'Time as a Source of Inequality within Marriage: Are Husbands More Satisfied with Time for Themselves Than Wives?' *Feminist Economics* 7, no. 2 (2001), 2.

same time, there was a market premium rather than a penalty associated with being a father. The ratio of income for fathers who worked full time in the paid labour market, compared to men who had never had children, was 133.6 per cent in 1996.[36] The authors characterized this as a marriage premium rather than a child premium. It works quite differently for women.

In further studies, these academics suggested that any women who had ever had a child earned less than women who had never had children. For example, in 1996 mothers (aged twenty-four to fifty-four) who worked full time in the paid labour market received 87.3 per cent of the income received by women who had never had children.[37] Research results suggested a 'human capital depreciation' for each year of absence from the paid labour market. The magnitude of the depreciation was substantial. What was lost from one year out of the paid labour force was equal to about 37 per cent of what was gained by one year in.[38] For women, the finding of a child penalty was consistent regardless of whether or not the researchers controlled for marital history.[39]

Related to this were the findings on leisure activities and the 'capacity to enjoy' this human right. With respect to this right, having a pre-school aged child in the household was important for men. A preschooler in the family reduced a husband's satisfaction with time for self by a small amount (about 7 percentage points); *any* child in the family reduced a wife's satisfaction with personal time by a much larger amount (almost 20 percentage points). For women, there was no difference between having a preschooler and having an elementary-school-aged child; having *any* children was the key variable. The researchers noted that, for men, making 'leisure time for one's spouse is a poor substitute for having such time for oneself.'[40]

In terms of hours worked, the unpaid household and community sector is the largest in all of Canada's economy. Canada's method of assessing the value of unpaid activities is one of the more conservative

---

36 Shelley Phipps, Peter Burton, and Lynn Lethbridge, 'In and Out Labour Market: Long-term Income Consequences of Child-related Interruptions to Women's Paid Work,' *Canadian Journal of Economics* 34, no. 2 (2001), 411–29. Based on 1995 Statistics Canada General Social Survey.
37 Ibid., 412.
38 Ibid., 420.
39 Ibid., 416–17.
40 Ibid., 18.

approaches, but even that gives a result of the value of unpaid work as being one-third of Canada's gross domestic product. What does that mean? Well, if you take a look at the monthly GDP figures for Canada in July 2006, unpaid work was equal to the total production from agriculture, forestry, fishing, hunting, mining, oil and gas extraction, manufacturing, the construction industries, utilities, and the information and cultural industries – and at that point it was still a few million short!

In New Zealand

In New Zealand, 60 per cent of men's work is paid, but almost 70 per cent of women's work is unpaid. The New Zealand time use survey of 1998–9 demonstrated how economically valuable the contribution of this work is to the nation's economy. 'In a year, the time spent by men and women on unpaid work in New Zealand as a primary activity equated, at 40 hours per week, to 2 million full time jobs. This compared with the equivalent of 1.7 million full time jobs in time spent in labour force activity.' [41]

New Zealand also chose the imputation method that delivered the most conservative sum of the value of unpaid work. The Department of Statistics in New Zealand justified its selection in a number of ways. It 'follow(ed) the guidelines in a Eurostat Working Paper.'[42] The next reason was that the replacement cost as the median housekeeper wage was 'relatively simple to apply.' Finally, the reader was advised that the median was chosen as opposed to the average 'because average wages tend to be higher than median wages due to the influence of those with very high wages.' At every point of making the imputation decision, the choice was the option which gave a lower percentage contribution to the whole economy. The sexist choice of the replacement housekeeper approach (despite the fact that New Zealand men claimed they did 36 per cent of all unpaid work) delivered a contribution from unpaid social capital of the equivalent of 39 per cent of the GDP. Using an opportunity-cost approach and the average weekly wage, the equivalent GDP contribution in the 1990 pilot time-use survey was 68 per cent.

41 Statistics New Zealand and Ministry of Women's Affairs, *Around the Clock – Findings from the New Zealand Time Use Survey 1998–99* (Wellington: Statistics New Zealand, 2001), 17–18.
42 Eurostat, *Proposal for a Satellite Account of Household Production,* Working Paper 9/1999/A4/11 (Luxembourg: Eurostat, 1999).

At a practical level, I can say that an hourly rate for housekeeping does not reflect the skill base of simultaneity of activity which most of us who have done it for years achieve in our unpaid household work. A chef does not also act as a tutor in Shakespeare or a music teacher, and the hourly rate for a chef exceeds that of a housekeeper. A nanny doesn't balance the monthly accounts while supervising a preschooler, and the hourly rate for a nanny in Auckland certainly exceeds that of a housekeeper. The cleaner does not confer with the children's doctor on the telephone while mopping the floor. In addition, the hourly rate for housekeeping does not reflect the conditions of work that are so often a feature of a rural housekeeper, which include accommodation, meals, or household overheads (electricity and maintenance, for example).

But there's an ideological agenda here that is consistently disturbing. There is a real resistance on the part of statisticians and economists to own up to the vital policy decision they are making in the choices they make about imputation. The policy consequences are omnipresent and serious, and there seems to me to be a conscious and constant effort to understate the contribution. It seems to me that there are very serious policy and budgetary considerations that threaten vested interests.

My own approach to that question has always been that the effects on the current budgetary distribution would be so revolutionary, and would fly in the face of the power and expectations of so many vested interests, that no one wants to know. What, for example, are the effects of thinking about the household as the largest single sector in the nation's economy, as Ironmonger demonstrated in Australia?[43] What is the result when it is demonstrated, as it has been in Nova Scotia, that people doing unpaid voluntary and community work not only donate their time but also spend more from their own pockets in carrying out this work than businesses claim as tax deductions for their contributions?[44] What are the consequences to the health budget if it is demonstrated that one-quarter to one-third of all primary health care is carried out by people called mum or dad, sister, neighbour, daughter,

43 See Duncan S. Ironmonger, 'Modelling the Household Economy,' in M. Dutta, ed., *Economics, Econometrics and the LINK: Essays in Honour of Lawrence R. Klein* (North Holland: Elsevier Science Publishers, 1995), 397–8; and Duncan S. Ironmonger, 'Why Measure and Value Unpaid Work?' *Conference Proceedings on the Measurement and Valuation of Unpaid Work* (Ottawa: Statistics Canada, 1993).

44 R. Colman, *The Economic Value of Civic and Voluntary Work in Nova Scotia* (Halifax: GPI Atlantic, 1998).

as it is in Canada? We are frequently told that the most efficient health economics is about the earliest possible diagnosis. But ancillary medical provision is almost non-existent. The general practitioner (GP) is thought of as the primary caregiver. The interruption to the working day of the unpaid to accompany the sick to visit the GP is seen as being the most 'productive' use of time, but I have serious doubts about that. In such a cost-benefit analysis, no account is taken of the productive and service work foregone by the 'unpaid' person in this scenario.

Have We Made Any Progress?

In reviewing where the feminist movement has got to with regards to unpaid work, its important to ask if we ever made some headway in respect of the power of definition.

In 1975, when I was elected to the New Zealand Parliament, our issues and situation were very different. But there was a consciousness about unpaid work. In a formal, international context, the first references to unpaid work were at the first United Nations World Conference for Women in 1975 in Mexico City. I was on the floor in the New Zealand delegation in Copenhagen in 1980 to extend those paragraphs, and references continued in major UN conferences in Nairobi, Beijing, Vienna, Copenhagen, and Rio de Janeiro. Through publications such as the UNDP *World Development Report* and *The World's Women*, commentary, statistics, and research kept up the pressure.

But the ideology of the New Right swept through our national and international movement post-Nairobi. The women's movement was caught between structural adjustment policies and the World Trade Organization's agendas. The market ruled our economic lives and the energy required for activism in the face of its power dominated the movement's activities. The feminist response and focus was to allow itself to be restricted to activity and energy around that debate – fostered, in part, by the Old Left approach about the exploitation of women only happening in the market.

Isabella Bakker has written that 'researchers have argued that gender-neutral macro-economic policy will only address women's needs and experiences to the extent to which they conform to male norms.'[45]

---

45 Isabella Bakker, *Unpaid Work and Macroeconomics: New Discussions, New Tools for Action* (Ottawa: Status of Women Canada's Policy Research Fund, 1998), 1.

Feminist advocates were overwhelmingly co-opted to work primarily on analysis and criticism of the dominating economic paradigms in their political and academic work, too, and, far from proposing alternatives, addressed women's needs and experiences in the realms in which women conformed to male norms, and could be measured against them.[46]

Now, I don't wish to set up an either/or or a dichotomous debate here: we have always needed both/and approaches to the issues of women in paid and unpaid work, but that has simply disappeared. For feminists actively concerned with the both/and approach, this has made us very wary of the kind of support we attract. Meg Luxton recollects that:

> The absence of much of the feminist movement from these debates was reflected in the discussion about whether or not unpaid work would be included in the 1996 Canadian census. With the notable exception of Mothers Are Women (MAW) and the Work is Work is Work coalition, the women's groups lobbying for its inclusion were non-feminist or explicitly antifeminist and represented women who were primarily homemakers themselves, or whose political activities focused on what they call 'the family.'[47]

Statistics Canada reported, 'Proponents for inclusion indicated that recognizing unpaid work promotes the status of those who choose to stay at home to look after young children, seniors or other family members,'[48] Luxton responded that what was missing was 'any recognition that most women, including those with paid employment, do domestic labour and would benefit from having its (and therefore their) status promoted. A bias in favour of women "who choose to stay at home" could have serious implications for policy development.'[49]

---

46 There have been a number of exceptions to this framework in Canada: Meg Luxton, Isabella Bakker, Shelley Phipps, Lynn Lethbridge, Peter Burton, Ron Coleman, Mark Anielski, Hans Messenger, Carol Lees, Evelyn Drescher, Beverly Smith, and others.

47 Leah Vosko and Meg Luxton, 'When Women's Efforts Count: The 1996 Census Campaign – From Nairobi to Beijing,' paper presented at the Non-Governmental Organizations Forum, The UN Fourth World Conference on Women, Beijing China, 1995, n.p.

48 Statistics Canada, *1996 Consensus Consultation Report*, No. 2 (Ottawa: Statistics Canada, 1994), n.p.

49 Meg Luxton, 'The UN, Women, and Household Labour: Measuring and Valuing Unpaid Work,' *Women's Studies International Forum* 20, no. 3 (1997), 436.

In addition, so many of the key policy agenda items have just made it easier for women to do two jobs more effectively, becoming the cohort group who work the most hours of any in the nation's economy. Further Canadian research found evidence that women in dual-earner households were more time-stressed than men, apparently as a result of the continued gendered division of housework, despite high levels of paid work by wives.[50]

If It's Not Work, What Is It?

What do we feel about these activities of ours? It's not leisure. But if it's not work, what is it, then? In the SNA rules, the household itself is not described as an enterprise. But if a household is a school and a school is an enterprise, why isn't the home schooler an unpaid worker in an enterprise? If the household happens to be the residence of a doctor, and the spouse has to constantly answer the telephone, is the spouse an unpaid worker in the enterprise?

If a woman or man is relieving an institution of the full-time responsibility of the care and attention of somebody, is she or he an enterprise or not? Are they an enterprise when the person in their care is not a family member, but not an enterprise when the person being cared for is a close relative? If the full-time caregiver wasn't 'working,' the service would have to be performed in an enterprise. There is no other place for it to be done.

Governments have no evidence on which to sustain any argument that dependents are better cared for in public or private institutions in Canada. Think about Ontario nursing homes. In 2004, local unions claimed these provided the least amount of resident care in the Western world. The Ontario government eliminated the minimum number of hours per day of nursing care, and did not require that residents have even one bath a week. Nursing homes allotted only $4.50 per resident per day for food. A registered practical nurse during a night shift might be responsible for the care of fifty or more residents. A personal support worker might be required to take care of fourteen residents at one time. That meant that some days, residents couldn't even get out of bed or get dressed.

And what about the following list of government or church 'enterprises' being in charge of the care of Canadians: Shelbourne Youth

---

50 Phipps, Burton, and Osberg, 'Time as a Source of Inequality within Marriage,' 1.

Centre, Nova Scotia School for Girls, Nova Scotia Youth Training Centre, Grandview Training School for Girls, St John's and St Joseph's Training Schools in Ontario, George Epoch's extensive sexual abuses in the Native communities, New Brunswick Training School, Mount Cashel Orphanage, Jericho Hill School in Vancouver, and the sexual and physical abuse of Aboriginal peoples while in residential schools as reported in the 1996 Royal Commission Inquiry?[51]

What's the situation for full-time, unpaid immediate family caregivers in Ontario? In 2004, if I was extremely ill or lived with a severe disability and I was not being cared for by an immediate family member, I would have been able to gather receipts for full-time attendant care, for supervision if I was residing in a home with a prolonged impairment, for sign language interpreter fees if I was deaf. The attendant care component would cover health care, meal preparation, housekeeping, laundry, a transportation driver, and security services where applicable.

In comparison, when my mother or father, or my sister or brother, or my daughter or son were doing this work full-time for months, if not years, they got to deduct 'reasonable expenses' associated with the cost of training required to care for me. They might have received a disability credit, as a caregiver, which varied according to whether the dependent was under eighteen, which could be claimed with other expenses to a maximum of $5,808. If the family income of my caregiver was less than $33,487 in 2003, they might receive another $1,600. Then there were personal credits for a relative over seventeen, caregiver tax credits of up to $587 – and the list goes on. Lord knows how you worked out what you were entitled to without an accountant – and that blew the credit right there. But one thing was for certain – this was, and is, an extraordinary exploitation.

We get some clues about this by examining the introductory speech of Chris Bentley, Ontario minister of labour, in moving the Employment Standards Amendment Act (Family Medical Leave) 2004 on 13 April 2004. The bill provided up to eight weeks of job protection for unpaid time off work in order to take care of seriously ill family members. He said:

It is clear that an aging population and significantly increasing workplace demands have contributed to growing levels of employee stress due to

---

51 The Government of Canada made a formal apology to survivors of these schools in June 2008.

work – family conflict … a recent Ipsos-Reid poll found that almost 32% of Canadian adults were now responsible for the care of older relatives … Most of our work life schedules do not include the additional time to provide the necessary care and support for seriously ill dependents … Employees making the impossible choice are less productive. They are often forced by circumstance into unplanned absences. When employees are forced to quit their job, the employees lose their skills, training and experience as well as their work. The costs to business are massive.

And finally at last he said: 'The availability of Family Medical leave will support our existing health services. In some cases, it might reduce the demand on these services.'

Unlike some of the other supposedly women friendly leave policies, this applied to all employees, including those working part time. Employees would not be required to have worked a specific length of time in order to qualify. Seniority and credit for length of service and length of employment would count as if they had been at work. Employer contributions to the premiums for pension plans, life and extended health insurance plans, accidental death plans and dental plans would have to be kept up.

But for those in the full-time unpaid workforce in the same circumstances, there was nothing.

The Human Rights Dimension

Canada: A major breakthrough in the human rights issues in this field was made when Cheryl and Philip Hutchinson took on the Ministry of Health and Senior Citizens of British Columbia and the Human Rights Commission of British Columbia on the validity of a ministry policy that prohibited the hiring of family members by adults with disabilities who qualified for and received ministry funding to cover the cost of long-term, in-home care services.[52] The policy constituted a blanket prohibition against hiring family members and applied regardless of whether the funding arrangement involved direct payment to the individual or payment through a homemaker agency as an approved service provider.

Ms Hutchinson was born with cerebral palsy, a condition that led to physical limitations in her childhood and to quadriplegia in her adult

---

52 *Hutchinson v. B.C.* (Min. of Health), 2004 BCHRT 58.

life. At the time of the case in 2004, Ms Hutchinson required assistance in all aspects of daily living, including bathing, dressing, toileting, transfers, mobility, and meal preparation, and used a wheelchair for mobility. Ms Hutchinson's father, Phillip Hutchinson, had been her primary caregiver since she was thirteen years old. In her view, her father was, and continued to be, her most appropriate caregiver and a major contributing factor to her success, accomplishments, and independence in the face of her disability. In order to provide his daughter with the care she required, Mr Hutchinson was forced to leave the workforce. The family had subsisted primarily on the limited funds available through social assistance since 1983. At the time of the hearing, Mr Hutchinson was seventy-one years old and continued to be his daughter's primary caregiver.

In 1998, Ms Hutchinson was accepted as a client of the Choices in Supports for Independent Living (CSIL) Program. CSIL was a ministry-funded program that provided funds directly to qualified adults with disabilities, allowing them some discretion to hire their own caregivers. However, the ministry policy prohibited Ms Hutchinson from hiring her father to provide for her care using CSIL funds.

Mr Hutchinson did not wish to be his daughter's sole caregiver as he realized that he would not be able to care for his daughter forever and he wanted her to be independent. He did, however, wish to be able to be hired as one of his daughter's caregivers under CSIL.

Cheryl Hutchinson and Phillip Hutchinson both filed human rights complaints alleging that the ministry's policy prohibiting the hiring of family members under CSIL was discriminatory. Ms Hutchinson alleged that the ministry's policy discriminated against her on the grounds of disability and family status contrary to section 8 of the Human Rights Code.[53] Mr Hutchinson alleged that the ministry's policy discriminated against him on the basis of family status contrary to section 13 of the Code in that it prohibited him from being hired by his daughter as her caregiver, purely on the basis that he was her father.

The case was tightly constructed, so it could not be seen as a universal remedy for all family members who are subject to this sort of discrimination. The complainants did not challenge the validity of a general prohibition against the hiring of family members. What was challenged was the blanket prohibition against the hiring of family

---

53   Human Rights Code R.S.B.C. 1996, c. 210 (as amended).

members, without an assessment of the individual circumstances, under CSIL.

The ministry argued that there was an expectation in (Canadian) society that families would look after other family members, and that many ministry programs operated on the basis that first and foremost it was the obligation of families to look after their own. In particular, family members had the primary responsibility to care for disabled family members. It was only when there was a shortfall in the care that the family and the community could provide that the ministry would step in to assist the family unit by providing funds to hire outside care-givers to supplement that care. The ministry argued that otherwise the policy would undermine the role and responsibility of families to look after their own. It would be contrary to the purposes of CSIL to pay family members for the care they were expected to provide for free, as CSIL was meant to be a supplemental program. Under CSIL, then, Ms Hutchinson was only eligible to receive public funds to hire care to the extent that her father (or other family or community supports) could not meet her needs. Accordingly, if Mr Hutchinson was able to provide care to his daughter, he would be expected to provide that care, to the extent that he was capable, for free. Integral to the ministry's argument with respect to the supplemental nature of CSIL, was that the cost of the care that was being provided for free in 2004 would be impossible for it to fund if they had to pay immediate family members providing such care.

Section 8 of the Code read as follows:

8(1) A person must not, without a bona fide and reasonable justification,
    (a) deny to a person or class of persons any accommodation, service or facility customarily available to the public, or
    (b) discriminate against a person or class of persons regarding any accommodation, service or facility customarily available to the public because of the ... family status, physical or mental disability ... of that person or class of persons.

Section 13 of the Code prohibited discrimination in employment. It stated:

13(1) A person must not
    (a) refuse to employ or refuse to continue to employ a person, or
    (b) discriminate against a person regarding employment or any term or condition of employment because of the ... family status ... of that person.

13(4) Subsections (1) and (2) did not apply with respect to a refusal, limitation, specification or preference based on a bona fide occupational requirement.

The judgment is very clear as to the part played by 'loss of dignity' in human rights cases. I will not dwell at any length on this here, but it is very instructive to any capability analysis. In Ms Hutchinson's case, the blanket policy against hiring family members had a significant adverse impact on her dignity, given her high care needs and her difficulties in hiring and retaining an appropriate caregiver. The policy did not address her actual needs as a vulnerable person with a severe disability. On the one hand, it offered her the opportunity to choose her own caregiver and, on the other, it denied her the opportunity to hire her father, her most appropriate caregiver.

The BC Human Rights Tribunal, which heard the case, found that the blanket prohibition against hiring family members impacted most severely on those, like Ms Hutchinson, who were severely disabled and required twenty-four-hour care with all of the intimate activities of daily living. It concluded that Ms Hutchinson had established a *prima facie* case of discrimination on the basis of disability, and found that the ministry's blanket prohibition against the hiring relatives offended the Human Rights Code on the basis of family status. It found that Mr Hutchinson had been discriminated against in seeking employment with no consideration of Mr Hutchinson's qualifications or suitability to do the job, and that both Hutchinsons had had their dignity violated. The Ministry of Health was ordered to cease and desist its discriminatory practice and to pay compensation of $105,000 to Mr Hutchinson for lost wages, and amounts to both Hutchinsons for loss of dignity.

While there is no doubt that this was a breakthrough case, its parameters were quite narrow, in that key points were the need for specialist care and the person best suited to provide it. The amount sought by Mr Hutchinson for lost earnings was curbed by the tribunal to allow for the amount of unpaid time a family member might reasonably have been expected to assist.

New Zealand: In New Zealand I have been following the human rights decisions and complaints of the full-time caregivers of members of their immediate families who are not remunerated or who are remunerated on a different basis from other caregivers. This situation was first covered in *Hills v. IHC* (6HRNZ 213). Two parents of a disabled child were found to have been discriminated against on the ground of family status (because they were the child's parents and related to him) because the IHC would not pay them to care for him in the same way they would pay caregivers who were not related to him to take care of him.

More recently, complaints have been made in regard to the government's policy of not contracting or paying parents to provide residential care to their disabled children. Although the complainants receive some income replacement from the government (in the form of NZ superannuation or the Domestic Purpose Benefit for care at home of sick or infirm), they are discriminated against in the government's disability services purchasing policy of not contracting/employing/paying parents for the provision of residential care services to their disabled children.

The response of the Crown Law Office to the Human Rights Commission of 30 June 2003 on this issue was most instructive. It wrote that the Government

> accepts ... that a discrimination issue is indeed raised; the Government's response is that the relevant differentiation is justified ... Government funded social assistance ... is framed as *assistance* rather than *payment* for the services provided by family members ... The Ministry of Health has, on an exceptions basis, approved payment to families for care where there are exceptional circumstances, e.g., in isolated rural areas where other care options are difficult to source, and for some Maori families where there are strong cultural reasons for requiring whanau (family) based care ... these payments have generally been at rates paid for homecare ... If the government were to have a general policy of paying parental caregivers of disabled persons for the provision of care provided to those disabled persons then this would have significant implications for similar government policies across the entire social assistance area ... the government considers that the current policy constitutes a justified limitation on the right to be free from discrimination.

The NZ government has no idea how many families are currently 'justifiably' subject to discrimination. As at 25 July 2003, there were 3,260 such people in receipt of the Domestic Purpose Benefit. No one knows how many people in receipt of NZ superannuation are full time caregivers for family members who are sick and infirm. If the majority of these older caregivers are women, they are likely to have fewer resources with which to carry out their care.

The rules and regulations governing any 'assistance' for caregivers have been a series of knee-jerk responses to differing circumstances over time that were sufficiently highlighted to demand political response. Caregivers are subject to different levels of funding and different assessment criteria, depending on whether the 'sick or infirm' person is the responsibility of the Department of Health or the IHC, or is an ACC client. The sickness community is not identified as part of the disability community. The rules are different, depending on whether the person being cared for is a partner, a parent, or a child. There are regional differences in the subsidies allowed and in the regionally available budgets, which will affect the benchmarks of assessors. Subsidies can range from $260 per week to $670 per week. Benchmarks are not about the quality or amount of care but about the nature of the disability of the person being cared for. 'Full-time care' is not about the amount of time the caregivers works. It is about the patient having access to twenty-four-hour care. The rule for those caregivers who receive any assistance at all is: 'A caregiver can be away from the home for a few hours per week'![54] When the patient needs twenty-four-hour continuous care, 'it is not reasonable to expect one person to manage. However, there is no provision to pay more than one Domestic Purposes Benefit in respect of the same patient.' Home help might be available temporarily and in an emergency to some caregivers, but 'generally home help should not be approved if able relatives other than primary or secondary school students live in the home.' Home-support services are different again, and may be available from a district health board assessor to provide relief for a caregiver.

Those who don't qualify for a Domestic Purposes Benefit might qualify, under special circumstances, for an Emergency Benefit, but if the person who is ill is a partner, there will be more stringent tests applied before the Emergency Benefit can be received.

You will recall that what is important in the capability model is not what people are or what they do, but what they can or cannot be and what they can or cannot do, given the opportunities or the freedoms.

These cases raise questions about many more potential complaints for lack of access to fundamental human rights. What of the family members who care full time for someone who does not fit into the current operative definition of 'disability' for the sake of a benefit? Should rights extend only to those full time caregivers whose work continues

---

54 See http://inet/tools/map/income_support/ma...benefit _-_care_of_sick_or_infirm.

for years and years without ceasing? Is there some time consideration that would mean that a parent stopping work to care for a child acci- dent victim or terminally ill parent for six to nine months is in a dif- ferent category from one who gives care for five years? What about grandparents who are full-time caregivers for grandchildren, in a Child Youth and Family situation where the child might otherwise be placed in foster care? [55] Do we think that their capability and freedom to func- tion effectively might be compromised? Do we think that the payment differential between their eligibility for assistance and that of foster par- ents might be discriminatory? Do we think that children who work long hours in unpaid work might be losing out on rights of access and oppor- tunities – to education, to leisure, and enjoyment of life?[56] Unpaid care of the sick is a critical part of the health care system that compromises the well-being of the caregiver – who is then further penalized by the system in terms of loss of earnings or is given no recognition at all. Do we recog- nize to what extent all this caregiving work undermines women's capac- ity to take an equal part in civil and political life?

In terms of a rights-based approach to those in the unpaid workforce – and, for example, for those in the 'unpaid' or underpaid or differently paid full-time caregiving role – we have to ask, to what extent does the discrimination and different treatment of family members in long-term caregiving (in terms of the legislation and regulations surrounding this) compromise or inhibit their capacity to participate effectively in political or community life, to attain the highest possible standard of physical and mental health, to exercise their right to opportunities of lifelong education, to enjoy safe and healthy working conditions?

We know that the movement of people between the paid and unpaid sectors has major economic ramifications. It was a joke once to repeat the old adage that when a man married his housekeeper the GDP went down. But governments are desperate to have those housekeepers back as engines of productivity in the market of the national economy.

---

55 Under section 3 of the Children Young Person's and their Families Act 1989, payments received by people in receipt of a social security benefit and providing foster care under the Act have all payments disregarded as income for benefit abatement purposes, but no one has been able to tell me what the position is in respect of superannuation.

56 The UK Census data 2001 gave rise to major policy issues around equal opportunity access to education status of the 175,000 children as carers, including 13,000 children under eighteen providing more than fifty hours of care a week.

They continue to legislate to assist this with parental leave provisions, flex time, childcare payments, and programs for 'work-life balance.' But those who work the longest and the hardest are still marginal and largely invisible, and the extent of this exploitation is a major human rights issue. Watch this space. The 'justified limitations' on the right to be free from discrimination were not supposed to extend to the servitude situations of the women and men who care for members of the family without recompense, twenty-four hours a day, seven days a week. The situation has arisen directly from the gendered discriminations of the definitions of work, and the drawing of the production boundaries around what is and is not economic activity. It's a barbaric nineteenth-century approach that needs to come to an end, so that the capacity of these workers to enjoy fundamental freedoms and human rights can be substantively improved.

5 Framing Dignity – Canada, New Zealand, and the Gay Marriage Debate

In 2006 I accepted a position at AUT University in Auckland, New Zealand, as professor of public policy. While I had held a personal chair for some time in my previous position, I had managed to avoid giving a Professorial Inaugural Lecture. But AUT University was determined I would 'perform.' I thought that people would expect something on unpaid work, development, or human rights issues. I wanted both to move away from those matters, yet demonstrate what my discipline of public policy analysis was about. I had spent months in Canada during the gay marriage debate, and had been so envious that the Charter of Rights *could deliver equality, in a situation where New Zealand continued to exercise discrimination by offering only the civil union alternative. I believed this difference was significantly influenced by how each of the main sectors – politicians, courts, the media, lobbyists – had framed the debate. The Professorial Inaugural Lecture offered the opportunity to explore this issue and to pay my respects again to Canada.*

In early 1993 I sat on the veranda of a house in Bogor, Indonesia, with the counsellor for the Canadian Embassy, Stan Moore, and his partner, Pierre Soucy. When Stan was posted, he and Pierre were in a committed relationship. When Stan arrived in Jakarta, he was not able to obtain the usual relocation assistance provided for spouses. When Pierre arrived in Jakarta, he arrived to a home in a state of disrepair. Stan had been allocated a home that would be sufficient for one person but not for a couple, and Pierre was not allowed to request any work orders from embassy maintenance staff, unlike other spouses. When the embassy issued a list of Canadian staff and their families, Pierre was not on the list. We sat there looking over the rice fields and planned the complaint they would make under their provincial human rights legislation.

Just these few characteristics of this story begin to demonstrate clear discriminatory treatment in access to services and outcomes that were unequal compared with other people who had access to those services. This was discriminatory behaviour in breach of human rights laws, on the grounds of sexual orientation. By way of an introduction to the legal framework that we are considering here, it serves a purpose for the key framing words 'human rights' and 'equality,' but there's a very important other word in this lecture: let me continue with Stan and Pierre.

One of the points I remember more than anything else was that Stan had been able to relocate Jasmine, the 'family' cat, and have this paid for by the Department of Foreign Affairs, but not Pierre's economy air ticket. The cat was family. Pierre was not.

At this point I can introduce the word 'dignity,' because now you have a very simple story about indignity to call on, and 'dignity' has always been at the forefront of the human rights discourse. We find 'dignity' in the preamble in the United Nations Universal Declaration of Human Rights and in the International Covenant on Civil and Political Rights (ICCPR). But do we ever find it in human rights discourse in New Zealand?

I'll get back to Stan and Pierre in a moment, but I want to explain what I am going to be doing in this lecture.

In public policy analysis we speak of how an issue is 'framed' by the political, judicial, and civil society leadership to explain how and why certain public policy outcomes are achieved. A 'frame' is an interpretation of a political issue. It establishes what an issue is about, and what has been left out. Analysis can often demonstrate that outcomes were completely predictable, in terms of the 'framing' of an issue, by the key words used at the very beginning of the public debate. A frame establishes what considerations are irrelevant or important to opinion-making on an issue. Exposure to a particular frame can alter the range of considerations people call to mind as they make their decisions on specific issues. I have a case study in which we are going to look at how one issue got framed.

Advocacy for equal rights for gay and lesbian people, and in particular the right to marriage, took place in Canada and New Zealand over the same decade. The countries share all the same key international human rights obligations. In particular, our domestic law uses exactly the same words in respect of 'unjustified limitations' for the full guarantees of rights and freedoms to all citizens. Section 15 of the Canadian Charter of Rights and Freedoms is very similar to article 26 of the International Covenant on Civil and Political Rights, which is the reference for the New Zealand Bill of Rights Act 1990. In this case study I want to compare the way party political leaders, the courts, and gay and lesbian advocates framed this issue in each country. Perhaps this can describe why Canada finished up with full equality in marriage and why New Zealand finished up with civil union – equivalence but not equality.

There have, of course, been cases of discrimination in marriage before. Different classes of people have been denied the human right to choose their marriage partners. We find this discrimination in Germany in the 1930s, when the anti-Semitic Nuremburg laws were enacted by the Nazis against the large German Jewish community, forbidding marriages between the Jews (deemed the *Untermenschen*, 'lower people') and German Aryans (deemed the *Ubermenschen*, 'higher people'). Many interfaith and intermarried couples committed suicide when these laws came into effect. Under the apartheid regime in 1949, the South Africa government enacted the Prohibition of Mixed Marriages Act, which outlawed marriages between members of different classified races. In the southern states in the United States various enactments contained the same sentiments, such as 'All marriages between ... white persons and Negroes are prohibited and declared absolutely void. Any person circulating printed matter presenting arguments or suggestions in favour of social equality or of intermarriage between whites and Negroes, shall be guilty of a misdemeanour ...'

In the context of these human rights cases, what is marriage? Marriage is a means of conferring the highest form of social approval, and in all these cases, it is the symbolic approval, the approval of dignity and self-respect, that those who do not have access to marriage desire. In the twentieth century and in my lifetime, perhaps the most significant court case in this respect was *Loving* v. *Virginia* (1967), which clearly articulated both the freedom to marry and the desire for racial equality. In its judgment, the U.S. Supreme Court wrote:

Marriage is one of the 'basic civil rights of man,' [*sic*] fundamental to our very existence and survival ... To deny this fundamental freedom on so unsupportable a basis as ... racial classifications ... so directly subversive to the principle of equality is surely to deprive all the state's citizens of liberty without due process of law.[57]

It was not until 2000 that Alabama became the last state to remove this law from its books.

Now, we need to look quickly at the political and legal structures in Canada to give us some more contexts for comparative purposes. Federally, there is a lower house (the House of Commons, which is elected) and an upper house (the Senate, which is appointed). The leader of the governing party in the House of Commons is the prime minister. Each province also has a legislature, cabinet, and a premier. The jurisdictions of the federal and provincial levels of government are set out in the Constitution Act (formerly the British North America Act). The provinces have wide jurisdiction. Human rights legislation is enacted at the provincial level. Canada's federal Parliament has responsibility for the constitution of which the equality law is part. Both the federal and provincial levels of government are bound by the equality law and cannot derogate from the Canadian Charter of Rights and Freedoms. That means the courts can rule that legislation is in breach of Charter rights and unconstitutional. Each province has two levels of trial court (a lower and higher court) and a court of appeal. The higher trial court sits as a divisional court and often hears appeals from administrative tribunals and the lower trial court. There is also a set of courts for matters related only to federal jurisdiction (e.g., taxation). For all courts, the highest level of appeal is to the Supreme Court of Canada.

The overarching protection of human rights is provided through the Canadian Charter of Rights and Freedoms, which was entrenched in 1982. The equality provision (section 15) came into effect three years later in 1985 (allowing governments a period of grace to bring existing laws and practices into compliance). The Charter applies to all legislatures (both provincial and federal) and to all government action. Anyone whose rights or freedoms under the Charter have been infringed or denied can go to court to seek 'such remedy as the court considers appropriate and just in the circumstances.' That means the courts – more or less at any level – can rule legislation or government action as being in breach of Charter rights and as unconstitutional. This can mean that the legislation can be struck down or suspended, government procedures

---

57 388 U.S. 1 (1967) Chief Justice Warren.

changed, and damages paid for the breach of rights. Charter rights can be subjected to 'reasonable limits prescribed by law as can be demonstrably justified in a free and democratic society' (section 1) and they can be over-ridden by explicit decision of a legislature through the 'notwithstanding clause' (section 33). The Charter is generally referred to as governing 'public action' between the state and its citizens.

The second layer of human rights protection is targeted at 'private actions' between citizens or related to arrangements respecting the provision of accommodation, goods and services, and employment. This layer is comprised of human rights legislation. Human rights legislation is passed at the level of provincial legislatures (and all provinces and territories in Canada have human rights legislation).

In New Zealand, the legislation we are principally concerned with is the New Zealand Bill of Rights Act. Although offering a mercifully straightforward structure in comparison to Canada, a principle difference is that it is not regarded as 'entrenched' or as giving (explicit) authority to courts to strike down legislation or government (public) practices that breach its provisions. There is a strong (and, unfortunately, somewhat ephemeral) presumption that Parliament will ensure conformity to the provisions of the Bill of Rights Act, but 'parliamentary supremacy' (or the law of the majority and the exigencies of political necessity) prevails.

But you want to know the end of the Stan and Pierre story. Stan and Pierre made a complaint under the Canadian Human Rights Act. On 13 June 1996, the Canadian Human Rights Tribunal found that there was a discriminatory impact on Stan and Pierre that was not trivial, that the federal government (Stan's employer) reinforced prejudicial attitudes based on faulty stereotypes, and that the effect of the impugned provision was clearly contrary to section 15 of the Charter's aim of protecting human dignity. The distinction amounted to discrimination on the basis of sexual orientation. The tribunal found that all of Stan and Pierre's complaint was substantiated. A payment was ordered for hurt feelings and self-respect. The tribunal gave the Department of Foreign Affairs sixty days to prepare an inventory of all legislation, regulations, and directives that contained definitions of common-law spouses which discriminated against same-sex common-law couples. The inventory was to be presented to the tribunal, and these practices were to be changed.

Stan and Pierre laid their complaint in 1993, the year that sexual orientation was added to the grounds of discrimination in New Zealand's

Human Rights Act, thanks to MP Katherine O'Regan, my successor in my old constituency.

At this time there was no way in which the Canadians could have been seen to be the comparative leaders in this area of discrimination. In 1983, 1985, 1986, 1989, and 1991, Sven Robinson, an MP in the federal Parliament and a member of the New Democratic Party (a centrist-left party), introduced bills into the federal Parliament to have sexual orientation inserted into the federal Human Rights Act. In 1991 and 1992, he tried to get the definition of spouse changed in the Income Tax Act and the Canada Pension Plan Act. A bloody battle had been fought in Ontario in 1987 over the inclusion of sexual orientation in the Ontario Human Rights Code. The decision of the Ontario Human Rights Tribunal in the complaint of *Michaels*,[58] decided in 1992, had struck down the exclusion of same-sex partners in provincial employment and benefit packages and ordered the provincial government to set up a parallel pension benefits structure for same-sex survivors if the federal government failed to change the Income Tax Act. Litigation to challenge the Income Tax Act was initiated by Nancy Rosenberg with the support of her union, following the *Michaels* decision. A number of provinces did not include sexual orientation as a protected ground in their human rights codes.

In 1993, polls showed that just 37 per cent of Canadians were in favour of extending the rights and entitlements associated with marriage to gay and lesbian couples. By 1995, both countries, New Zealand through legislation and Canada through the courts, recognized sexual orientation as grounds for discrimination. Yet both countries retained in excess of 100 pieces of law that discriminated against same-sex couples on their statute books. It is worth noting that several 'early' marriage cases brought by gays and lesbians in Canada under provincial human rights codes had been lost.

The courts made the running in Canada and they played a major role in the framing discourse. In *Haig and Birch v. Canada* in August 1992, the Ontario Court of Appeal (note this Ontario jurisdiction – we'll hear a lot from them) ruled that the failure to include sexual orientation in the Canadian Human Rights Act was discriminatory.[59] Notice that there is no judicial kick for touch here – no 'leave it to the legislators' – and for good reason.

---

58 Fore more information, see http://en.wikipedia.org/wiki/Michael_Leshner.
59 *Haig v. Canada* (1992) 16 C. H.R.R. D/226 (Ont. C.A.).

Federal justice minister Kim Campbell had promised that the government would introduce legislation to add sexual orientation to the Canadian Human Rights Act, but this did not pass the first reading. We then have to look at the Canadian courts again for the case of *Egan & Nesbit v. Canada*,[60] which concerned spousal benefits of same-sex partners under the federal Old Age Security Act. In May 1995, all nine judges agreed that sexual orientation was a protected ground and that protection extended to partnerships of lesbians and gay men. The decision affirmed clearly that the equal rights provisions contained in the Charter demanded that gay and lesbian couples be treated the same as opposite-sex couples. The right established didn't lead to a remedy however, as the majority of the Supreme Court in the *Egan* case said that this violation was a 'reasonable limit' under subsection 1 of the Charter. Mr Justice Sopinka argued that Parliament had to contend with fiscal constraints and the implications of these for the scope of social programs. He wrote that same-sex spouses were a 'novel concept' and that discrimination on this basis was not an unreasonable restriction on equality.[61]

The decision in 1995 had a very cooling effect on the movement to reform human rights and other legislation. *Egan* was interpreted by federal departments and ministers as removing pressure for immediate legislative reforms, and it had a similar effect for provincial jurisdictions. In 1994, for instance, the Ontario New Democratic Party government failed to secure large-scale reforms in the interests of lesbian and gay rights in the face of strong opposition from both inside and outside the government, and risk-averse politicians were keen to avoid gay rights reform. The court's message in the early and mid-nineties was an ambiguous one, and the legislatures were loathe to clarify it. But this gave the gay and lesbian movement, especially in Toronto, time, strategy, and organization, as we will see.

Although Quebec had included sexual orientation in its human rights legislation, not all provinces had followed suit. The Alberta Individual Rights Protection Act did not cover discrimination based on sexual orientation. An academic – Delwyn Vriend – who was fired in 1991 because he was gay, pursued the case through the whole court hierarchy, and on 2 April 1998, the Supreme Court of Canada unanimously ruled that the

---

60 *Egan v. Canada* (1995) 2 S.C.R. 513.
61 Ibid.

exclusion of homosexuals from Alberta's Individual Rights Protection Act was a violation of the Charter of Rights and Freedoms. The Supreme Court said that the Alberta Act would be interpreted to include homosexuals even if the province didn't change it. The Alberta government did not use the notwithstanding clause despite pressure from conservative and religious groups. (Just to catch up, the Canadian Parliament finally added sexual orientation to the Canadian Human Rights Act in 1996.)

Before we move on, I think it's important to think about the notion of equality. What was happening in Canada was the extension of the meaning of the word equality from the old Aristotelian notion that all men are born equal, to the concept of substantive equality. The clearest definition of substantive equality I have ever come across was that set out in an amicus brief presented by the Legal Education Action Fund (LEAF) that made submissions in another very important Canadian Charter case, *Andrews v. Law Society of British Columbia*.[62] This definition operationalizes well and is easily tested. LEAF argued that equality should be understood as a matter of socially created, systematic, historical, and cumulative advantage and disadvantage. Any of us who have a lifelong minority experience can embrace this definition and feel no strain to be comfortably accommodated by it. Although this approach was not totally embraced by the court in the *Andrews* case at the time, it is now a very good definition of how equality is applied in the Canadian courts with an emphasis on 'purposive,' substantive, positive equality rights focused on outcomes rather than technicality or form.

But not in New Zealand.

While everyone has the right to freedom from discrimination on the grounds laid out in the Human Rights Act of 1993, our law does not express a positive equality provision in its domestic legislation. So, for example, we are not guaranteed the equal benefit of the law without discrimination. This is despite our acceptance of the Optional Protocol of the International Covenant on Civil and Political Rights (ICCPR), our heaviest international legal human rights obligation where our rights are supposed to be 'immediately enforceable.'

We've seen lots of activity in the Canadian courts, so how were the New Zealand courts dealing with full human rights for gay and lesbian people? And what human rights discourse were they 'framing'?

---

62 *Andrews v. Law Society of British Columbia* (1989) 1 S.C.R. 143.

In 1998, the *Quilter*[63] case was brought by three lesbian couples who had applied for registration of their marriages or for licences to marry. They took a case to the high court of New Zealand for a declaration that the inability to register or to have a licence for a marriage was a breach of the discrimination sections in the New Zealand Bill of Rights Act. In particular, they were concerned with section 6: 'whenever an enactment can be given a meaning that is consistent with the rights and freedoms contained in this Bill of Rights, that meaning shall be preferred to any other meaning.' The Crown argued that even if the court found that it was discriminatory to refuse the issue of licences for same-sex marriage, and if the court found it was possible to give the act a meaning which was consistent within the Bill of Rights Act, then it would argue that this limitation of rights was reasonable and demonstrably justifiable in a free and democratic society.

Basically, the Crown's case was that by not being a man and a woman – and they contended that the Marriage Act was clear about this – the couple lacked the capacity to marry. And since procreation was important to marriage – yes, the New Zealand Crown case argued this in 1996 – that this was not a ground for discrimination. Similarly, if the present state of the law was unsatisfactory, then the court ought not to 'create a manifest absurdity to alleviate the situation' but should leave the question to Parliament. The high court judge concluded that marriage was limited to a union between a man and a woman. He did hold that the Marriage Act discriminated against same-sex couples who wished to marry. He also held that the Marriage Act could not be given a meaning consistent with the rights and freedoms contained in the Bill of Rights Act. Limiting marriage to a union between a husband and a wife could be regarded as a demonstrably justified and reasonable limitation prescribed by the law. He concluded that enabling marriages between same-sex couples to take place must be left to Parliament and not be made by a New Zealand court by 'strained interpretation.'

In the Court of Appeal, the majority found that the Marriage Act had a central premise that partners in marriage were of the opposite sexes, and that Parliament would have to effect such a major change to a fundamental institution and legal system with the great number of consequential changes where the law depended on marital status. The courts couldn't do this indirectly. The majority on the bench did not

---

63   *Quilter v. Attorney General* (1998) INZLR 523.

question whether or not the law should be concerned with the outcome, rather than the purpose of the Act, or that the real effect of the Marriage Act was to treat the appellants as not equally deserving of respect with other citizens. Mr Justice Keith stressed 'that this is not an area that can be captured by neat formulas.' In this New Zealand decision, you do not find any discussion at all of the word 'dignity' in the majority opinion. In respect of New Zealand's international legal obligations and, in particular, article 26 of the ICCPR, the majority stated 'a differentiation based on reasonable and objective criteria does not amount to prohibited discrimination within the meaning of article 26.' This is essentially the New Zealand legal framing that remains in place throughout the whole period of comparison.

The decision of then president of the Court of Appeal, Mr Justice Gault, added that the differentiation of gender characteristics of marriage 'has long been conventional and should be ruled unjustifiable only by the legislature because of the social policy implications.' Even the judgment of Mr Justice Tipping – who does find, in fact, that the marriage act is discriminatory – has no discussion at all of dignity.

The considerations of equality and dignity are only found in the minority judgment of Mr Justice Thomas. This will be the sole time in the comparative period when a New Zealand 'leader' uses the same framing of the issue as Canadian leaders. He quotes the dignity and worth provision from the Preamble to the Universal Declaration on Human Rights. He quotes from the Supreme Court of Canada's judgment in the *Egan* case: the existence of discrimination or otherwise can only be found by 'assessing the prejudicial effect (i.e., the outcome), of the distinction against the fundamental purpose of preventing the infringement of essential human dignity.'[64] He made the point that the essence of discrimination must be the impact of the law and not the intention behind the law. He found that based on sexual orientation, the distinction inherent in the Marriage Act and in the many enactments which conferred rights and benefits on married persons undoubtedly discriminated against gays and lesbians. He wrote:

> the concern, respect and consideration implicit in the goal of equality before and under the law is lacking. In the result gays and lesbians do not receive equal treatment under the law or the equal benefit of the laws of

---

64 Dissenting Judgment Thomas J. CA 200/96.

this land. My conclusion is that as a matter of law as well as logic, gay and lesbian persons and couples are discriminated against contrary to section 19 of the Bill of Rights.[65]

In consideration of the reasonable limits in section 5, Justice Thomas said:

> differentiations which are discriminatory cannot be reconciled with the democratic ideal of equality before and under the law. Discrimination in all its forms is odious. It is hurtful to those discriminated against and harmful to the health of the body politic. As such, it is, or should be, repugnant in a free and democratic society. There are, in other words, no reasonable limits prescribed by law which could be demonstrably justified in a free and democratic society. Whatever justification is advanced to justify the exclusion of gays and lesbians from the status of marriage therefore cannot be properly attached to the criterion in section 5.[66]

But later he says:

> I am unable to interpret the Marriage Act in the manner sought by the appellants. The Bill of Rights is not a supreme law. The legislative history of the Bill of Rights is well known. Parliament expressly rejected a Bill of Rights Act which would enable the courts to strike legislation down as invalid on grounds contrary to the Bill of Rights. Parliament or legislative supremacy was deliberately retained by the legislature. This court has an interpretative role, and while it must, in accordance with parliament's directions, prefer a meaning to any statutory provision which is consistent with the Bill of Rights, it cannot adopt a meaning which is clearly contrary to parliament's intent. No other meaning is possible without usurping parliament's legislative supremacy. It does not mean this court is shirking its responsibility to apply section 6 in declining to strain the meaning. That section does not authorize the court to legislate.[67]

So, the legal situation for gays and lesbians in New Zealand in 1996 could be compared with the situation of Canadian gays and lesbians

---

65 Ibid.
66 Ibid.
67 Ibid.

after the *Egan* case. In fact, in their submission to the Select Committee on the Civil Union Bill in New Zealand, the Human Rights Commission advised that the number of complaints of discrimination on the grounds of sexual orientation fell away after *Quilter*. More than 100 pieces of legislation effected different treatment, but the New Zealand courts were not going to do anything about it.

The *Quilter* couples then pursued the complaint to the United Nations Human Rights Committee using the Optional Protocol. The committee came to the same conclusion as the majority in the Court of Appeal, but they were working with very similar wording to that in the Canadian Charter, and it's to Canada and Ontario that we now return.

The Ontario Supreme Court's 1999 decision in *M v. H* was a crucial turning point. The case concerned the post-breakup support in same-sex relationships with M seeking support from H, her lesbian partner. Two features of the Court's rulings are important. First, the Court affirmed its position that the principle of equality demanded that same-sex and opposite-sex couples received the same legal treatment. Secondly, and most important, the Court came to a different conclusion about when violation of gay and lesbian equality rights was justified as a reasonable limit under section 1 of the Charter. That the case revolved around a 'private dispute' (support and property division) rather than public money (as in a pension plan) may have been a key difference. The decision was upheld in the Ontario Court of Appeal. At a stroke, the courts made compulsory what most Canadian legislatures had understood to be voluntary. Legislative activity to implement the decision quickly followed at a federal level, and in Ontario, British Columbia, Quebec, and Nova Scotia, with changes in Saskatchewan, Manitoba, and Alberta not far behind.

The Ontario Attorney General was granted leave to appeal the decision of the Ontario Court of Appeal to the Supreme Court of Canada. In May 1999, the Supreme Court of Canada ruled that the Ontario Family Law Act definition of spouse as a person of the opposite sex was unconstitutional, as was any provincial law that denied equal benefits to same-sex couples. Ontario was given six months to amend the Act.

In June 1999, although many laws were going to have to be revised to comply with the Supreme Court's May ruling, the federal government voted 216 to 55 on a motion in favour of preserving the definition of marriage as the union of a man and a woman.

Meanwhile, back in New Zealand, in 1999 the Ministry of Justice noted in its post-election briefing for incoming ministers that 'same-sex couples are frequently treated differently from opposite-sex couples across the statute book.' A government discussion paper highlighting significant instances of same-sex couples being treated differently was released and sought public feedback by 31 March 2000. The two countries were wrestling with very similar situations with scores of statutes breaching sexual-orientation equality rights.

Canada's Parliament moved first. In February 2000, Prime Minister Jean Chrétien's liberals introduced the Modernization of Benefits and Obligations Act in response to the Supreme Court's May 1999 ruling (and another omnibus law suit filed by a gay and lesbian advocacy group). In total, the bill affected sixty-eight federal statutes relating to a wide range of issues such as pension benefits, old age security, income tax deductions, bankruptcy protection, and the Criminal Code. The definitions of marriage and spouse were left untouched, but the definition of a common-law relationship was expanded to include same-sex couples.

In New Zealand nothing was happening, but in Canada the courts were about to take off again.

In July 2000, British Columbia's Attorney General Andrew Petter (in an NDP government) announced he would ask the courts for guidance on whether Canada's ban on same-sex marriage was constitutional. Meanwhile, Canadian activists had been using their imaginations strategically. On 10 December 2000, Reverend Dr Brent Hawkes of the Metropolitan Community Church in Toronto, read the first banns – an old Christian tradition for publishing or giving public notice of people's intent to marry – for two same-sex couples. Hawkes's research had found that if the banns were read on three Sundays before a wedding, he could legally marry the couples without a state-sanctioned marriage licence. He'd found this old alternative still mentioned in the statute. The reading of the banns was an opportunity for anyone who might oppose the wedding to come forward with objections before the ceremony. No one came forward on the first Sunday, but the next week two people stood to object. Hawkes dismissed their objections and read the banns for the third time the following Sunday. He married the two same-sex couples on 14 January 2001. These were two of the cases that went to court in Ontario.

I asked Michelle Douglass, who was then chair of the Gay and Lesbian Task Force in Ontario, how the movement held in check those in the community who wanted to go for same-sex recognition which was not marriage. She said that across the country they had interpreted civil union very early as a form of domestic apartheid. They called it the 'separate but equal' solution. Two provinces did forge ahead with civil unions or domestic partnerships: Nova Scotia and Quebec. The Quebec activists were explicit that they were doing what was possible at the time and within their sphere of influence to recognize and value same-sex relationships until the time came for formal marriage recognition. The debate, which coined the phrase, in fact occurred in the federal Parliament subcommittee on justice. The question of marriage was about principles of justice, human rights, and equality and dignity, and equality and dignity were not about creating a separate but equal regime. This was the language adopted for use, the framing position of the leadership of the advocacy groups throughout the movement. It was a very different language and a very different framing from that used in New Zealand.

Meanwhile, back in New Zealand late in 2000, nine people, six men and three women, began working with government gay MP Tim Barnett to develop a legislative model for legal recognition of same-sex couples. In all these notes and copies of minutes and correspondence that I have from this group, it is clear that the principle of equal treatment was never the key concern. The key concern was that there should be recognition of something that would pass. Lack of political consciousness about the great human rights activities of the twentieth century appeared to be completely lost on the authors of much of this work. Some of the language took my breath away.

> The Civil Union Bill proposes to provide state recognition for same-sex and different-sex couples who have registered their relationship. It will preserve the perceived historical definition of marriage as being between a man and a woman. The bill will preserve the existing perceived status of marriage by creating *an equal* and parallel *but separate* system of registration for civil unions. (My emphasis.)

We have all seen and we have lived through 'separate but equal.' Let me frame that for you.

It's the photo of the bus with the sign that says *Juden Verboten*. It's the sign outside the Memphis Zoo that says Whites Are Not to Visit the Zoo on Tuesdays – the only day blacks were permitted to go. It's the entranceway, the bathroom, the seating labelled *Net Nieblankes*, and the Colored Waiting Room, the White's Dining Room and Restaurant. It's the Prohibited Areas for all Persons of the Japanese Race, and the wall through the Occupied Territories. This is what separate but equal looks like. It's not pretty ... it's not over ...

In their letter dated 28 February 2001 to a number of activists asking for feedback, the Civil Union Bill team (CUB team) wrote, 'We are seeking a model that is acceptable to our communities and is likely to receive political support in the House. (This necessarily excludes the option of seeking same-sex marriage at this time).' The next letter went out to six men and to five women. I have copies of the responses from nine of them. Only one of these, a female student, gets to grips with the problem. She wrote that the proposed bill suggested a 'separate but equal regime. A similar argument on the grounds of race would not be acceptable.' She continues, 'Furthermore, I question whether the Civil Union Bill does, in fact, fulfil the requirements of the Bill of Rights Act and the Human Rights Act.' At this time, two women and one man resigned from the original CUB committee, leaving five men and one woman. The reasons for the resignations were quite clear, as one wrote, 'The bill would signify that it is permissible under New Zealand law to provide a lesser status for same-sex couples as compared with marriage for different-sex couples. A degree of equality is no equality at all. It is not possible to be partly equal.'

The April 2001 memo from the CUB team framed the registration of civil unions as the preferred model for New Zealand for the following reasons: (1) it was pragmatic; (2) it was internationally compatible; (3) it claimed human rights consistency; (4) it streamlined processes; and (5) it was politically achievable.

Now we are starting to get a very different picture of the decisions made around framing by the activist and lobby group in New Zealand and Canada. By this time the CUB team had pretty much dropped the word 'equality,' certainly in any sense of substantive equality, and dignity seldom got a mention in all the correspondence, memos, and draft bills that I have seen, except when they quoted Ted Thomas.

Meanwhile, back in Canada in 2001, the action was again in the courts. In Ontario, the Divisional Court unanimously held in the *Halpern* case, that the common-law definition of marriage as 'the lawful and voluntary union of one man and one woman to the exclusion of all others' infringed equality rights under section 15(1) of the Charter in a manner that was not justified under section 1 of the Charter. The panel's ruling on a remedy was not unanimous. One of the panel members said that Parliament should legislate the appropriate remedy and that it should be given two years to do so. If it didn't do this, the parties could return to the court to seek an appropriate remedy. Another member favoured a more immediate amendment by the court which would alter the common-law definition of marriage by substituting the words 'two persons' for 'one man and one woman.' (Remember that in the New Zealand Court of Appeal, Justice Keith thought that this was not an area that could be captured by neat formulae.) The third member adopted a middle position: he would allow Parliament two years to amend the common-law rule, failing which the reformulation remedy would be automatically triggered. This last option became the formal judgment of the court. The Attorney General of Ontario and the clerk of the City of Toronto took no position in the court with respect to the issues raised by the appeal and stated they would abide by any order made by the court.

That's pretty cool – the Crown standing aside – or even the Attorney General in BC going to the court for a declaratory judgment. I wish I could imagine that happening in New Zealand!

Meanwhile, back in New Zealand in early June 2001, Labour MP Tim Barnett released a press statement saying that Prime Minister Helen Clark had approached him in November 2000 to set up an advisory group of mostly gay people to come up with a proposal which would give relationship recognition and gain similar rights to married couples. The framing took place immediately. In Barnett's interview with *Express* (a NZ gay newspaper), published on 7 June 2001, he said that while there were many good arguments for same-sex marriage, civil unions were currently the preferred model as they were more politically achievable. 'The reality is that marriage is not what many people in our community want and it's not really politically achievable.'[68]

In 'our' community?

In material that my academic colleague Dr Mark Henrickson was pulling from his major Lavender Islands survey[69] (which was supplied to Labour ministers at the time) of gay communities in New Zealand (which received more than 2,200 responses), it was interesting to note that marriage was supported by 42.7 per cent of females and 34.9 per cent of males. Civil union was supported by 43.5 per cent of males and 27.3 per cent of females. This might be further analysed in noting that 37 per cent of the women respondents and 14 per cent of the men reported having some kind of parenting relationship with children. There was a very clear gender distinction around support. But Barnett

68 Helen Robinson's interview with Tim Barnett, *Express*, 7 June 2001, 3.
69 Dr Mark Henrickson, personal communication with author.

claimed throughout the debate that civil union was the preferred option among the gay community he moved in! Well of course, that's stating the obvious. But it had the effect of silencing the frame of many women in my gay community.

Apart from the inclusion of Helen Clark's name in the June 2001 press statement, the prime minister remained effectively silent on the issue throughout this period. From 2002 the New Zealand government was going to be forced to comply with provisions under the New Zealand Bill of Rights Act and the Human Rights Act of 1993 that outlawed discrimination by reason of marital status or sexual orientation. An omnibus companion piece of legislation was prepared that would effect major changes across many of those areas of discrimination, and this would go hand in hand with the civil union legislation. The *Express* newspaper continued to run with the 'best option right now politically achievable approach' and quoted and ran interviews with the remaining woman on the original CUB committee and with the men who supported civil union who had also been on that committee.

Dignity, equality, and human rights pretty much left the frame in New Zealand but not in Canada. On 12 July 2002, the Ontario Supreme Court ruled that prohibiting gay couples from marrying was unconstitutional and violated the Charter of Rights and Freedoms. The court gave Ontario two years to extend marriage rights to same-sex couples. The Government of Ontario decided not to appeal the court's ruling, saying only the federal government could decide who could marry. On 29 July 2002, the federal government announced it would seek leave to appeal the Ontario court ruling, to seek further clarity on these issues. This approach of the federal government was designed to seek clarification and not to oppose.

But nobody in New Zealand was watching, and on 14 May 2003 the cabinet policy committee noted that neutral laws on relationships whether married, de facto, or same-sex should be applied across the board and agreed that a civil union registration scheme should be established to provide a mechanism for adult couples to register their relationships. Just of minor interest is the fact that, on a full-cost-recovery basis, the fees for civil union registration were to be higher than those for marriage registration. The fees for civil union registration would be set at a level higher to ensure a full cost recovery of the registration services. So, it was to cost more to be less than equal, too!

Let us now turn to the judgment in the Court of Appeal for Ontario delivered on 10 June 2003. Remember, the Attorney General of Ontario had appealed to seek clarification. Prior to the Court of Appeal hearing, the Supreme Court in Quebec and in British Columbia had both declared that the common-law definition of marriage was unconstitutional and that they contravened section 15(1) of the Charter. Both courts gave a two-year suspension to the judgment. At the beginning of the judgment in *Halpern et al. v. the Attorney General of Canada et al.*, it read:

> The central question in this appeal is whether the exclusion of same-sex couples from this common law definition of marriage breaches sections 2a, or 15(1) of the Canadian Charter of Rights and Freedoms in a manner that is not justified in a free and democratic society under section 1 of the Charter. The case is ultimately about the recognition and protection of human dignity and equality in the context of the social structures available to conjugal couples in Canada.[70]

It went on:

> Human dignity means that an individual or group feels self-respect and self-worth. It is concerned with physical and psychological integrity and empowerment. Human dignity is harmed by unfair treatment, premised upon personal traits or circumstances, which do not relate to individual needs, capacities or merits. It is enhanced by laws which are sensitive to the needs, capacities and merits of different individuals taking into account the context underlying their differences. Human dignity is harmed when individuals and groups are marginalized, ignored or devalued, and is enhanced when laws recognize the full place of all individuals and groups within Canadian society.
>
> Marriage is without dispute one of the most significant forms of personal relationships. For centuries, marriage has been a basic element of social organization. Through this institution society publicly recognizes expressions of love and commitment between individuals granting them respect and legitimacy as a couple. This can only enhance an individual's sense of self-worth and dignity. The ability to marry and to thereby participate in a fundamental and societal institution is something most Canadians take for granted. Same-sex couples do not. They are denied access to this institution simply on the basis of their sexual orientation.

---

70 (2003) 225 DLR (4th) 529, para. 1.

The question at the heart of this appeal is whether excluding same-sex couples from one of the most basic elements of civic life, marriage, infringes human dignity and violates the Canadian constitution.[71]

The court found that the claimant was subject to differential treatment. It found that there was a formal distinction between the claimant and others, and a failure to take account of the claimant's already disadvantaged position resulting in substantively different treatment between the claimant and others, and that that differential treatment was discriminatory. The analysis was concerned with substantive, not formal equality, and the emphasis was on human dignity. The court made the following considered comments:

The assessment of whether a law has the effect of demeaning a claimant's dignity should not be undertaken from a subjective objective perspective. The relevant point of view is not solely that of a reasonable person but that of a reasonable person dispassionate and fully appraised of the circumstances, possessing similar attributes to, and under similar circumstances as, the group of which the rights claimant is a member. This requires a court to consider the individual or group's traits, history and circumstances in order to evaluate whether a reasonable person, in circumstances similar to the claimant, would find the impugned law differentiates in a manner that demeans his or her dignity.

The court then moved to determine whether this violation might be a reasonable limit prescribed by law that could be demonstrably justified in a free and democratic society.

Stating that marriage is heterosexual because it has always been heterosexual is merely an explanation for the opposite sex requirement of marriage. It is not an objective that is capable of justifying the infringement of a charter guarantee. It is not disputed that marriage has been a stabilizing and effective societal institution. The couples are not seeking to abolish the institution of marriage; they are seeking access to it. Plus the task of the Attorney General of Canada is not to show how marriage has benefited society as a whole, which we agree is self-evident, but to demonstrate that maintaining marriage is an exclusively heterosexual institution is rationally connected to the objectives of marriage which, in our view, is not self-evident.

---

71   Ibid., para. 8.

The opposite sex requirement in the definition of marriage does not minimally impair the right to claim this. Same-sex couples have been completely excluded from a fundamental societal institution. Complete exclusion cannot constitute minimal impairment.[72]

The court held that the common-law definition of marriage was inconsistent with the Charter. It declared invalid the existing definition of marriage and reformulated it as the voluntary union for the life of two persons to the exclusion of all others. It went on:

This remedy achieves the equality required by section 15(1) of the Charter but ensures that the legal status of marriage is not left in a state of uncertainty. Given that the common-law rule was fashioned by judges and not by parliament or a legislature, judicial deference to elected bodies is not an issue. If it is possible to reformulate to common law rules so that it will not conflict with the principles of fundamental justice, such a reformulation could be undertaken. We are also of the view that the argument made by the Attorney General of Canada that we should defer to parliament once we issue a declaration of invalidity is not apposite in these circumstances. The role of the legislator and legislative objectives is to be considered at the second step of the remedy analysis when a court is deciding whether severance or reading in is an appropriate remedy to cure a legislative provision that breaches the Charter. There is no evidence before this court that a declaration of invalidity without a period of suspension will prove any harm to the public, threaten the rule of law or deny anyone the benefit of legal recognition of their marriage. In our view, an immediate declaration will simply ensure that opposite-sex couples and same-sex couples immediately receive equal treatment in law in accordance with section 15 of the Charter.

We reformulate the common-law definition of marriage as the voluntary union for life of two persons to the exclusion of all others.

We decline to order a suspension of the declaration of invalidity or of the reformulated common-law definition of marriage.

We make orders requiring the Clerk of the city of Toronto to issue marriage licences to the couples and require the Registrar-General of the Province of Ontario to accept for registration the marriage certificates.[73]

---

72 Ibid., para. 139.
73 Ibid., para. 154.

Seven days later, on 17 June 2003, Prime Minister Jean Chrétien announced that the government would introduce legislation to make same-sex marriages legal, while at the same time permitting churches and other religious groups to sanctify marriage as they saw it. The federal government would not appeal the provincial court rulings allowing same-sex unions.

All of this completely passed by the New Zealand parliament, and the activity there remained framed by 'it's not marriage' and 'it's the best that we can get politically.'

In February 2004, Prime Minister Helen Clark was asked why New Zealand wasn't seeing the full equality of an amendment to the Marriage Act. She replied that we 'were moving in line with mainstream western countries.' She said that in Canada 'the issue was bogged down in state law.'[74] Well actually by then, February 2004, no one was bogged down at all. The process was very clear, and the framing meant the outcome would be equal marriage.

We have had a look at the kind of leadership that was evident in the courts, and that of the key lobbyists, in the framing of the issues. Now, let's have a look at the politicians. In June 2003, after Chrétien announced that the Canadian government would introduce legislation to make same-sex marriages legal, there was a huge uproar inside his Liberal Party because Chrétien made this proposal without caucus consultation. However, in both Canada and New Zealand, there had been years of investigations and reports about the nature of the discriminations. But something else that is also very important to understand is that, in Prime Minister Chrétien, we had a political leader who was about to retire.

As Chrétien was about to retire, there was a Liberal Party competition for who would succeed him as leader, and in September 2003, Canada found itself in the middle of an election campaign. The key parties concerned were the Liberal Party in government, the Canadian Alliance Party, the New Democratic Party (NDP), and the Bloc Québécois. The NDP was the only federal party that had a policy supporting legalizing same-sex marriage and it had had this since 1999. During the campaign, NDP leader Jack Layton said: 'This isn't a question of personal views or personal morality; it's an issue of rights. Our policy is

74 *Express*, 11 February 2004, 16.

very, very clear'. 'We don't have free votes on human rights issues.'[75] The opposition Canadian Alliance Party countered with a motion in Parliament to reaffirm the heterosexual definition of marriage and to state that Parliament would take all necessary steps to protect it. This was the same motion as that which was passed by over 200 votes only four years earlier.

On 16 September this was defeated 137 against and 132 in favour. In the debate, Justice Minister Martin Cauchon told Commons: 'in 1999 I voted with the majority in this House, but let me remind parliamentary members that our attachment to long-cherished traditions and conventions is not the only, or even the best, measure of what is just or what is right.'

I was in Canada during this period in 2003 and I distinctly remember how the news media framed the Liberals' annual caucus retreat. Spokespeople for Paul Martin, the leadership contender, were quoted as saying it was the sort of issue which should be sent to a nationwide referendum. Chrétien immediately responded that the reason why a country committed itself to human rights as found in the Charter was so that majorities could not impose discriminatory situations upon minorities via referendums.

At every point at which any internal criticism was made of the Liberal prime minister, he and his justice minister, Martin Cauchon, responded in terms of human rights. From the very beginning, the Liberal Party leadership framed the issue in terms of human rights and at no time did it derogate from that position. In this comparative analysis, it does matter and it is important to point out that both Chrétien and Cauchon were Catholic, French speakers, and married men with families. Both were lawyers. Cauchon, in particular, had focused on international and human rights law in his student years. Paul Martin was also a staunch Catholic who went to church most Sundays. He dropped the referendum position, but aides and spokespeople continued to do the running for him throughout this period. At the Liberal Party caucus meeting, Martin had said that he wanted to replace civil marriages with civil unions. In September 2003, his aides indicated that he intended to 'rework' the same-sex legislation before it was introduced.

---

75 Kim Lunman, 'Layton Warns NPD Maverick,' *Globe and Mail*, 9 September 1993, A5.

But the tide was going out on the positions Martin ran around and the media framing was very focused on human rights.

Following from the Ontario decision, on 8 July 2003, British Columbia lifted its ban, giving gay couples the right to marry immediately. On 19 March 2004, Quebec affirmed its earlier ruling that homosexuals had the right to marry and that the traditional definition of marriage was discriminatory and unjustified. Quebec took the opportunity provided by this later case to revoke its earlier moratorium on marriage. This was very important as Quebec was a province with civil unions for gays and lesbians, and the courts held that this was not equality. In terms of dignity, civil union was not equal with marriage. This was followed by courts in Manitoba, in Nova Scotia, and in the Yukon. None of these cases were further appealed to the Supreme Court of Canada, a point of both legal and political significance.

On 17 July 2003, the federal government referred draft legislation entitled 'An Act Respecting Certain Aspects of Legal Capacity for Marriage' to the Supreme Court of Canada for review. The Supreme Court was being asked whether or not Parliament had the exclusive legal authority to define marriage; if the proposed act was compatible with the Charter of Rights and Freedoms; and whether or not the constitution protected church authorities who refused to sanctify the same-sex marriage.

I need to explain what a reference to the Supreme Court of Canada is. It's a way for the government to get the Court's opinion on major legal factual questions before they become law. The aim is to make sure potentially contentious legislation would survive a challenge under the constitution. It's not an unusual practice. The federal government of Canada has taken this action more than seventy times since 1872. First, the government files the question it wants answered, and then the Court decides the issues and the list of interveners it is willing to hear on the issues. Usually, when all the arguments are heard, the Court takes several months to render its decision.

This was a unique circumstance, as the raft of decisions on the marriage question across the country was having a major effect on politicians. By early June 2004, Paul Martin was saying that the verdicts of the Court were clear and that disallowing marriage would clearly be discriminatory. Clearly, his framing was changing. He now said that 'it was absolutely a question of human rights and under those circumstances there is no way that anybody should be allowed to discriminate or prevent same-sex marriage,' and that 'Canada is a nation of minorities and we cannot take away the Charter of Rights, it is so fundamental'.[76]

At almost the same time, civil union legislation was being prepared for introduction as a government bill in New Zealand. On 29 April 2004 the Crown law office advised the Attorney General that the Civil Union Bill was consistent with the New Zealand Bill of Rights Act.

For further analysis of the framing in New Zealand, you could go to the website of the minister of justice, the Honourable David Benson-Pope, to find answers on civil union relationship matters. Do these bills undermine marriage? Are these just proposals for same-sex couples? As I read through these I found little evidence of equality and dignity and human rights. Most of the framing from the government's point of view was about what the civil union legislation was not about.

Two months later, on 22 June 2004, I had the opportunity to spend some time with the by then retired minister of justice, Martin Cauchon, who had led the political framing of the debate with Jean Chrétien. He had always taken the position that 'anything less than equal is less than adequate.' His key framing around the issue was that equivalence is not equality. He had seen it necessary as minister of justice to take a very clear position early on. He told me he was a minister of justice who belonged to the first student generation of the Charter. He said the leadership of Chrétien was absolutely vital and without that prime ministerial leadership and focus on equality, dignity, and human rights the situation would have been very different. He said:

> The Charter of Rights should be respected and practised, not just believed in as some esoteric threshold. Marriage was an institution, a very strong institution, and therefore it had to reflect who we, Canadians, are. It had to be free, it had to be open and that this will make it a stronger institution.[77]

He described the use of the notwithstanding clause to deprive people of their rights as 'simply dreadful.' He said, 'Canada is leading the world and my vision of Canada is a vision that is inclusive. My

76 Bill Curry, 'Same-sex Marriage Shouldn't Be Stopped,' *Globe and Mail*, 5 June 2004, B1.
77 Martin Cauchon, personal communication with author.

kids will look at our country and when the world talks about human rights, the reference in the world will be Canada.'[78]

While Martin Cauchon, although retired from Parliament, was still giving leadership around the issue, the Civil Union Bill had been sent to a select committee in New Zealand.

You might remember that the *Halpern* decision from the Ontario Court of Appeal was given on 10 June 2003. When I made my submission to the New Zealand parliamentary Select Committee on the Civil Union Bill on 23 August 2004, no member of the committee had read the *Halpern* decision, no one had asked for it, no departmental adviser had drawn the attention of the committee to the judgment, so I supplied it to them. Only five out of the thousands of submissions that were made opposed the bill because it was not an approach of fundamental human rights or a question equality and dignity. These were the submissions of the three early CUB members who walked out, my own submission, and that from the Human Rights Commission, which made the dignity argument, but then was very conciliatory and adopted 'the best we can get' approach in the end.

Prime Minister Helen Clark had anticipated with precision the nature of much of the debate in the New Zealand Parliament. This was epitomized by the interventions of Opposition MP Nick Smith, which were frequent and which led the personal attack on the prime minister and her views on marriage. For pages and pages of the parliamentary debate there is debate about marriage. The numbers of those who use the words 'human rights' are obviously in two camps. Right-wingers spoke about human rights being 'handed out like Christmas presents.' The tone was extremely offensive. When the strongest supporters spoke about human rights, and even when they moved into the areas of equality and dignity, they fell short of the notion of substantive equality and the essence of dignity in human rights outcomes. A number of MPs tried the Paul Martin escape position and called for a referendum on the issue. No one talked about substantive equality and few used the equality words. The debate in the House again and again held up the framing, or the lack of it, that had been in evidence throughout the whole debate. No one said – hold it folks – you can't have half a human right, and if you think you can for gay and lesbian people, just who might be next?

---

78 Ibid.

On 9 December 2004, as the New Zealand parliamentary debate on the Civil Union Bill rambled to its vitriolic end, the Supreme Court of Canada delivered its judgment on the marriage reference. It held that the capacity to marry persons of the same sex was consistent with the Canadian Charter of Rights and Freedoms. And let me just quote one or two sentences from that judgment:

> The frozen concept (of marriage) reasoning runs contrary to one of the most fundamental principles of Canadian constitutional interpretation, that our constitution is a living tree which by way of progressive interpretation accommodates and addresses the realities of modern life. Read expansively, the word marriage does not exclude same-sex marriage.

And later,

> With respect to the effect of section 1, the mere recognition of the equality rights of one group cannot in itself constitute a violation of the section 15(1) rights of another, and a furtherance of those rights cannot undermine the very principles the charter was meant to foster.[79]

So let's see where this has left everybody in law, and let's have a look at some of the instances that people are afraid of. We begin with some photographs of the marriage of Brettel Dawson and Angie Macdonald held in Ontario on 22 August 2003. Now, Brettel has dual citizenship. She is a professor of law at Carleton University. Brettel and Ange were in New Zealand for four months in 2008, and we were never able to establish which half of Brettel Ange was married to whence in New Zealand. Was NZ law effectively questioning the validity of a marriage under Canadian law? That they were married while in Canada but not in NZ? Did that mean heterosexual Canadian marriages – or all South African or Spanish marriages were at risk of being declared invalid in NZ?

Let's move on to another wedding, that of my extraordinarily resilient friends Jenny Rowan and Jools Joslin. I attended their first wedding in 1995. I worked with them to assist their case (the *Quilter* case) in the New Zealand courts and their 'communication' with the United Nations Human Rights Committee. And I attended their wedding in

---

79 2004 S.S.C. 79. Available online at www.cbc.ca/news/background/samesexrights/2004ssc079.wpd.txt.

Quebec in August 2006, when they were married under Canadian law in the garden of Brettel and Ange's home. Their marriage is not recognized in New Zealand.

I concluded the Professorial Inaugural Lecture with a memory of my interview for the position of professor of public policy at AUT University. In the summer of 2006, I had met with Vice-Chancellor Derek McCormack and Professor Ian Shirley to discuss my appointment to this position. I had furnished them with the usual academic curriculum vitae. Among the items listed was one which read 'action research: gay marriage.' One of them asked me very genuinely, 'What's that about?' I was able to advise, 'Vice-chancellor and professor, this is what it's about, and for equal marriage in New Zealand, there is still some way to go.'

So, we are working on that. And thank you, Canada.